100 THINGS SPURS FANS SHOULD KNOW & DO BEFORE THEY DIE

Mike Monroe

TRIUMPH
BOOKS

Library of Congress Cataloging-in-Publication Data

Names: Monroe, Mike, author.
Title: 100 things Spurs fans should know & do before they die / Mike Monroe.
Other titles: One hundred things Spurs fans should know and do before they die
Description: Chicago, Illinois : Triumph Books LLC, [2016]
Identifiers: LCCN 2016003185 | ISBN 9781629371931
Subjects: LCSH: San Antonio Spurs (Basketball team)—History. | San Antonio
    Spurs (Basketball team)—Miscellanea.
Classification: LCC GV885.52.S26 M64 2016 | DDC
    796.323/6409764351—dc23
LC record available at http://lccn.loc.gov/2016003185

This book is available in quantity at special discounts for your group or organization. For further information, contact:

Triumph Books LLC
814 North Franklin Street
Chicago, Illinois 60610
(312) 337-0747
www.triumphbooks.com

Printed in U.S.A.
ISBN: 978-1-62937-193-1
Design by Patricia Frey
Photos courtesy of AP Images unless otherwise indicated

For Spurs Fans

Contents

Introduction

When someone asks you to come up with a list of 100 things Spurs fans should know and do before they die, the knee-jerk response is: that's a lot of things.

It doesn't take long before one realizes 100 things may not be enough to capture everything that fans of the San Antonio Spurs ought to know and do.

Indeed, there are dozens of things Spurs fans should know about the five most important players in franchise history, not to mention the most important head coach. Tim Duncan, Manu Ginobili, Tony Parker, David Robinson, George Gervin, and Gregg Popovich are the primary subjects of 23 of the 100 Things you'll find in this book. If that seems excessive consider the fact that the 19 Duncan-Popovich years comprise 44 percent of the team's history in San Antonio. Of course, it also includes the six trips to the NBA Finals and the five championships that stamp it as one of pro basketball's greatest dynasties.

The team's history is colorful and includes many personalities and quirky moments that are essential to understanding how one of the smallest markets in all of pro sports managed to become one of its most successful, a model for how to succeed in any circumstance.

Ordering the sequence wasn't easy and many changes were made along the way. Putting Duncan at the very top of the list is unassailable, though a few million Argentines might disagree.

Feel free to dispute any of the rankings but remember: difference of opinion is what makes a horse race.

Researching and writing the book wasn't easy but it never seemed like a chore. I believe even the most avid Spurs fans will learn a few things. The most casual may learn nearly 100.

No. 1 awaits.

1 Tim Duncan

When the Spurs won the 1997 NBA Draft lottery, the entire basketball loving world knew they would make Tim Duncan the No. 1 overall selection. The NCAA Division I Player of the Year had just set an all-time NCAA record for career rebounds (1,570) that would last until 2011. He was a can't-miss prospect, a franchise changer, the best big man to come out of the college ranks since Shaquille O'Neal in 1992.

Even with such high expectations, nobody could have predicted the run of excellence that would make Duncan a member of the NBA's mythical All-Time top 10, a list that includes legends like Michael Jordan, Magic Johnson, Larry Bird, Bill Russell, Oscar Robertson, Wilt Chamberlain, Kareem Abdul-Jabbar, and Elgin Baylor.

Spurs fans should make the case that he belongs in the All-Time top five.

What no one attending the draft at Charlotte Coliseum on June 25, 1997, knew about Duncan was the competitive fire that stoked his approach to the game nor the self-discipline that would allow him to drive himself through 19 seasons at a level of excellence never seen in a player of his age.

Consider: as a 21-year-old rookie in 1997–98 Duncan produced a Player Efficiency Rating of 22.6, a number that clearly identified him as an All-Star-caliber performer. Seventeen years later, as a 39-year-old veteran in 2014–15, he produced an identical PER, 22.6, and was named third-team All-NBA and made the All-Defensive second team.

The longevity of Duncan's excellence is unparalleled in NBA history.

The native of St. Croix, U.S. Virgin Islands, benefited from playing alongside former NBA Most Valuable Player David Robinson from the very beginning of his career. Recognizing Duncan's superior offensive skills, Robinson shared his go-to role on the Spurs with the rookie; the veteran led the team in points scored at 21.6, the rookie averaged 21.1. Duncan also averaged a team-high 11.9 rebounds per game and was named to the All-Defensive second team.

He was a unanimous choice as Rookie of the Year.

It took only one exhibition game against the Houston Rockets, in which Duncan scored 17 points and grabbed 17 rebounds while playing less than 30 minutes, for eventual Hall of Fame power forward Charles Barkley to declare: "I have seen the future and he wears No. 21. He was quite impressive, better than I expected, and I expected a lot. He's polished. Very polished."

Duncan was disappointed he was not able to push the Spurs past their playoff nemesis, the Utah Jazz, in that rookie season, the Spurs falling to Karl Malone, John Stockton, and Co., in five games.

He would not have to wait long to taste true playoff success.

An NBA championship, the Spurs' first, in 1999, also produced the first of Duncan's three Most Valuable Player performances in the Finals.

Taking over as the Spurs' leading scorer in the lockout-shortened 1998–99 season, Duncan again made first-team All-NBA and first-team All-Defensive, but his dominant performance in the Spurs' 4–1 NBA Finals triumph over the New York Knicks was even more impactful than what he had done in the regular season. He averaged 27.4 points, 14.0 rebounds, and 2.2 blocked shots per game and was a unanimous choice as the MVP of the series.

Duncan had to suffer through the disappointment of missing the playoffs with a knee injury in 1999–2000. It was bad timing for

After being selected No. 1 overall in the 1997 NBA Draft, Tim Duncan became the face of the Spurs franchise and the centerpiece of five championship teams.

him and the club, as it preceded his first free-agent summer. He re-signed with the Spurs despite a serious push by the Orlando Magic to make Duncan and Pistons forward Grant Hill a free-agency package for the ages.

There would be more playoff disappointment—back-to-back losses to the Lakers in the 2001 and 2002 Western Conference semifinals, including being swept in 2001 with blowout losses (by 39 and 29 points) in Games 3 and 4.

Duncan won the first of his two regular-season Most Valuable Player Awards in 2001–02, when he averaged 25.5 points and 12.7 rebounds per game and was, once again, an All-Defensive first-team pick. None of that helped the Spurs in another disheartening loss to the Lakers in the conference semifinals.

When the Spurs met the Lakers in the 2003 semifinals, Duncan was a man on a mission. With a chance to close out the series in the Lakers' Staples Center in Game 6, he poured in 37 points and grabbed 16 rebounds.

Duncan was a clear choice as league MVP that season, as well, with averages of 23.3 points and career highs of 12.9 rebounds and 2.9 blocks per game. When he led the Spurs to a 4–2 Finals win over the New Jersey Nets in the 2003 NBA Finals, he won his second Finals MVP Trophy, punctuating his domination with a near-quadruple double in the championship-clinching Game 6: 21 points, 20 rebounds, 10 assists, and eight blocks, one of the most dominant close-out games in Finals history.

The 2002–03 championship was a fitting punctuation to David Robinson's Hall of Fame career; after he retired, even more of the Spurs' scoring burden fell on Duncan's shoulders. Though he would never again win another regular-season MVP Award, there was one more Finals MVP Trophy in his future. A thrilling, seven-game triumph over the gritty Detroit Pistons in the 2005 NBA Finals earned him the trophy in a close vote over teammate Manu Ginobili.

Hurricane Hugo

As a youngster, Tim Duncan put his competitive drive and athletic discipline into competitive swimming. Growing up on St. Croix, in the U.S. Virgin Islands, he had learned to swim at an early age, like nearly every youngster in the islands. He found that he loved competitive swimming and, by age 13, he had put up some of the best times in the United States in the 400-meter freestyle. He dreamed of representing the United States in the Olympics.

Then, on September 17, 1989, Hurricane Hugo, a Category 4 storm, slammed into St. Croix on a path that would make it one of the most deadly and destructive hurricanes ever. Duncan and his family survived its landfall but the pool at which he trained was ruined.

Forced to give up his Olympic swimming dream, Duncan channeled his athletic pursuits to basketball.

The rest is history.

Duncan would earn a fourth championship ring on the 2007 Spurs team that swept young LeBron James and the Cleveland Cavaliers in the Finals, point guard Tony Parker taking Finals MVP honors.

Four titles, two MVPs, and three Finals MVP Awards in 10 seasons would have stamped Duncan as a megastar, but what followed in the next eight seasons would solidify his legacy as an all-time Top 10 player. Though he never again would average 20 or more points per game in the regular season, he continued to play at an All-Star level, even through the 2011–12 season, when he was omitted from the All-Star Game for the first time in his career. (There was no All-Star Game in the 50-game 1998–99 season.)

The Spurs would conclude that season on a 10-game win streak and then win their first 10 playoff games to take a 2–0 lead over the Oklahoma City Thunder in the Western Conference Finals. Four straight losses would spoil the great playoff run and lead to speculation that Duncan's career might have come to an end. After all, he was 36 and at the end of a contract.

Instead, Duncan re-dedicated himself to an off-season conditioning program that includes various forms of martial arts training and re-signed with the Spurs for a 50 percent pay cut from the NBA-maximum $21.4 million contract on which he had played.

He made his fifth trip to the NBA Finals in 2013, only to suffer the heartbreak of a crushing defeat in Game 6 when the Spurs, leading the Miami Heat 3–2, blew a five-point lead with 28 seconds left.

When he missed a layup—and then a point-blank putback—that could have tied Game 7 with 41 seconds left, he said the game "will always haunt me."

Duncan helped the Spurs exorcise the demons of that 2013 disappointment when he averaged 15.4 points and 10.0 rebounds in the Spurs' resounding 4–1 2014 NBA Finals victory over the Heat.

Opting to return for a 19th season at age 39, Duncan finished the 2015–16 Spurs season with career totals that make him a sure-fire first-ballot Hall of Famer: 26,496 points (14th all time), 15,091 rebounds (sixth all time), and 3,020 blocks (fifth all time). He ranks first in Spurs history in games played, points scored, rebounds, and blocks.

After the Spurs were dismissed in the second round of the playoffs by the Oklahoma City Thunder, Duncan announced his retirement July 11, 2016, in typically low-key fashion: via a 543-word press release.

Redemption: The 2014 NBA Championship

After the 112–107 overtime victory over the Oklahoma City Thunder in Game 6 of the 2014 Western Conference Finals put the Spurs in an NBA Finals rematch with the same Miami Heat team that broke their hearts in the 2013 Finals, Spurs captain Tim Duncan expressed what every Spurs fan knew: the Spurs were thrilled to have a shot at redeeming themselves for having blown a title shot the previous June.

"We're happy to be back here this year. We're happy to have another opportunity at it," Duncan said. "We're happy that it's the Heat again. We'll be ready for them. We've got some experience, obviously, from last year against them, and we'll go back and look at some film. And we've got that bad taste in our mouths still.

"Hopefully, we'll be ready to take it this time."

This was perceived by some in Miami, LeBron James in particular, as proof the Spurs didn't like the Heat, an assertion coach Gregg Popovich called "silly."

In truth, the Spurs had dedicated their entire season to redeeming themselves by proving they were still capable of winning another championship.

That they got the chance to do so against the Heat was just a bonus.

The process of redemption actually began when Gregg Popovich's daughter, Jill, grew tired of his moping around in the weeks that followed the Game 6 collapse and Game 7 loss that cost the Spurs a chance to be a perfect 5–0 in trips to the NBA Finals.

Popovich admitted he just couldn't stop thinking about Game 6 of the 2013 Finals, when the Spurs blew a 94–89 lead in the final 28.2 seconds of regulation time.

His daughter made him stop fretting and start planning a way for his players to get past the crushing disappointment.

Popovich recalled his daughter's admonishment to *San Antonio Express-News* columnist Buck Harvey: "'OK, Dad, let me get this straight: you won four championships, and you go to a fifth Finals. Other coaches lose all the time. But poor Greggy can't lose because he's special. Can you please get over yourself? End of story.'"

Popovich stared at her, then started laughing. Hadn't his daughter told him the same "get-over-yourself" line he's told so many others?

"That started me on the path to recovery," he said.

Popovich's response was to begin planning his annual retreat with his assistant coaches, this time in San Francisco, around a play-by-play analysis of Game 6. By pinpointing every single mistake that led up to the final 28.2 seconds he was able to show his players that it had not been the cruelty of "the basketball gods" that had "screwed" the Spurs. It had been all that had gone *before* those final 28.2 seconds that allowed the collapse to occur.

"We hit them right between the eyes with what we could have done better," Popovich said. "That's a whole lot better than 'The basketball gods did it to us.'

"That doesn't help anybody."

The entire 2013–14 season was dedicated to getting back to the Finals, and when the trip finally was ticketed with the 4–2 elimination of a very good Thunder opponent, Duncan simply stated the truth: the Spurs were happy they were playing the Heat.

The regular season had produced an NBA-best record of 62–20, assuring the Spurs home-court advantage in every round of the playoffs, including the Finals. Their playoff run had begun with a reality check: a first-round series against the Dallas Mavericks that extended to seven games, a reminder that their standout season guaranteed nothing.

They regained their footing with a 4–1 second-round domination of a very good Portland Trail Blazers team and then prevailed in the Western Conference Finals against the Thunder and Kevin Durant, the regular-season scoring champion and Most Valuable Player.

By the time the Finals arrived, their "beautiful game" offense, with an emphasis on ball movement, player movement, and going from a good shot to a great shot, was working to perfection.

Game 1 produced a 110–93 win that was tougher to secure than the final score made it appear. The team's Big Three—Tim Duncan, Manu Ginobili, and Tony Parker—combined for 56 points but the outcome was not secured until the final two minutes, when the Spurs scored 11 unanswered points.

Game 2 was a reminder of how things could unravel if the Spurs did not adhere to their season-long philosophy. Making only 43.9 percent of their shots as the ball too often got "stuck" in a non-existent offensive flow, the Spurs dropped a 98–96 decision that cost them home-court advantage and had Spurs fans fearing another heartache against the Heat.

Afterward, Popovich summed up the game and his team's season-long offensive approach: "You move it or you die."

Popovich then made a strategic move that changed the series. Replacing Tiago Splitter with Boris Diaw, one of the game's best interior passers, in the starting lineup re-ignited the share-the-ball

Playing with Pain

Nearly as amazing as the Spurs' domination of the Heat in the 2014 NBA Finals was the fact that two of the stars of the series completed the team's triumphant playoff run with significant injuries.

Manu Ginobili, whose powerful dunk over Miami's shot-blocking star, Chris Anderson, late in Game 5 was one of the highlights of the series, was discovered to have a stress fracture in his right leg. Turns out Ginobili had played with the ailment throughout most of the playoff run, a remarkable turn of events considering how well he played during the postseason.

The play of backup point guard Patty Mills, who averaged 10.0 points per game and made 13-of-23 three-pointers during the Finals, was even more remarkable considering the fact he was found to have a torn rotator cuff in his right shoulder that required surgery a few days after the conclusion of the series. Recovery from the operation forced him to miss the first 31 games of the 2014–15 season, but his willingness to play with the discomfort through the bulk of the season and into the playoffs was vital to the team's fifth championship run.

offense and produced 59.4 percent shooting. The move translated into a 111–92 win that was even more dominant than the score made it seem.

When the Spurs followed with a 107–86 victory in Game 4, the series returned to San Antonio for a chance to secure the championship in front of their fans.

In Game 5, Kawhi Leonard broke out for 22 points and 10 rebounds while also defending Miami star LeBron James with minimal double-team help. The result: another blowout victory, 104–87.

The Spurs' overall margin of victory, 14.0 points per game, made the series the most dominant Finals in NBA history. They shot a Finals record 52.8 percent and made a record 55 three-pointers despite playing only five games.

Most remarkably, they did it without the kind of singular scoring star that has typified the majority of champions throughout league history; five players averaged between 10.2 and 18 points per game in the series. They completed their run with the lowest leading postseason scorer (Tony Parker at 17.4 points per game) of any NBA title winner since the 1951 Rochester Royals.

Leonard was named Finals MVP but both Duncan and Diaw received votes from the nine-person media panel, clear indication the triumph had been a team accomplishment.

"We're a true team, and everybody contributes," Parker said. "Everybody did their job. We did it together, and that was the whole key."

Even the Miami players understood that what the Spurs had accomplished was transformative.

"That's how team basketball should be played," said James, the four-time league MVP. "Guys move, cut, pass. You've got a shot, you take it, but it's all for the team and it's never about the individual."

In his post-championship address to his team, Popovich revealed precisely what the series had meant to him and, by extension, to all of Spurs Nation:

"I've never been prouder of a team, nor have I ever gotten as much satisfaction from a season in all the years I've been coaching. To see the fortitude you guys displayed, coming back from that horrific loss last year and getting yourselves back in position and doing what you did in the Finals. You are really to be honored for that and I just can't tell you what it means."

That's enough to make it the most meaningful of the five championships the Spurs have won since entering the NBA in 1967.

3 The Admiral

Ten years before lottery luck put the Spurs in position to make Tim Duncan the No. 1 overall pick of the 1997 NBA Draft, they had landed the first pick of another draft that featured a franchise-changing big man.

David Robinson, a 7-foot-1 center with the athleticism of a small forward, had earned NCAA Player of the Year honors at the United States Naval Academy, where he had averaged 28.2 points and 11.8 rebounds despite being double-teamed nearly every time he touched the ball.

But there was a catch: the military obligation owed by anyone who graduates from one of the U.S. military academies and receives a commission as a junior officer in the Army, Navy, Air Force, Marines, Coast Guard, or Merchant Marines.

Robinson was worth waiting for, so the Spurs never hesitated to make him their selection in 1987, even though the wait carried a huge risk.

Because he was too tall to serve as a line officer aboard ship, Robinson was commissioned as a reserve officer (Lieutenant, Junior Grade) in the Navy's Civil Engineering Corps, a military stint for just two years, rather than the five years most military academy graduates bear.

The risk for the Spurs? NBA rules in 1987 allowed Robinson to re-enter the draft, rather than sign with the Spurs, when he finally became eligible for the NBA.

To avoid what would have been a horrendous embarrassment for the franchise, Spurs general manager Bob Bass, with the approval of owner Red McCombs, agreed to guarantee that Robinson never would be paid less than the average of the two highest-paid players in the league if he agreed to sign with the Spurs rather than re-enter the draft.

The team had been in a competitive malaise for four seasons, with three different coaches, bottoming out at 21–61 in 1988–89 after Larry Brown had been lured away from the University of Kansas shortly after leading the Jayhawks to the NCAA championship.

Failing to get Robinson on board for 1989–90 would have been a disaster, but the costly salary guarantee turned out to be money well spent.

Once he was under contract, it didn't take long for Robinson to win over Spurs fans. He agreed to play in the annual Midwest Rookie Review, one of the NBA's first summer leagues, hosted by the Spurs at Blossom Athletic Center.

It was standing room only for every game played by the Summer Spurs and Robinson did not disappoint with his ability to run the floor and finish fast breaks with powerful dunks.

He had amazed the coaches on the first day of summer practice.

David Robinson's military obligation to the U.S. Navy delayed his Spurs debut by two years. He proved to be worth the wait.

"Players were just shooting around before practice," recalled Gregg Popovich, then one of Brown's assistants, "but everything stopped when David did a handstand and then walked from one end of the court to the other—on his hands. Nobody had ever seen anything like it."

Robinson was an instant success on the court. He averaged 24.3 points and 12.0 rebounds as a rookie, earning Rookie of the Year honors. More importantly, he led the Spurs to a record of 56–26, at the time a franchise best. It gave the Spurs an NBA record for biggest improvement from one season to the next, 35 more wins than in 1988–89.

Despite his solid scoring and rebounding—he averaged no fewer than 23.2 points and 11.7 rebounds in his first four seasons—Robinson was not able to get the Spurs past the second round of the playoffs, a fact that played heavily into Brown's dismissal midway through the 1991–92 season.

Under head coach John Lucas in 1993–94, Robinson put up the best numbers of his career, winning the NBA scoring title with an average of 29.8 points per game. With the Spurs locked into their playoff position, Lucas orchestrated Robinson's pursuit of the title in the final game of the regular season. "The Admiral" became just the fourth player in NBA history to score 70 or more points in a game, totaling 71 against the Clippers on April 24, 1994. Earlier that season he had become just the fourth player in league history to post a quadruple-double when he posted 34 points, 10 rebounds, 10 assists, and 10 blocks against the Detroit Pistons.

Robinson would have his lone MVP season under coach Bob Hill in 1994–95, when he averaged 27.6 points, 10.8 rebounds, and 3.2 blocks and led the Spurs to a league-best 62–20 record. He became the franchise's first MVP but his dream season ended with a thump when Hakeem Olajuwon and the Houston Rockets outplayed Robinson and the Spurs in the 1995 Western Conference Finals, winning in six games.

Tim Duncan's arrival in 1997 gave the Spurs the best low-post tandem in the league and Robinson finally earned a championship ring when the Spurs won the 1999 NBA Finals against the New York Knicks.

While Duncan won the Finals MVP Award, he and his teammates understood that Robinson's willingness to cede the role of "go-to" scorer to his young teammate, right from the start of Duncan's career, had been a show of selflessness and leadership that could not be overstated.

Robinson had no problem giving way to the budding superstar who played beside him.

"Whatever it takes to make this team better, that's what we have to do," Robinson had said when the issue of Duncan's taking over as primary scorer was raised during Duncan's rookie season. "You've got to put your ego aside. I don't care. If we're better with him scoring down the stretch, I have no problem with that at all. If we get the wins, I go home with a smile on my face."

Injuries, including repeated bouts with back spasms, plagued Robinson in his final five seasons and he announced before the 2002–03 season that it would be his last. At age 37 he would go out in a blaze of glory, scoring 13 points and grabbing 17 rebounds in an 88–77 Game 6 NBA Finals victory that sent him off to retirement with a second NBA championship.

Robinson ranks first in franchise history in blocked shots (2,954), free throws made (6,035) and attempted (8,201), and steals (1,388). He is third in points scored (20,790) and seventh in assists (2,441).

Robinson remained in San Antonio after retirement and focused his attention on Carver Academy, a nonprofit private school he funded and opened in 2001 to provide opportunities for inner-city children. A role model for all NBA players, Robinson's name is attached to the NBA's annual Community Assist Award.

Named one of the 50 greatest players in NBA history as part of the NBA at 50 celebration in 1997, Robinson was elected to the Naismith Memorial Basketball Hall of Fame, inducted in 2009. He was inducted a second time, in 2010, as a member of the 1992 U.S. Olympic "Dream Team."

A three-time member of U.S. Olympic teams, he won two gold medals (1992 and 1996) and a bronze medal (1988) and has been inducted in the U.S. Olympic Hall of Fame.

The Spurs retired his No. 50 in 2003.

Robinson joined the Spurs ownership group in 2004 and regularly attends Spurs games, sitting in the second row, opposite the team bench.

4 Gregg Popovich

Nobody could have known that Gregg Popovich's addition to new Spurs coach Larry Brown's staff in 1988 ultimately would lead to one of the most successful head coaching careers in NBA history.

Since assuming command of the Spurs bench on December 10, 1996, Popovich has amassed 1,089 wins, coached the Spurs to five championships, and been named Coach of the Year three times. His win total going into the 2015–16 season ranked ninth all time, just 20 behind Rick Adelman, who retired from coaching after the 2013–14 season.

Popovich's regular-season winning percentage, 68.5 percent through the 2014–15 season, ranks third all time among those who have coached at least 500 games, trailing only Phil Jackson (70.4) and Billy Cunningham (69.8). His playoff winning percentage,

61.8, is fifth all time, behind only Jackson, Butch Van Breda Kolff, John Kundla, and Cunningham.

Not bad for a guy who insists he would have been blissfully happy making a lifelong career of coaching Pomona-Pitzer, an NCAA Division III team that combines two of the five colleges comprising the Claremont Colleges, located on a one-square-mile campus between Los Angeles and San Bernardino in Claremont, California, and self-described as "reminiscent of the Oxford-Cambridge model."

A 1970 graduate of the U.S. Air Force Academy, Popovich had landed at Pomona-Pitzer in 1979 after resigning his commission as an officer in the U.S. Air Force and then serving as an assistant coach at the Air Force Academy under Hank Egan.

Don't doubt Popovich's assertion that he could have been happy staying at Pomona-Pitzer. He loved the academic life and the free thinking that characterized the Claremont Colleges experience. There were no scholarships for players, who had to meet the rigorous academic standards of the schools. It was a pure athletic endeavor he appreciated but he coached his teams with the same intensity and demands that has characterized his career with the Spurs.

At Pomona-Pitzer, Popovich was an active member of the academic community, working as an associate professor, chairing the college's student life committee, serving on the women's commission, and even living in a dorm with his family for one year.

It was the opportunity in 1986 to take an academic sabbatical—a paid year away from campus to explore other academic pursuits—that changed Popovich's career path. He began his sabbatical by heading to Chapel Hill, North Carolina, to explore the coaching methods that had made Dean Smith one of college basketball's most successful coaches. He ended it by spending a season as an unpaid assistant on Brown's coaching staff at the University of Kansas.

Brown recognized Popovich's people skills and coaching acumen and knew there would come a day when he would try to lure him away from Pomona-Pitzer.

"We spent so much time together and there was a lot of exchange of ideas and it was easy to see he has qualities that make him special," Brown said. "My whole thing is I can teach anybody all the basketball I was taught but you can't teach loyalty. I always tell guys I can't teach them to love me, so if they care about me that's really important. I just loved him as a person. I respected his knowledge, obviously, but he's also one of the most decent, loyal guys I've ever been around and I just wanted to be connected."

After Brown coached the Jayhawks to the 1988 NCAA championship, Spurs owner Red McCombs lured him to San Antonio to coach the Spurs. Brown brought with him from Kansas assistant coaches Ed Manning, Alvin Gentry, and R.C. Buford. Then he told McCombs he wanted a fourth assistant: Popovich. McCombs gave him the green light and Brown made a call to Pomona-Pitzer and talked Popovich into joining his staff.

Brown's tenure in San Antonio lasted only three and a half seasons. He was dismissed 38 games into his fourth season, with GM Bob Bass taking over on the bench with Brown's assistants, including Popovich, still in place. After the 1991–92 season, Popovich departed San Antonio for a job as an assistant on Don Nelson's Golden State Warriors staff. He spent two seasons under "Nellie," where he gained an appreciation for Nelson's "out of the box" thinking.

On May 13, 1994, Spurs chairman Robert McDermott, who had been permanent Dean of Faculty at the Air Force Academy and knew Popovich from his four years at USAFA, brought him back to the Spurs as executive vice president of basketball operations and general manager.

The Spurs went 121–43 under head coach Bob Hill in the 1994–95 and 1995–96 seasons but with Robinson out with back spasms at the start of the 1996–97 season, the Spurs got off to a 3–15 start. On December 9, 1996, Popovich, in his capacity as GM, fired Hill and took over as head coach.

Criticized roundly for timing the move just as Robinson was to return to the lineup, Popovich endured the critics and then suffered through a rough season of his own when Robinson's return lasted only six games before he suffered a broken left foot. The Spurs won only 17 of 64 games under Popovich but the payoff turned out to be a spot in the NBA draft lottery that ultimately landed the No. 1 overall pick, Tim Duncan.

Gregg Popovich, seen here with Spurs chairman Peter Holt, has presided over one of the true dynasties in modern sports since becoming San Antonio's head coach in 1996.

With Duncan and Robinson as his team's anchors, Popovich coached the Spurs to championships in 1999 and 2003. The Admiral retired after the 2003 Finals, but there were two more championships soon after, in 2005 and 2007.

After significant rules changes turned the NBA into a more perimeter-oriented, fast-paced league, Popovich adapted his offense and got the Spurs back to the Finals in 2013 and 2014, when they won a fifth championship behind an offensive approach that came to be called "the beautiful game."

Popovich ended his dual role as head coach and general manager in the summer of 2002, turning over the basketball operations department to R.C. Buford, whom he had brought back to San Antonio in 1994 as the team's head scout. However, he retained a title as president of Spurs basketball and remains the final voice in most basketball decisions.

Popovich's record since Duncan's arrival is 1,072–438, a winning percentage of 70.9. He was named Coach of the Year in 2002–03, 2011–12, and 2013–14.

5 Breaking Through

It seems hard to imagine, but Gregg Popovich was in danger of being fired as Spurs head coach early in the season that produced the Spurs' first championship.

A stalemate in collective bargaining talks between the NBA and its players' union had produced a lockout that delayed the start of the season until February and shortened it from 82 to 50 games. The Spurs won their first two games but dropped eight of the next 12. With a two-game road trip to Houston and Dallas on the

Victory Parties

About 20,000 fans greeted the Spurs at San Antonio International Airport on their arrival the day after the victory at Madison Square Garden that clinched the 1999 NBA title. A day later, an estimated 230,000 fans turned out for a parade along the San Antonio River.

Approximately 40,000 fans later filled the Alamodome when the championship was toasted. Avery Johnson introduced each player with the fervor of a revival preacher and had the crowd in the palm of his hand.

schedule, Spurs fans were restless and there was talk that losses in those two might prompt the ownership group to demand a coaching change.

"Yes, the fans were upset about our lack of production in that lockout season but we were able to weather that storm," recalled point guard Avery Johnson. "We just weren't going to let Pop get fired. That just wasn't going to happen. I was prepared to quit if he got fired—he meant that much to me."

The Spurs followed their halting start by winning nine straight to calm the doubters, finishing the season with the league's best record, 37–13. They followed with a playoff run that produced the first of the five championships they would win under Popovich, and it was Johnson who hit the championship-clinching shot in Game 5 of the NBA Finals against the Knicks at Madison Square Garden.

"He was a great example to me, especially when I became a head coach, that when life deals you a bad situation, keep your composure, keep your character, and be true to yourself," said Johnson, who would go on to become head coach of the Dallas Mavericks and the New Jersey/Brooklyn Nets and then move to the college ranks as head coach at the University of Alabama. "That is one of his greatest attributes."

The Spurs closed out the season by winning 19 of their final 22 games, heading into the playoffs with home-court advantage assured throughout. They would not need the additional edge, closing out all four of their playoff series on the road—at Minnesota (3–1), the Lakers (4–0), Portland (4–0), and New York (4–1).

The Spurs went into their first NBA Finals on a high note, sweeping the Portland Trail Blazers in a Western Conference Finals series that included forward Sean Elliott's amazing "Memorial Day Miracle" shot, a three-pointer that completed a comeback from 18 points down in the second half and gave them an 86–85 Game 2 win that preserved home-court advantage.

The 1999 NBA Finals against the Knicks suffered from the absence of Knicks center Patrick Ewing, who sustained a partial tear of his left Achilles tendon during the Eastern Conference Finals. Nevertheless, it was a matchup that featured some of the best big men in the game: Duncan, Robinson, and the Knicks' Larry Johnson and Marcus Camby.

In the end it was Johnson, the 5-foot-10 point guard, who hit the championship-clinching basket in Game 5 at Madison Square Garden, an 18-footer from the left corner.

"That's my shot," Johnson said. "I love corner shots. My teammates believe in me, Pop believes in me, and the Lord Jesus believes in me, and that gives me a lot of confidence."

The Spurs' defensive excellence, with Robinson and Duncan dominating the interior, was on display throughout the playoffs. They gave up more than 89 points in only two of 18 playoff games, and one of those was in a 118–107 close-out win over the Lakers in the Western Conference semifinals. In the NBA Finals they allowed the Knicks an average of just 80 points per game.

The interior defensive tandem of Robinson and Duncan dominated, averaging 5.2 blocks per game in the Finals. It was a vindication of Robinson's career, a first championship after the frustration of seven disappointing playoffs, including being outplayed by Hakeem Olajuwon in the Western Conference Finals in his MVP season of 1994–95.

"David Robinson has been taking a lot of flak throughout his career," gritty shooting guard Mario Elie said after Game 5. "I told him, 'Dave, you just shut everybody up.' I'm glad the good guys finally got one."

Popovich, a championship coach in just his third season, didn't know quite what to say.

"It's kind of stunning," he said. "You wonder if it's really true. You wonder what you're doing here. I just feel real grateful."

Duncan was named Finals MVP after averaging 27.4 points, 14.0 rebounds, and 2.2 blocked shots per game.

Backup guard Steve Kerr became just the 11th player in league history to win four consecutive titles, having won three in a row as a member of the 1996, 1997, and 1998 Chicago Bulls.

The Iceman

Long before the arrival of David Robinson or Tim Duncan, the Spurs had a superstar.

Nicknamed "The Iceman," or simply "Ice," George Gervin came to the team midway through its first season in San Antonio, filling the need for a star presence that was especially important to primary owners Red McCombs and Angelo Drossos. They acquired him from the financially floundering Virginia Squires for $225,000 cash.

"From the Yankees on down, the teams that make it work have a star or more than one star," McCombs said, "so we had to get Gervin. This is an entertainment business and you've got to have stars."

Getting Gervin wasn't as easy as it initially seemed. Squires owner Earl Foreman already had traded Julius Erving to the New York Nets for money. To keep the Squires from destroying their fan appeal, ABA commissioner Mike Storen tried to block the Gervin deal.

Undeterred, Drossos and McCombs flew Gervin to San Antonio, stashed him in a hotel not far from the Alamo with orders not to leave his room, and sued Storen and the ABA.

The fact Drossos managed to have the case heard in San Antonio before a judge who was a personal friend was no coincidence. Lo and behold, the judge ruled in the Spurs' favor and the Iceman era was free to begin.

Joining the team in mid-January of the 1973–74 season, the Iceman became the team's first superstar, winning four NBA scoring titles and helping engender the love affair between the city and the Spurs that continues today.

Spurs fans immediately embraced Gervin's game but it took a while for him to warm up to San Antonio. Unsure about living in a community with a small African American populace, Gervin eventually was won over by the passion of fans who turned out to watch him and his teammates play at HemisFair Arena.

"I didn't know what kind of relationship I would have with the city," he said. "Once I started playing—once I got out of that hotel—I was able to see the city and then put on a Spurs uniform and be around as many fans as we had coming to the arena. The relationship was starting to grow on me because they had that passion. They showed that they loved the team."

"We all talk about how the fans love the team today," Gervin said in an interview conducted for the *San Antonio Express-News* in 2015. "Well, they loved it yesterday, too. That was the beauty of it."

George Gervin, popularly known as "The Iceman," was the first superstar in franchise history.

The beauty of Gervin's game was one of the most effortless jump shots in basketball history and, of course, the finger roll, which he called "my patented shot."

Combining speed and athleticism with an amazing basketball IQ, Gervin produced offensive statistics for the ages:

- 26,595 points, 16th on the all-time NBA-ABA list
- 23,602 points as a Spur (ABA-NBA), second only to Tim Duncan
- 26.2 points per game NBA career scoring average, ninth all time

Famous Spurs Nicknames

There have been a lot of colorful nicknames for Spurs players over the team's long history and many of them are universally recognized. Is there a basketball fan alive that doesn't know that George Gervin is "The Iceman" or David Robinson "The Admiral"?

There are many more Spurs nicknames, some of which are nearly as recognizable as those two:

The Big Fundamental (Tim Duncan); Dr. K (Larry Kenon); Captain Late (James Silas); The Little General (Avery Johnson); Big Shot Rob (Robert Horry); El Contusion (Manu Ginobili); The Whopper (Billy Paultz); The A-Train (Artis Gilmore); Cadillac (Greg Anderson); Slo-Mo (Kyle Anderson); Bobo (Boris Diaw); Bones (Brent Barry); The Bruise Brothers (Dave Corzine, George T. Johnson, Mark Olberding, Kevin Restani, Reggie Johnson, and Paul Griffin); The Claw (Kawhi Leonard); The Rifleman (Chuck Person); The Red Rocket and Red Mamba (Matt Bonner); Flipper (Mike Gale); Big Bird (Kevin Restani); Tinkerbell (Gene Banks); The Truth (Walter Berry); Brick (Frank Brickowski); Pooh (Johnny Dawkins); Mad Max (Vernon Maxwell); Pops (Caldwell Jones); Hot Rod (Rod Strickland); Doc (Glenn Rivers); Sweet Pea (Lloyd Daniels); Mr. Mean (Larry Smith); Sleepy (Eric Floyd); Amigo (Carl Herrera); Nique (Dominique Wilkins); Speedy (Craig Claxton); Nick the Quick (Nick Van Exel); and Dice (Antonio McDyess).

- The three highest single-season scoring averages in Spurs history: 33.1 (1979–80); 32.3 (1981–82); 29.6 (1978–79)
- Career shooting percentage of 50.9, remarkable for a perimeter player

It was after Spurs general manager Bob Bass hired Doug Moe to coach the Spurs into the NBA in 1976–77 that Gervin's scoring prowess really came to the fore. Moe wanted the fastest offense in basketball—his benchmark for offensive pace was a minimum of 100 shots per game—and recognized Gervin's unique ability within his offensive system.

"He moved so easily and could take it to the hoop," Moe said. "Just an ability that certain players have to get themselves open and then he could shoot it. He just had that great, great touch and ability to get his shots off."

Gervin recognized instantly that Moe's system was perfect for his game.

"He helped make me who I was because of his style of play and he trusted me with the basketball," he said.

Gervin's production began to slide after he turned 31 in 1983, his scoring average dropping by 11.1 points per game from 1981–82 to 1984–85. The Spurs traded him to the Chicago Bulls in exchange for forward David Greenwood a week before the start of the 1985–86 season.

Gervin, who continues to work for the Spurs as a community relations representative, became the first Spur elected to the Naismith Memorial Basketball Hall of Fame, entering in 1996.

His No. 44 jersey was retired in 1987.

7 Duncan's Dominant 2003

The three seasons that followed the Spurs' first championship in 1999 were frustrating. Tim Duncan missed the 2000 playoffs after suffering a left knee injury in mid-April and the Spurs were eliminated in the first round. They followed that season by running up the NBA's best record in 2000–01, only to be swept, in embarrassing fashion, by the Lakers in the Western Conference Finals. Duncan won the regular season MVP Award in 2001–02 but the playoffs ended with another Western Conference semifinals loss to the Lakers.

Things were different right from the start of the 2002–03 season. The Spurs moved from the multi-purpose Alamodome into a new home, then called the SBC Center, a basketball-first arena. They also added Argentine rookie Manu Ginobili, a second-round draft pick from 1999, the MVP of the Italian League. Duncan became a back-to-back MVP, averaging 23.3 points, 12.9 rebounds, and 2.9 blocked shots per game, and the Spurs earned home-court advantage throughout the playoffs with a record of 60–22.

Just before the start of the season, Robinson, who had turned 37, announced his intent to retire at its conclusion. He had played through back spasms and assorted nagging injuries for several seasons but had missed only 18 games since the 1996–97 season, when he played only six games before suffering a broken left foot.

Wanting to limit Robinson's playing time to keep him as healthy as possible for the playoffs, Spurs coach and GM Gregg Popovich signed 18-year NBA veteran Kevin Willis to fill a backup role. The 40-year-old 7-footer became a valuable reserve, playing in 71 regular-season games. Robinson's playing time was cut to just 26.2 minutes per game and 64 games played.

The playoffs began with a jolt, as the Suns stole home-court advantage in Game 1 of the first round when Stephon Marbury banked in a long three-point shot that beat the overtime buzzer. With the Spurs ahead 95–93, Duncan had missed two free throws with 5.1 seconds left to open the door for Marbury's winner.

Outplayed by Marbury in Games 1 and 2, 20-year-old point guard Tony Parker dominated Marbury in Game 3 in Phoenix, scoring 29 points as the Spurs regained home-court advantage. They closed out the Suns in Game 6 in Phoenix to set up another matchup with the Lakers.

It was a home-court series until Game 6. Ahead in the series 3–2, the Spurs, especially Duncan, dominated. The regular-season MVP made 16-of-25 shots, scored 37 points, and grabbed 16 rebounds, dominating Lakers center Shaquille O'Neal. The Spurs won the most lopsided game of the series, 110–82.

Awaiting the Spurs in the Western Conference Finals were the Dallas Mavericks, who had matched their regular-season record of 60–22. The two teams had tied in head-to-head competition so

What Could Have Been

When New Jersey Nets point guard Jason Kidd, widely regarded as the NBA's best through much of his playing career, became a free agent a few weeks after the Spurs defeated his Nets in the 2003 NBA Finals, the Spurs made a hard run at signing Kidd.

While there was widespread speculation the Spurs would jettison Tony Parker if Kidd agreed to come to San Antonio, Gregg Popovich has made it clear he had no intention of trading his young French point guard. Instead, he has said, his intent was to play both Kidd and Parker at the same time, a prospect that many believe could have produced even more titles for the Spurs.

After he became head coach of the Milwaukee Bucks in 2014, Kidd admitted that every time he has walked into AT&T Center since spurning the Spurs' offer to re-sign with New Jersey, he wonders about what might have been had he opted to become a Spur.

home-court advantage had gone to the Spurs because of their better record within the Western Conference. The Mavericks stole it back by winning Game 1 but the Spurs won the next three games before dropping yet another game on their court in Game 5.

When Tony Parker turned up ailing with stomach problems before Game 6—some bad crème brûlée was blamed—the Spurs struggled in Game 6 in Dallas. They trailed by as many as 15 points in the third period and were down 71–58 with just 10:53 left in the game. But Stephen Jackson got hot from behind the three-point line and 37-year-old Steve Kerr made three long-range shots as the Spurs scored 23 unanswered points to secure a 90–78 win and a spot in the Finals. Jackson finished with a career playoff high of 24 points.

"I couldn't remember the last time I played," Kerr said afterward. "It's been a long time but tonight Tony was sick and the team needed me."

The opponent in the 2003 NBA Finals was making its second straight trip to the championship round. Led by All-NBA point guard Jason Kidd, the New Jersey Nets were intent on atoning for their loss to the Lakers in the 2002 NBA Finals.

The teams split the first two games in San Antonio and the next two in New Jersey before Duncan dominated Game 5, when he scored 29 points and grabbed 17 rebounds, abusing Nets power forward Kenyon Martin in a 93–83 Spurs win.

Duncan next put together one of the greatest close-out performances in NBA Finals history, barely missing the first quadruple-double in Finals history. He scored 21 points, grabbed 20 rebounds, handed out 10 assists, and blocked eight Nets shots.

When it came time for presentation of the Larry O'Brien Trophy, it first was handed to Robinson, whose 13 points and 17 rebounds represented his best game of the entire postseason run, and the final game of his stellar career.

Manu Ginobili

Spurs general manager R.C. Buford still recalls seeing Manu Ginobili for the very first time. Scouting the FIBA Under-22 World Championships in Australia in 1999, he was impressed by several members of the Argentine team. Ginobili, though, was little more than an afterthought and Buford isn't sure why he included him on a list of players to keep track of. His first take on the skinny swing man from Bahia Blanca included the observation that he "couldn't guard anyone" and that his 0-of-8 shooting (including 0-of-6 from three-point range) in the bronze medal game hinted of a streakiness that might make him a big risk in the NBA.

Nonetheless, there was something about Ginobili's competitiveness and aggression that intrigued Buford.

"I wish I could tell you I knew Manu would be what he turned out to be," Buford told *San Antonio Express-News* beat writer Johnny Ludden years later, "but the less you know about a player the more you can dream. With international players you're dreaming on guys with size and skills that a lot of players with size from the U.S. don't have."

Buford's conflicted conviction about Ginobili's potential manifested when he waited all the way to the team's second selection in the second round of the 1999 draft (No. 57 overall) before selecting the Argentine dynamo. He also acquired Croatian swing man Gordan Giricek in a deal with the Dallas Mavericks.

Ginobili nearly got passed over at No. 57, too. Buford admits he strongly considered his Argentine teammate, point guard Lucas Victoriano. Fearing he could never convince Popovich to take an international point guard, he used the pick on Ginobili.

Several million Argentines and at least an equal number of Spurs fans forever are grateful he did because Ginobili turned out to be one of the team's all-time greats and one of its most popular players. Certainly he is the most popular player among the Hispanic population of San Antonio, the largest city in the United States with a majority Hispanic population (59.5 percent according to the 2010 United States census).

After drafting Ginobili the Spurs observed the development of his game as a star for Kinder Bologna of the Italian League, where he played for eventual Spurs assistant coach Ettore Messina.

The Spurs signed Ginobili in July 2002, and Popovich got a hint of what he could be as an NBA player during the 2002 FIBA World Championships in Indianapolis. An assistant coach for Team USA, Popovich sat alone in near-empty stands at Conseco Fieldhouse for an early morning game between Argentina and Russia and tried to suppress the smile on his face as Ginobili dominated, end to end.

"I think we may have found a player," he said to a friend afterward.

What Popovich and the Spurs found was a player who knew only one way to play: attack mode from start to finish. He was an athletic slasher able to finish at the rim. He paired his drives with a good three-point shot that got better in the clutch, a combination that made him a nightmare to defend.

As a facilitator, he never met an easy pass he could not convert to a work of basketball art. He threw passes behind his back, between opponents' legs, and on the bounce from half a court away. He introduced NBA fans to the Euro-step, though it took several seasons before NBA referees adjusted to the fact the move was not, in fact, a travel.

The verve with which he played was infectious. He was part Maradona, part El Cordobes, 100 percent Ginobili.

Popovich would have to wait a while to put Ginobili to use as a rookie because he suffered a severe ankle sprain in Argentina's semifinal victory over Dirk Nowitzki and his German team. Able to play just a few halting minutes in Argentina's overtime loss to Yugoslavia in the gold medal game, Ginobili came to Spurs training camp still suffering the effects of the sprain. He missed most of the first month of his rookie season.

Manu Ginobili developed into one of the NBA's most unlikely stars after being drafted by the Spurs with the 57th pick in the 1999 NBA draft.

By playoff time, though, Ginobili had become a key reserve for the 2002–03 champion Spurs. He played in all 24 playoff games, averaging 9.4 points, 3.8 rebounds, and 2.9 assists per game.

When Stephen Jackson, the starter at shooting guard through most of the season and all 24 playoff games, bolted the Spurs in a contract dispute after the 2003 title run, Ginobili's role became more prominent. By the end of the 2003–04 season he had become a starter and was named to the All-Star team in 2004–05, when he averaged 16.0 points per game. He made an even bigger impact in the run to the 2005 NBA title, averaging 20.8 points per game and coming within one vote of being named MVP of the 2005 Finals.

Popovich began fiddling with Ginobili's role during that playoff run, bringing him off the bench in eight games as a "change of pace." In the playoff run to the 2007 championship, Ginobili came off the bench in all 20 postseason games and he continued in a "sixth man" role the following season, when he averaged 19.5 points per game and earned the NBA's Sixth Man Award.

Both Popovich and Ginobili understood Ginobili was a bench player in name only, and Popovich joked that his ultra-competitive guard probably had a very insulting place where he wished he could put the Sixth Man Award after it was presented to him.

Ginobili's competitive intensity and pedal-to-the-metal style led to many injuries and teammate Brent Barry gave him an appropriate but linguistically tortured nickname: El Contusion (pronounced Cone-TOOZ-ee-own). In the lockout-shortened 2011–12 season he missed 32 of 66 games with a variety of injuries, including a fractured right hand. Heading into the 2016–17 season, at age 39, he had missed 22, 14, 12, and 24 games in the previous four seasons.

Amazingly, Ginobili played the five games of the 2014 NBA Finals with a stress fracture in his right leg, which kept him from playing for Argentina in the 2014 FIBA World Cup tournament in Spain.

Ginobili's play for his native country has been equally as important as his role with the Spurs and he is considered one of the greatest international players in basketball history. He earned a gold medal at the 2004 Olympics, a bronze medal at the 2008 Beijing Games, and a silver medal at the 2002 FIBA World Championships. He participated in his fourth Olympic tournament in Rio de Janeiro in 2016.

9 Tony Parker

The first time Gregg Popovich saw Tony Parker with his own eyes, he was not impressed.

The Spurs had arranged a private workout with Parker in Chicago, where the 19-year-old point guard, a professional since age 15 for Paris Basket Racing, often spent summers with relatives. This time, however, he flew to the Windy City from France, with a change of planes, and went directly to the workout from O'Hare International Airport.

Waiting to compete against Parker in the workout was 34-year-old Lance Blanks, a Spurs front office employee eight years removed from a three-year NBA career but still in terrific physical condition, at 6-foot-4 and 190 pounds.

By all accounts, Blanks dominated the workout, embarrassing Parker in the process.

Afterward, Popovich minced no words in assessing the workout for Parker and his agent.

"I told both of them that he's too soft and I'm looking for someone with more fiber and grit," Popovich recalled in a 2013 interview with Jan Hubbard, author of *The History of The Spurs.*

Worse than his performance against Blanks was Parker's casual acceptance of Popovich's criticism.

"He was nonchalant, like he was in a cafe outside Montmartre in Paris having a glass of wine and a croissant. It didn't seem to matter to him any more than that," Pop said.

Popovich returned to San Antonio believing his team's search for its next Avery Johnson would have to focus elsewhere.

But Parker had fans in the Spurs basketball operations department; chief among them was the most recent hire. Sam Presti, all of 24 years old, had worked as an intern for general manager R.C. Buford the previous season and then been hired as a scout. He had studied hours of video of Parker and had seen him at the 2000 Nike Hoop Summit tournament. He was convinced that he would be perfect for Popovich's offense and had the potential to be a star.

When Popovich rattled off all the reasons Parker was wrong for the Spurs after the Chicago workout, Presti put together a videotape of Parker that refuted, one by one, each of Popovich's concerns.

Popovich agreed to give Parker a second chance, this time in San Antonio. Rested this time, Parker had a brilliant workout and Popovich was won over totally.

Parker, he told the entire basketball operations staff, would need no more than 10 games as a rookie before he would be starting for whichever team was fortunate to get him.

On draft night, however, each team that seemed primed to pick Parker passed on him. The Spurs made him the final pick (28th overall) of the first round of the 2001 draft and quickly made Presti look so good that Popovich began calling him the Spurs' "boy genius." In fact, it didn't take Parker 10 games to move into Popovich's starting lineup. He was on the court for an opening tip in the fifth game of his rookie season and has been the team's starter and one of its key players for 14 seasons.

A six-time All-Star and four-time All-NBA selection, Parker has been a key contributor on four of the Spurs' five championship teams. He was named MVP of the 2007 NBA Finals, when he made 42-of-74 shots (56.8 percent) and averaged 24.5 points per game and led the Spurs to a 4–0 Finals sweep of LeBron James and the Cleveland Cavaliers.

Parker came into the league as one of the fastest players ever to suit up in the NBA but he was hardly a polished point guard. Finally convinced that Parker had the desire to be great, Popovich challenged him to learn the nuances of playing the position and rode him hard. Parker accepted Popovich's "tough love" coaching and improved, season by season.

Far from a natural perimeter shooter, Parker re-made his shot under the instruction of Spurs shooting coach Chip Engelland, considered one of the game's best "shot doctors." After making only 41.9 percent of his shots as a 19-year-old rookie, he has had five seasons in which he shot better than 50 percent (and one at 49.9 percent) and has a career shooting percentage of 49.4.

Still, the essence of Parker's offensive game is penetrating into the painted area and creating shots for himself and others. Through most of his career he has ranked among the NBA leaders in points in the paint, a category traditionally dominated by centers and power forwards. His most productive season came in 2012–13, when he made a career-high 52.2 percent of his shots and averaged a career-high 20.3 points while handing out 7.6 assists per game.

Heading into the 2016–17 season Parker ranks as the all-time Spurs assist leader (6,349). He ranks second in Spurs history in games played (1,080), fourth in points scored (17,884), and seventh in steals (970).

Born in Bruges, Belgium, Parker was raised in Paris, where his father, Tony Parker Sr., a European professional player who had played at Loyola of Chicago, made sure he had a basketball in his hands as soon as he could walk.

"I was two," Parker recalled. "My dad played basketball so I was following him everywhere, trying to do the same moves and everything."

Just as important to Parker's basketball development were summers spent in Chicago at the home of his father's parents. There Parker learned that if you wanted to fit in on the playground, it was a good idea to wear a No. 23 Michael Jordan jersey.

Parker vividly recalls the 1991 NBA Finals, which he watched in his grandparents' living room. He declared: "I'm going to play in the NBA some day."

His childhood boast came true and he even matched Jordan's accomplishment of being named MVP of an NBA Finals.

Parker also has been the driving force behind the French national team as it has become one of the top teams in international competition. In 2013 he was MVP of the Eurobasket tournament in which France defeated archrival Spain for the first time (in the semifinals) and claimed its first Eurobasket championship. He also was named FIBA's European Player of the Year for 2013.

10 The Big Three

After including Tim Duncan, Manu Ginobili, and Tony Parker among the top nine things Spurs fans need to know, it might seem redundant to make "The Big Three" No. 10.

Au contraire!

What the Spurs' Big Three have done has made them the greatest trio of teammates in NBA history, and that deserves its own mention.

The Spurs' "Big Three"—Manu Ginobili, Tony Parker, and Tim Duncan—are the winningest trio of teammates in NBA history.

There have been plenty of dominant trios since the NBA began in 1946–47, beginning with Bill Russell, Bob Cousy, and Bill Sharman, the three stars who led the Celtics to four titles in five seasons, from 1957–61, and continuing in Boston with the trio of Russell, Tom Heinsohn, and John Havlicek. In the 1980s, the Lakers (Kareem Abdul-Jabbar, Magic Johnson, and James Worthy) and Celtics (Larry Bird, Kevin McHale, and Robert Parish) trios ruled, as did the Michael Jordan-Scottie Pippen-Horace Grant Bulls of the 1990s and, for a brief run, the much-trumpeted Miami threesome of LeBron James, Dwyane Wade, and Chris Bosh.

But no three players ever enjoyed as much success together as the Spurs' Big Three. Following the 2015–16 season, the three Spurs have played more games together (730) than any trio in league history and surpassed Bird, McHale, and Parish as the winningest trio (575). They have been together in five NBA Finals and won four of them. Their playoff win total together (126) also is an NBA record. At various times all three have been All-Stars and members of the All-NBA team and all three likely are destined for the Naismith Memorial Basketball Hall of Fame after retirement. And they have played the entirety of their individual careers for the Spurs.

Just before the start of the 2011–12 NBA season, Jeff McDonald, Spurs beat writer for the *San Antonio Express-News*, and I sat down at the Four Seasons Hotel in Houston for an interview with the Big Three. The Q&A ran in the newspaper under a headline that, four years later, is laughable: SPURS BIG THREE: THE LAST RIDE.

Here are excerpts from that Q&A session that describe the relationships that helped make them the best teammate trio in basketball history:

Duncan, asked to recall his first thoughts about Tony Parker, who joined the team in 2001: "I think it's pretty well documented that I wasn't too sure about what to expect from him. With his age, with his inexperience, with his lack of knowledge of the language...all those things went into it."

Duncan, on his first impressions of Ginobili, who joined the Spurs in 2002: "I think it was the same thing, on a different level with him. With French Boy, it was about him being, whatever, 13 years old and asking him to start for a team that's been doing pretty good. With Crazy Boy, it was just getting used to playing with someone like that, taking some of the shots that he does.... I think luckily we went through a process with him on the practice squad where Bruce (Bowen) just beat the crap out of him for a couple of weeks. We learned to respect him along those lines before we ever had to play with him on the floor."

Ginobili, on adjusting to playing alongside Duncan: "It took me three or four months to even understand what he was saying. I was from overseas. I couldn't understand anybody. When I got here, I was trying to understand what he wanted, and how to make him be comfortable around me. That was a big key for me to get on the court. I knew I had to convince him that I was good, and could help him win."

Parker, on his adjustment to playing alongside Duncan: "For me, he didn't talk to me for the whole first year (laughing). It was kind of tough at first, because you want to earn his respect. He was our franchise. It was hard at the beginning, because he doesn't talk. I would have Pop scream at me and tell me to go talk to TD, and I didn't want to. I was scared of TD. He always looked like he was mad. As the years went by, it got better."

Ginobili, on winning a championship in his very first season with the Spurs: "My first year, I was too new. I didn't know how hard it was. I had come from winning in Europe, and winning championships with the (Argentine) national team. I came here and we won, and I said, 'Oh. Good.' I really started learning how hard it was with the next two."

Duncan, on the transition to the Big Three Era that began after David Robinson retired following the 2003 championship run: "I was thinking if we can get better players than this, it would be easier next time. It's fun to think about it, winning in '99, and '03, and '05, and '07. I remember in '05 (against Detroit), any one of us could have won the MVP that year. We all played pretty well that series. It's fun to think about what level everyone was playing on to win those championships."

Parker, on where the Big Three should rank among the league's greatest trios: "Yeah, that's a great question, because I'm watching the game last night (Miami's Big Three had played its preseason opener the night before) and it shows all the best Big Threes—Chicago, Boston, the Lakers. After that, there's a hole and it goes straight to Miami. I don't know why they never put us on that list. It's not like it's going to bother me, because I have the rings and I'll sleep well at night. But they just don't want to put us up there. I always said if we did what we did in New York we'd be gods right now."

11 The 2005 NBA Championship

It took seven grinding NBA Finals games and one amazing, game-winning three-point shot for the Spurs to secure the franchise's third NBA championship.

All the hard work made it especially satisfying.

The victory over the defending champion Detroit Pistons required a second-half comeback in Game 7, an amazing three-point shooting display by "Big Shot Rob" Horry in Game 5, lock-down Game 7 defense by Bruce Bowen on Pistons star Chauncey Billups, some electric performances by Manu Ginobili, Tim Duncan's typically clutch play, and a hilarious, tension-relieving film clip that lightened the mood after back-to-back disheartening losses in Michigan.

Just getting to the Finals was an interesting journey. The previous season's playoff run had ended in the Western Conference semifinals, forever remembered for Lakers guard Derek Fisher's three-point shot that won Game 5 at AT&T Center on a play triggered with four-tenths of a second remaining.

The Spurs tweaked the roster in the off-season, signing free agents Brent Barry, a long-range shooting guard-forward, and veteran big man Tony Massenburg, and drafting Croatian point guard Beno Udrih. Then, at the February trade deadline, they dealt forward-center Malik Rose, a fan favorite and Tim Duncan's favorite teammate, along with two future first-round picks, to the New York Knicks for center Nazr Muhammad.

The deal outraged most Spurs fans who adored Rose's work ethic and his bubbly personality. Dozens of them showed up to "protest" at the Philly cheesesteak restaurant Rose had opened in the Quarry Market shopping center.

In the end, the Rose-aholics got over their pique when Muhammad replaced Rasho Nesterovic in the Spurs' starting lineup for the playoffs and put up solid numbers throughout the grind to the team's third title.

The regular season produced the second-best record in the league, 59–23, with a franchise-best 38–3 record at home. Tim Duncan and Bruce Bowen became the first teammates named to the NBA's All-Defensive first team since Michael Jordan and Scottie Pippen (1997–98) as the Spurs allowed just 88.4 points per game, a league low.

Duncan and Ginobili made the Western Conference All-Star team and Gregg Popovich coached the Western All-Stars for the first time in his career.

Still, it took the Spurs a while to adjust after the Rose-for-Muhammad trade. They finished the season losing nine of their last 11 road games, so when they dropped Game 1 of their first-round series to the Denver Nuggets at AT&T Center—their first home loss in more than five weeks—the loss of home-court advantage seemed especially troubling.

Popovich responded with a lineup change that altered the series. Barry replaced Ginobili in the starting lineup and the Nuggets did not know how to adjust. Barry responded by making all four of his three-point attempts and scoring 16 points, and Ginobili scored 17 off the bench.

The Spurs then regained the home-court edge when Ginobili exploded for 32 points in a Game 3 win in Denver. They secured a 3–1 edge with an overtime win in Game 4 that featured 11 points from Tony Parker in the extra period.

The second-round matchup against the Seattle SuperSonics was a home-court series until the Spurs broke through at Seattle's Key Arena. Tim Duncan, a 67 percent free-thrower during the regular season, made 14-of-17 foul shots and scored 26 points in the close-out game.

The Western Conference Finals pitted the Spurs against a Phoenix Suns team that had electrified the league with Mike D'Antoni's "seven seconds or less" offense that averaged an NBA-best 110.4 points per game and produced a 62–20 record, the league's best. Point guard Steve Nash, the league leader in assists (11.5 per game) ran the offense and was named league MVP. Big man Amar'e Stoudemire averaged 26.0 points per game and was an All-NBA second team selection.

The Suns entered the series with home-court advantage but without guard Joe Johnson, who suffered a fractured orbital bone near his left eye in Game 2 of Phoenix's second-round series against Dallas.

The Spurs quickly stole home-court advantage, winning Game 1 in Phoenix when they outplayed the Suns at their own breakneck

The Fateful Finals MVP Vote

There were three worthy candidates for Finals MVP after the Spurs defeated the Detroit Pistons in seven games in the 2005 NBA Finals: Tim Duncan, the top scorer and rebounder in the series, whose 17 points in the second half of Game 7 were vital when the Spurs staged a rally from nine points down with less than 20 minutes left; Manu Ginobili, who averaged 18.7 points per game in the series and scored 23 in Game 7; and Robert Horry, whose game-winning three-pointer in Game 5 was the shot of the series.

As it turned out, the vote was one of the closest in Finals history, Duncan barely edging Ginobili, 6–4.

Orlando Sentinel NBA writer Tim Povtak polled the 10 media members who voted for Finals MVP and there was outrage in Argentina when he published the tally and revealed that yours truly, then in his second season covering the Spurs and the NBA for the *San Antonio Express-News*, had voted for Duncan, rather than Ginobili.

With 20-20 hindsight, I wish I had voted for Ginobili so he could have shared the honor with Duncan.

game, winning 121–114. Four Spurs, including Barry (5-of-8 from long range), scored at least 20 points.

A 4–1 series win put the Spurs back in the NBA Finals, this time facing Popovich's friend and onetime mentor Larry Brown and his Pistons team trying to defend their 2004 NBA title.

The Spurs' air-tight defense was on display in Games 1 and 2, when they held the Pistons to 69 and 76 points in victories at AT&T Center that may have seemed too easy.

Once the series returned to the Palace of Auburn Hills, the Spurs discovered there would be no easy path to another title. Detroit blew them out in Game 3, 96–79, then dominated them so thoroughly in Game 4, 102–71, that the momentum shift could be felt at the Alamo. Reserve point guard Lindsey Hunter, a defensive menace, so thoroughly intimidated Spurs backup point guard Beno Udrih that Popovich had no choice but to replace him with ailing backup Devin Brown. Udrih would play only one minute in the remainder of the series.

Popovich had to find a way to ease the tension that gripped his team after the disheartening losses. He discovered it when someone produced a grainy film of assistant coach Brett Brown playing in the 1979 Maine high school championship game, complete with the very short basketball shorts that were worn back in the day.

Splicing the footage of Brown early in a review of the horrendous loss resulted in uproarious laughter that changed the mood of the team.

Lightened up and ready for Game 5—with Brown (Devin, not Brett) getting all the backup minutes behind Parker—the Spurs regained control of the series with the most dramatic Finals win in club history, thanks to Horry.

One of the greatest clutch shooters in NBA history, Horry scored 18 of his 21 points in the fourth quarter and overtime, making 4-of-5 three-point attempts during that stretch.

He saved the best for last, a dramatic three-pointer that gave the Spurs a 96–95 overtime victory in Game 5 and a 3–2 lead in the best-of-seven series.

Horry's game-winning shot equals Sean Elliott's "Memorial Day Miracle" three-pointer from 1999 as the greatest clutch shot in franchise history.

This is how the shot came about:

During a timeout with 9.5 seconds left in overtime, Popovich had diagrammed a play for Horry to inbound the ball to Manu Ginobili, then cut for the basket. Ginobili was to get the ball back to Horry, a give-and-go play designed to get a shot for Horry going toward the hoop.

When Horry's defender, Pistons defensive standout Rasheed Wallace, left Horry to double-team Ginobili, Horry stopped at the three-point line and called for a pass. Ginobili got him the ball and Horry rose and lofted his fifth three-pointer of the final 17 minutes.

It dropped through the net with 5.8 seconds remaining, silencing the partisan crowd.

When Richard Hamilton missed a well-defended shot with 1.9 seconds left, the Spurs had a victory, a 3–2 series lead, the momentum of the series, and the knowledge that Games 6 and 7 would be played at AT&T Center.

The gritty Pistons forced Game 7 with a 95–86 Game 6 win and then had a nine-point lead, 48–39, with 7:44 remaining in the third quarter of Game 7. With Rasheed (not Ben) Wallace and Antonio McDyess taking turns frustrating Duncan, the Spurs captain had missed 10 of his first 13 shots, including eight in a row.

But Duncan's teammates never lost faith and kept feeding him in the post. He erupted to score 17 of his 25 points in the final 18 minutes to spark a Spurs rally.

"My teammates were more confident in me than I was," Duncan said. "That is more appreciated than they will ever understand. I got on a roll there for a little while. It wasn't the greatest of games but there was a stretch when I felt really good."

Horry made another three-pointer in the fourth quarter, giving the Spurs a 64–59 lead with 8:23 left.

Popovich also made a defensive switch that made a major impact. Switching defensive ace Bowen onto Pistons star Chauncey Billups—Tony Parker handled shooting guard Rip Hamilton—disrupted Detroit's offense.

Bowen's block of Billups' three-point try with 56 seconds left blunted Detroit's comeback attempt; Ginobili and Horry made six-of-six free throws in the final 22 seconds to secure an 81–74 win and the team's third championship.

After sparking the Spurs' second-half rally, Duncan was named Finals MVP for the third time, joining Michael Jordan, Magic Johnson, and Shaquille O'Neal as the only players to have won three Finals MVP Awards up to that time.

12 Memorial Day Miracle

Over the years, the number of Spurs fans who claim to have witnessed, firsthand, Sean Elliott's three-point winner over the Portland Trail Blazers in Game 2 of the 1999 Western Conference Finals has grown to hundreds of thousands.

In fact, "only" 35,260 were at the Alamodome when Elliott made perhaps the most famous shot in franchise history, though hardly the most clutch shot. (See Horry, Robert, and 2005 championship).

Elliott's shot on that Memorial Day was certainly amazing. The Spurs forward took an in-bounds pass from Mario Elliott with 12 seconds remaining, nearly fell out of bounds before tight-roping along the right sideline to re-set his feet, and launched a perfect, high-arching three-point shot over the outstretched hand of Portland's Rasheed Wallace to give the Spurs an 86–85 lead that would hold up for a victory. The win gave them a 2–0 lead in the best-of-seven series that would ultimately send them to the franchise's first NBA Finals.

Those who weren't actually inside the Alamodome may even believe Elliott's shot barely beat the final buzzer. In fact, he let it fly with about 10.5 seconds left; when the ball went through the basket, a full nine seconds remained for the Trail Blazers to score and relegate it to one of the most amazing feats nobody recalls.

Bob Costas, calling the game for NBC-TV, was incredulous that Elliott even attempted the shot.

"That's a shot you take with the clock running out, not with nine seconds left," he said.

The great game analyst and former head coach, Doug Collins, agreed.

"That fooled me," Collins said. "I didn't think they'd shoot a three right there. And he was actually covered pretty well."

Even Elliott's teammates were shocked to see him rise up for the shot.

"I started to yell, 'No! No!'" Malik Rose told the *San Antonio Express-News* after the game. "But before I could, it went in. So I just screamed, 'Great shot! Great shot!'"

Elliott already had made 5-of-6 three-pointers and helped the Spurs rally from an 18-point second-half deficit to put themselves in position to steal the win. His rationale for attempting the shot despite the nine seconds it left the Trail Blazers? "I thought I had one more three left in me," he said.

Elliott then made the defensive play that secured the win, combining with David Robinson for a block on Jimmy Jackson's shot with two seconds left.

Elliott finished the game with 22 points, 18 of those from beyond the three-point arc.

The effect of the shot, and the Spurs' win, was profound. Disheartened, the Trail Blazers lost both home games when the series shifted to Portland and the Spurs eased into their very first NBA Finals with a few days to rest up for their Eastern Conference opponent, the New York Knicks.

Years later, Popovich would put the shot in perspective as he discussed the little things that make the difference for any team that wins a title.

"I didn't know Sean was going to make that stupid shot from the corner," he said. "If we lose that game, maybe we don't even get through that series."

13 28.2 Seconds

How can the most painful moment in franchise history be placed so high on this list of 100 things Spurs fans should know and do before they die?

As with many national and personal tragedies, most Spurs fans can tell you exactly where they were and what they were doing during the final 28.2 seconds of Game 6 of the 2013 NBA Finals, when a Spurs championship seemed so certain the NBA ordered ushers at Miami's American Airlines Arena to begin the process of roping off the first row of fans from the court.

No one could have imagined that Game 6 also would serve as the impetus for the team's triumphant 2013–14 season that culminated in a fifth NBA title, a championship most Spurs fans regard as the most satisfying moment in club history.

But in the immediate aftermath of the game—which set up a Game 7 loss—even the players joined the fans in trying to forget what had just happened.

But forgetting was difficult.

Three days after Game 7, Manu Ginobili, his wife, Marionela, and their four-year-old identical twin sons, Dante and Nicola settled into a beach resort hideaway in the Caribbean.

One of the most competitive athletes in NBA history, Ginobili, a professional basketballer since age 15 in his native Argentina, wanted nothing more than to laze away the days in an idyllic setting and bury the most painful defeat in his long basketball career.

"It would have been easier," he said, "if every waiter and employee or visitor at that hotel hadn't watched the Finals. But we all know the NBA Finals are really popular and hundreds of millions of people watch every game, so I understood it was a big thing and they appreciated what you did and wanted to say something about the games.

"I really didn't appreciate it, but I understood it. It made me remember way more often than I wanted."

What Ginobili could not erase from his memory was the free throw he missed with 28.2 seconds remaining, when a made foul shot could have given the Spurs a six-point lead.

It was not the only mistake made by the Spurs in those final moments. Six events had to occur in that short span for the Heat to send the game into overtime.

All six occurred, beginning with Ginobili missing the first of two free throws he was awarded after drawing a foul from Miami's Ray Allen.

Here is a brief synopsis of the 28.2 seconds that will live in franchise infamy:

- 28.2 seconds: With the Spurs ahead 93–89, Ginobili misses his first free throw and makes the second. Spurs 94, Heat 89.

- 27.0: Miami's LeBron James, with Spurs guard Danny Green contesting, air-balls a three-point attempt from the left quadrant.
- 25.0: James' miss clanged so hard off the backboard that Spurs forward Kawhi Leonard was unable to grab it. Miami's Dwyane Wade got a fingertip on the ball to help tip it up and away, right back into James' hands.
- 21.0 seconds: Given a second chance at making a three-pointer, James drains the shot. Spurs 94, Heat 92.
- 20.1 seconds: Popovich calls his final timeout and draws up a play.
- 19.4 seconds: Duncan inbounds the ball to Leonard, who is immediately fouled by Mike Miller.
- 7.9 seconds: James misses another three-point attempt, also from the left wing.
- 6.3 seconds: Chris Bosh rebounds James' miss and funnels a pass to Allen, who dribbles to the right corner.
- 5.2 seconds: Allen turns, sets his feet perfectly, and launches a three-pointer that hits nothing but net. Spurs 95, Heat 95.

Sebastian De La Cruz

When 11-year-old Sebastian De La Cruz, wearing the traditional mariachi attire he wears in numerous performances as San Antonio's "Little Mariachi," rendered an electrifying version of "The Star-Spangled Banner" before Game 3 of the 2014 NBA Finals, he got a standing ovation from the crowd at AT&T Center and ugly commentary on social media. When the racist comments were relayed to Gregg Popovich, the Spurs coach defended Sebastian during a pregame press conference before Game 4 and invited him to sing the anthem a second time.

Actress-producer (and former wife of Tony Parker) Eva Longoria produced a short film about Sebastian titled *Go Sebastian Go!* that aired on ESPN in 2015.

- 0.6 seconds: Tony Parker misses a 12-foot shot and time expires.

The Spurs actually had a 100–97 lead with 2:42 remaining in overtime, but Allen and James scored the final six points of the game to give the Heat a 103–100 win that forced Game 7, when Miami claimed its second straight NBA title.

Everything about Game 6 was impossible to forget, from the seemingly safe lead the Spurs yielded to the team dinner that followed.

Popovich had arranged to dine at Il Gabbiano, Miami's best Italian restaurant. The hope, of course, was for a celebratory feast but Popovich believes in nothing quite so much as fine dining, always with the right bottle of wine.

"You play the game. You win. You lose. You have dinner," Popovich reminds prying reporters seeking to distill something philosophical from defensive rotations, offensive schemes, or motivational speeches.

So the dinner was on, win or lose.

Some 90 minutes after the crushing defeat, the Spurs players filed into Il Gabbiano and sat down for the private feast.

"For at least an hour," said Parker, "nobody said a word."

Eventually, players and coaches discussed the game that had slipped away, and it was from that most painful of moments that the San Antonio Spurs started formulating a response that ultimately would lead to one of the most perfect playoff performances in NBA history: a five-game demolition of the same Miami Heat a year later in the 2014 NBA Finals.

You play the game.

You win.

You lose.

You have dinner.

Buon appetito!

14 Sweeping LeBron

The 2006 playoffs had ended with one of the most crushing defeats in franchise history up to that point. (That was seven years before Game 6 of the 2013 NBA Finals). A season that saw the best record in franchise history, 63–19, was derailed when the Dallas Mavericks outlasted the Spurs in overtime in Game 7 of the Western Conference semifinals. The Mavericks had finished with the league's second-best record (60–22) and only a quirk in the league's playoff format, later acknowledged as a mistake and changed, had forced a matchup one round too early.

The club's response was to return the bulk of the roster for another run at a title in 2006–07. Free-agent center Francisco Elson was signed to replace Nazr Muhammad and free-agent guard Jacque Vaughn signed to back up Tony Parker, but the rest of the roster returned intact.

Twenty-five wins in the final 31 games got the Spurs the No. 3 seed in the Western Conference, behind the 67–25 Dallas Mavericks and the 61–21 Phoenix Suns.

What followed was a seemingly pre-destined path to their fourth title. A first-round matchup against the sixth-seeded Denver Nuggets, led by mercurial guard Allen Iverson, produced a 4–1 series win and a matchup against the Suns in the semifinals. But that was hardly the most important occurrence of the first round: The Mavericks, who had beaten the Spurs three times in four regular-season games while rolling up the sixth-best record in league history, were shocked by the No. 8 seed Golden State Warriors in the first round, eliminating the odds-on Western favorite.

Still, the Spurs had to face the 61–21 Suns in the second round and appeared to be in big trouble when Phoenix, led by two-time MVP point guard Steve Nash, erased an 11-point fourth-quarter deficit in Game 4 at AT&T Center. The Suns led 100–97 with just 22.9 seconds left and in possession of the ball.

With orders from Gregg Popovich to take a quick foul, Robert Horry then body-checked Nash into the scorer's table, a category-two flagrant foul so egregious that Suns coach Mike D'Antoni and Phoenix guard Raja Bell charged at him. Horry was ejected for the flagrant foul and Bell was given a technical.

Video also showed that Suns star Amar'e Stoudemire and backup forward Boris Diaw rose from their bench and took a couple of steps in the direction of the melee. After reviewing the incident, NBA commissioner David Stern suspended Horry from Game 5 in Phoenix as well as Stoudemire and Diaw, for violating the league's restriction on players leaving the bench during games.

The Spurs went on to win Game 5 88–85 behind Manu Ginobili's 26 points, regaining home-court advantage, then closed out the series at AT&T Center with a 114–106 victory.

After their upset of the Mavericks the Warriors were handled easily in their semifinals matchup with the Utah Jazz, falling in five games. The Jazz and the Spurs had split their season series, 2–2, but Utah was no match for the more experienced Spurs in the Western Conference Finals, falling in five games.

The storyline of the 2007 NBA Finals was evident: could Cavaliers superstar LeBron James, in just his fourth season, drag the Cavaliers to Cleveland's first pro sports championship since the Browns won the 1964 NFL title?

The Spurs made it clear from the start that the 22-year-old James was not yet capable of dominating an NBA Finals by himself. They rolled to relatively easy wins in Games 1 and 2 at AT&T Center and then took a 3–0 series lead when James needed 23 shots to score 25 points in Game 3.

In Game 4, the closest game of the series, James took 30 shots and scored 24 points but Tony Parker's 10-of-14 shooting (24 points) made him Finals MVP and led the Spurs to just the eighth Finals sweep in league history.

15 Pro Basketball Comes to San Antonio

In the summer of 1973, San Antonio businessmen Angelo Drossos and B.J. "Red" McCombs put together a group that leased the Dallas Chaparrals for the season, with an option to buy. Everyone involved in the transaction knew the San Antonians would ultimately exercise the option because the Dallas owners wanted nothing more to do with the team.

San Antonio sports fans welcomed the team with open arms at HemisFair Arena, the beginning of a love affair that continues to this day.

But there would have been no San Antonio Spurs if not for the badly mismanaged Chaparrals, one of the original teams in the American Basketball Association.

Owned by a group of wealthy Dallas businessmen who knew plenty about making money but almost nothing about running a professional sports franchise, the Chaparrals were a box-office bust.

Exasperated by crowds so small the reporters who covered the team's games could count the fans, one by one, the Chaps ownership group put the team on the sales block, and it's hard to blame them. The official crowd count for the team's final home game of the 1972–73 season was 130.

Initially, the Dallas owners found a buyer in Newark, New Jersey, agreeing to a sale that would relocate the team to the East coast. That deal was put on hold after ABA officials began their due diligence of the new owners, reputed to have ties to mob figures.

"I had a contract to broadcast the games the next season and was ready to move to Newark," said Terry Stembridge, the Chaparrals assistant general manager and the play-by-play announcer on the team's radio broadcasts. "One of the (Chaparrals owners) said, 'Terry, you'd better pack your bags and a Tommy gun.'"

Eventually, ABA commissioner Mike Storen refused to approve the deal.

"So there we were," Stembridge said in an interview with the *San Antonio Express-News* in 2015. "(Chaparrals general manager) Robert Briner called me and said, 'What are we going to do?' I said there's a guy in San Antonio that I don't know but he owns the Toros and his name is Red McCombs and I could call him. Robert said, 'Why not?'"

In fact, McCombs had not owned the San Antonio Toros, a semipro football team. His sports ownership experience had come with a Class AA baseball team in Corpus Christi for more than a decade. But McCombs was a civic-minded San Antonian who had come to the conclusion that if San Antonio wanted to attract Fortune 500 companies, it first needed a major league sports franchise.

"There was no question that was the surest way to get national exposure to get Fortune 500 companies even to have interest in what we were trying to do here," McCombs said. "Of the CEOs of the Fortune 500 companies at that time, only eight or nine of those guys had ever been to San Antonio. Their idea was more like we were Laredo or Abilene."

When Stembridge called McCombs to see if he might be interested in buying the Chaparrals, he found the buyer the Chaps needed.

It was a call that forever would change the San Antonio sports scene. Stembridge laid out a scenario McCombs found more than appealing.

"I got this phone call out of the blue and the guy told me the Chaparrals were for sale and then he said, 'Red, these guys are desperate to sell. They're not even drawing 400 or 500 people and they've been at it for four or five years.'"

McCombs enlisted his friend, Angelo Drossos, a San Antonio stockbroker who had previously worked as a salesman for McCombs' car dealership and had a reputation as a brilliant negotiator. The two arranged a meeting with the Chaparrals owners.

"We started talking to them and one thing led to another and I had done enough business in my own world to tell when someone was desperate to sell something," McCombs said.

Initially, McCombs figured on a purchase price of $800,000, the amount the Chaps owners had lost the previous two years. Drossos figured they might be able to do better.

"Angelo and I were closest of friends and after we met them Angelo said, 'They'll do anything to get rid of that team.'"

McCombs thought things over for a few days, then came up with an idea that produced a deal: lease the team with an option to buy, guaranteeing $800,000 in operating expenses for two years. Anything above $800,000 would have to be made up by the Dallas group.

"There were a lot of other things that happened on the way but that's how we got the deal done," McCombs said.

Cost of the lease: one dollar.

McCombs took on about a third of the operating expenses and Drossos found other investors. He agreed to run the club without a salary.

One investor, an oilman named Wayman Buchanan, resisted signing up after seeing how much the Chaps had been losing annually. Drossos leaked his name to one of San Antonio's two daily newspapers and he signed on to avoid embarrassing Drossos, one of his closest friends.

"Angelo was my best friend and he was a heck of a salesman and he had put my name at the top of his investor list," Buchanan said. "My name came out in the paper that I was in on the deal and that's how I ended up as one of the owners."

Buchanan said he and the other local businessmen McCombs and Drossos lined up each paid between $10,000 and $15,000.

"We didn't put up that much money," he said, "but we signed a note guaranteeing repayment of a loan with Frost Bank. I had 5 percent but it seemed like I had to sign a note every month for some more operating money."

In charge of day-to-day operations, Drossos hired former Virginia Squires general manager Jack Ankerson. McCombs and Drossos wanted a new identity for the team, including a new name and colors. They hired ad man Jack Pitluk Jr. to help, and he suggested a contest among potential fans to rename the team. "Spurs," suggested by Mrs. Eulalia Ramon, of San Antonio, was Pitluk's choice. Drossos and McCombs agreed.

Ankerson, an avid fan of the NFL's Oakland Raiders, suggested silver and black for the colors and Drossos liked the idea. McCombs gave his approval, and that was that.

McCombs focused his attention on lining up community support for the team, especially from the news media.

"Everybody was on board and the media played a tremendous role with it," McCombs said. "I visited with (publisher) Charlie Kilpatrick at the *Express-News* and (publisher) Frank Bennack at the *Light* and told them they had to be on board with us. Both of them told us, 'Look, if you've got a team that is horseshit we can't pretend it's good.' But they told us they would try to help us with it in any other way they could and they did.

"We got great coverage. About six weeks into our first season we were doing better than we thought we would. I was walking into the St. Anthony Hotel and saw a newspaper rack, and on the front page of the *Express*, in color, there was an action shot of the game the night before. I ran inside and got a handful of quarters to get all the papers with that action shot in color. I sent those papers to all my friends."

On October 10, 1973, the Spurs played their first game in their new home city against the San Diego Conquistadores, coached by Wilt Chamberlain. James Silas was the team's leading scorer in that first season. Midway through the season, McCombs and Drossos orchestrated a trade that would bring the team its first superstar, a skinny scorer named George Gervin. Gervin brought some star appeal and helped solidify the love affair between city and team.

"The Spurs have made a difference here," Gervin told the *San Antonio Express-News* in a 2015 interview. "If you mention San Antonio anywhere in the world—I don't care if you're in Paris or Tokyo or anywhere else—the response is always, 'That's where the Spurs play.'

"It used to just be the Alamo. But with TV and all those championships we're now known worldwide as the home of the Spurs."

16 Iceman's Scoring Title

In the closest scoring race in NBA history, George Gervin won the 1977–78 scoring title on the final day of the season by scoring 63 points against the New Orleans Jazz. His nemesis, Denver's David Thompson, had scored 73 against the Detroit Pistons earlier that same afternoon, upping his average to 27.15 points per game.

Gervin's 63 points brought his average to 27.22 points per game.

The Iceman gives most of the credit to his Spurs coach at the time, Doug Moe. The Spurs star and Denver's Thompson were neck-and-neck all season for the scoring lead, separated by less than a point. When the final day of the regular season arrived, both teams were locked into playoff spots and playing non-playoff teams.

Those final games became quests to get the scoring title for their respective stars, the NBA schedule playing an unwitting role. It had the Nuggets playing the Pistons in an afternoon game; the Spurs faced New Orleans at night.

Thirty-three in the Second

George Gervin's 33 points in the second period of his 63-point game was an all-time NBA record until Carmelo Anthony matched it in the third quarter of a Denver Nuggets game against the Minnesota Timberwolves on December 10, 2008.

Anthony made four three-pointers in his 33-point quarter, and the record he shared with Gervin lasted until Golden State's Klay Thompson scored 37 in the second quarter of a game against the Sacramento Kings on January 23, 2015.

Though Gervin didn't seem to mind sharing the record with Anthony, Thompson's 37-point quarter compelled him to point out a big difference between his achievement and those of both Thompson and Anthony: there was no three-point line in 1976–77. Thompson, after all, had made nine three-pointers in his 37-point period, accounting for 27 of the 37 points. Afterward, Gervin offered congratulations but also pointed out that his record was established without benefit of a three-point line. The NBA didn't adopt the long-distance line until the 1979–80 season.

"First, I said, 'Wow, that's pretty impressive,'" Gervin told Bleacher Report after Thompson's performance. "But I'd like to see him try to get 33 or 37 in a quarter when there wasn't no three-point line."

Gervin's contention is that Thompson didn't break his record; rather, that he established a new one.

"I'm saying, like, wait a minute, y'all," he said. "Y'all are making it seem like what I did was just regular. I ain't mad at the kid doing what he did. But what I'm saying is, let's let the fans know what really happened, and let them be the judge of it."

Thompson struck first, scoring 73 in Detroit, the third-highest total in league history. That upped his average to 27.15 points per game, slightly better than Gervin's 26.8.

Thus, Moe knew that Gervin needed 59 points against New Orleans to pass Thompson. His pregame instructions to his players: Gervin was to take every shot until he had the points he needed.

Admitting later that he had a case of the nerves because of the plan, Gervin missed his first six shots. He called a timeout and told his teammates to forget about Moe's plan.

"I said, 'Hey, guys, I need 59. I just ain't getting 59,'" he said in a 2015 interview with the *San Antonio Express-News*.

But Moe overruled his reluctant star and the plan continued. When Larry Kenon put up a shot after Gervin's timeout, Moe called another and told Kenon he would take him out of the game if he did it again. Kenon took another shot and Moe made good on his threat, removing him from the lineup.

Gervin finally got over his jitters and the rest is part of Spurs lore.

"I scored 20 in the first quarter," he said. "Then I got in a zone and got 33 in the second, and I only needed 59."

Early in the third quarter, Spurs athletic trainer John Anderson told Gervin he had the 59 points he needed.

"I said, 'Wait, John, let me go on and get a couple more points just in case they miscalculated,' and that's how I ended up getting 63 points in 33 minutes and winning my first scoring title.

"It was special."

17 Duncan's Dynasty

Since arriving in San Antonio for the 1997–98 season, Tim Duncan played in 1,001 winning regular-season games, 158 winning playoff games, and won five championships in six trips to the NBA Finals. The team's winning percentage since Duncan arrived is 70.9 percent and the Spurs have compiled the longest streak of 50-win seasons in NBA history (17).

It is the best 19-year stretch in NBA history, surpassing that of Bill Russell's Boston Celtics that ran from 1957 through 1975. True, those Boston teams won 12 championships, albeit in a much smaller league with fewer great teams.

The Duncan Dynasty can be so named because advanced analytics back the assertion. Nate Silver, the renowned numbers cruncher who worked for *The New York Times* and now runs FiveThirtyEight for ESPN, ranked the 16-year Duncan-Spurs run that began with the 1999 championship as the best in NBA history, based on longevity and sustained excellence.

In 2015, the *San Antonio Express-News* asked some longtime NBA observers and experts to weigh in on the merits of a Duncan Dynasty. Their opinions were telling.

Former Phoenix Suns owner Jerry Colangelo, 76, now serves as chairman of basketball operations for the Philadelphia 76ers but began his NBA career in Phoenix in 1968 and before that was a scout for the Chicago Bulls in 1966.

Former Hawks, Knicks, and Grizzlies head coach Hubie Brown, 82, was a high school coach in the mid-1950s, a college coach in the 1960s, and began his NBA coaching career as an assistant with the Milwaukee Bucks, beginning in 1972. He has strong opinions and expresses them in a forthright manner.

Sacramento Kings coach George Karl, 65, was a star at North Carolina from 1970 to 1973, then began a five-year pro playing career with the Spurs. A head coach for 30 years in the NBA, he took his 1995–96 Seattle Supersonics teams to the NBA Finals, where they fell to the Chicago Bulls in Michael Jordan's first season back after playing minor league baseball for two years.

All three have distinct notions of the debate.

"To me the Michael Jordan Bulls over those eight years (1991–98) and the Lakers during that period of time with Magic (Johnson) and Kareem (Abdul-Jabbar) and (James) Worthy were a dynasty," said Brown, 82. "You could also include the Celtics in that period because they got there five times and won it three times.

"Do we say San Antonio is a dynasty because of the every-other-year championships and, more important, the amount of years they made the playoffs and the amount of years they won 50-plus games?

"Going all the way back you have to remember that off that Celtics team during that period of time I don't know how many made the Hall of Fame, but then the Hall of Fame was easier to make then than it is today."

While the early Celtics dynasty was the most dominant in league history—11 titles in 13 seasons—detractors point out there were only eight NBA teams when the run began, only 14 by the time it ended.

Said Colangelo: "I don't want to say it was easier to dominate but the circumstances were so different that if you had the dominant center and maybe the greatest of all time, along with a great cast of terrific players the Celtics had assembled under Red Auerbach, there was an easier path to dominate at that time.

"Fast forward to the modern era and it's much more difficult to dominate to that degree. But having said that, maybe not consecutive Final Fours, but San Antonio has put together a pretty good era of domination, winning championships and getting there. Maybe they missed out a year or two but they kept coming back."

Karl, fifth on the list of winningest NBA coaches (1,175), ranks the Duncan Spurs right behind the Michael Jordan Bulls of the 1990s.

"I don't think there is any question I might even put the Spurs ahead of the (Russell) Celtics," Karl said, citing the difficulty of thriving in a league with many more competitive teams than the early Celtics faced. "Players today are so much bigger, stronger, faster, quicker. We train them at a higher level. So I would have the Bulls being No. 1, the Spurs No. 2, the (Larry Bird) Celtics and (Magic Johnson) Lakers over the longevity of the '80s and into the '90s next. They also had some failure in there that the Spurs and Bulls didn't have."

18 MVP Admiral

Despite putting up gaudy numbers in the 1994–95 season—27.6 points per game, 10.8 rebounds, 3.23 blocks, 2.9 assists, and 1.65 steals—one can argue that the 1994–95 season was not the best of David Robinson's Hall of Fame career.

Robinson had a higher scoring average the previous season, an NBA-high 29.8 points per game that included a 71-point game, at the time the seventh-highest-scoring game in NBA history.

In four other seasons he had higher rebound averages, including a league-best 13.0 per game in 1990–91.

Four times he blocked more shots per game, including a league-best 4.5 per game in 1991–92.

He wasn't even the Spurs' top rebounder in 1994–95, trailing league-leading teammate Dennis Rodman by six per game (16.8 to 10.8).

Nevertheless, the totality of Robinson's play, combined with the Spurs' NBA-best and franchise-record 62 wins, resulted in his becoming the first Spurs player voted Most Valuable Player, either in the ABA or NBA.

It was a huge story for both Robinson and the Spurs. The fact there were other worthy candidates made Robinson's selection more gratifying for the Spurs and their fans. Shaquille O'Neal, especially, was a major contender as the league scoring leader (29.3 points per game) for an Orlando Magic team that had the best record in the Eastern Conference.

The final MVP tally wasn't really close. Robinson received 73 first-place votes from a media panel of 105 voters. Utah's Karl Malone received 14, O'Neal 12. Robinson's point total was nearly 300 more than that of second-place O'Neal.

Houston's Hakeem Olajuwon, the 1994 MVP, finished fifth in the voting, receiving only one first-place vote after a season in which his impact had diminished and the Rockets had struggled to a 47–35 record. But when the Spurs met the Rockets in the Western Conference Finals, Olajuwon dominated Robinson and led the Rockets to a second straight NBA title.

Olajuwon averaged 35.3 points, 12.5 rebounds, and 4.2 blocks in the series; Robinson averaged 23.8 points, 11.3 rebounds, and 2.2 blocks per WCF game.

The MVP results were announced the day before the series was to begin and Robinson was presented the MVP trophy by commissioner David Stern in a ceremony at the Alamodome before tipoff, a mostly partisan Spurs crowd of 33,337 roaring its approval.

The Rockets had gone back to their locker room during the ceremony, and the story goes that Olajuwon told his teammates "they are giving that man my award."

Some of Olajuwon's teammates have turned that tale to near-legend. However, in an interview with the Rockets website in 2015, Olajuwon asserted that he never said anything about Robinson and never believed he should have won the MVP Award.

"I want to correct everybody," Olajuwon told Rockets.com. "David deserved the MVP. I wasn't having an MVP year that year and David was having a great year. The motivation was knowing we can win but it had nothing to do with being mad at losing the MVP to David Robinson."

In all likelihood, Robinson would gladly have swapped honors with Olajuwon, giving up the trophy for a championship ring.

19 Sean Elliott

One of the most popular players in Spurs history, Sean Elliott made one of the most dramatic shots in club history while playing with a disease that would require a kidney transplant weeks after the championship conclusion of the 1998–99 season.

That sounds more like the plot of a Hollywood movie than part of an athlete's biography.

The beginning of Elliott's career in silver and black was almost an afterthought despite his having been the No. 3 overall pick in the 1989 draft.

Mention the Spurs' jump from 21 wins in 1988–89 to 56 wins in 1989–90 and most casual fans attribute the improvement to the arrival of David Robinson after the conclusion of his two-year stint in the United States Navy.

While it is true that Robinson was a unanimous choice as NBA Rookie of the Year after averaging 24.3 points and 12.0 rebounds per game, the Spurs also got a major contribution from Elliott. He became a starter for Spurs coach Larry Brown at the beginning of the season and he put up solid numbers while splitting time at small forward with Willie Anderson and David Wingate. He also gave a hint of things to come when his play improved during his first playoffs, shooting 55.2 percent from the field and averaging 12.7 points per game.

Already a fine perimeter shooter, Elliott adapted quickly to the NBA three-point line and benefited immediately from playing alongside Robinson, a supreme creator of shots for all of the Spurs' perimeter players. By his second season Elliott was the full-time starter at small forward, averaging 37 minutes per game, his scoring average jumping to 15.9 points per game.

Elliott made the All-Star team for the first time in 1992–93, his fourth season, and averaged 17.2 points per game. However, he had begun to experience some physical ailments that affected his energy. Tests revealed a problem with his kidneys, ultimately diagnosed as focal segmented glomerulosclerosis, a dangerous condition that ultimately would require a transplant.

After the 1992–93 season, the Spurs did not know how much longer Elliott would be able to play. The decision was made to trade him and they found a willing partner in the Detroit Pistons, who had concluded that NBA rebound leader Dennis Rodman had become a distraction who needed to be moved. The Spurs revealed Elliott's condition to the Pistons but the deal went through anyway.

Elliott didn't take to Detroit at all and clashed with Pistons leader Isaiah Thomas. His scoring average plummeted from 17.2 points per game to 12.1. He was miserable.

The Pistons weren't happy either, and just before the 1994 trade deadline Detroit sent him to the Houston Rockets for Robert Horry. After the Pistons' medical report on Elliott was confirmed by the mandatory physical exam given all traded players, the

Rockets backed out of the deal. Horry went back to Houston and helped the Rockets win the 1994 NBA title.

Elliott missed the final four games of his one season in Detroit with pneumonia and the Pistons went into the off-season desperate to get something for him. They called the Spurs and returned him to San Antonio for Bill Curley, the Spurs' first-round pick (No. 22 overall) in the 1994 draft and a future second-round pick.

Elliott was elated and in his first season back in silver and black his scoring average jumped back to 18.1 points per game, a career best at the time. The next season, 1995–96, he made his second appearance in the NBA All-Star Game and averaged 20 points per game for the season.

His kidney condition worsening, Elliott was told before the lockout-shortened 1998–99 season began that medications no longer were enough to control the effects of his ailment. A transplant would be required.

Even as Elliott began the process of finding a donor with a kidney that was a match for his—his older brother, Noel, would volunteer—he and the Spurs made the decision that he would play the 1998–99 season and keep the pending transplant a secret.

"I had a responsibility to those guys on the team, to the people who came to watch the games, and to the coaching staff not to bring my problems to the court," he would later tell NBA.com.

He started all 50 games of the lockout-shortened season and 17 more in the Spurs' run to the franchise's first championship. He averaged 30.2 minutes per game in the regular season and 33.8 in the playoffs, when he made his Memorial Day Miracle three-pointer that won Game 2 of the Western Conference Finals against the Portland Trail Blazers.

Elliott received a kidney from his brother on August 16, 1999. Amazingly, he returned to the court just six months later, playing 12 minutes in a home game against the Atlanta Hawks on March

14. The Alamodome crowd gave him a standing ovation when he checked in.

He explained his decision to continue his career after the transplant.

"By going out and playing, I can wipe away a lot of misconceptions people have," Elliott told the *Austin American-Statesman* before his return to the lineup. "I'm not coming back just for me, but for people who had transplants like this, to give them hope.

"Maybe I'll be the guru, the Dalai Lama of kidney transplants."

After playing 52 games and 12 playoff games of the 2000–01 season, Elliott announced his retirement, at age 32.

Elliott's broadcasting career began shortly after his retirement when NBC-TV hired him as an analyst on their broadcasts of NBA games. He moved to ABC Sports and ESPN for the 2003–04 season. He took over as analyst on locally produced telecasts of Spurs games beginning with the 2004–05 season and, as of the 2016–17 season, continues in that role.

Elliott's No. 32 jersey was retired by the Spurs near the end of the 2005 season. The University of Arizona also retired his No. 32 in 2006.

20 Captain Late

When the Spurs arrived in San Antonio in 1973–74, they brought with them some exciting stars, none of whom were named George Gervin. "The Iceman" would not join the team until February of 1974 after the team's new ownership acquired him from the Virginia Squires for $225,000 cash.

They did, however, bring with them James Silas, a scoring point guard with a flair for the dramatic. He was such a reliable clutch shooter that he earned the nickname "Captain Late" for his ability to hit big shots when games were on the line in the final minutes.

A native of Tallulah, Louisiana, Silas played college ball at Stephen F. Austin College in Nacogdoches, Texas, where he was a two-time NAIA All-American. He averaged 30.7 points per game as a senior, leading the Lumberjacks to a 29–1 record.

Despite his gaudy scoring average he was not drafted until the fifth round of the 1972 NBA Draft, No. 70 overall, by the Houston Rockets. He thought he proved himself worthy of a spot on the Rockets roster during training camp but believed he never had a chance because of where he had played college ball.

In an article from *Pro Basketball Weekly* by renowned ABA sportswriter Dan Pattison, Silas discussed being overlooked because of where he played.

"No one heard of Stephen F. Austin even though we were a good team," Silas told Pattison, who interviewed him late in the 1975–76 Spurs season for his ABA column. "I think scouts should look to NAIA schools more.

"There are good players in the NAIA who don't even get a chance. Coming out of the NAIA hurts a guy. If you have a big name like a Travis Grant or Elmore Smith it doesn't hurt, but it has hurt others. There is no recognition. The bigger schools get the ink and television exposure.

"I thought I was as good as anyone I read about. I always thought I was as good as the big college guards. Now I'm getting my chance to prove it."

By then Silas had proven he was one of the best guards in either the ABA or the NBA. By then he was a two-time ABA All-Star and had been a second-team All-ABA selection the previous season,

If injuries had not derailed his career, original San Antonio Spur James Silas might be remembered today as one of the best point guards in ABA/NBA history.

when he had shot 50.9 percent from the field and averaged 19.3 points and 4.9 assists per game.

Ultimately, his play in his four ABA seasons would land him a spot on the All-Time ABA Top 30 team that was selected for a 30-year ABA reunion in Indianapolis in 1997.

Silas got his chance in the ABA in 1972 when Dallas Chaparrals coach Babe McCarthy took a chance on him after the Rockets waived him just before the start of the 1972–73 NBA season. It was the final season for the ill-fated Chaparrals, who would draw so few fans in Silas' rookie season in Dallas that team ownership would subsequently lease the team, with an option to buy, to a group from San Antonio.

Silas became McCarthy's starting point guard as a rookie and averaged 13.7 points and 3.1 assists per game and made the ABA's All-Rookie team.

Once the team moved to San Antonio and replaced McCarthy with Tom Nissalke, Silas solidified his role, leading the team in points scored (1,321) in his first season in San Antonio. Gervin had a higher scoring average (19.7 points per game) once he finally joined the team on February 7, 1974, but played in only 25 games and scored only 486 points.

It was after Bob Bass replaced Nissalke midway through the Spurs' second season in San Antonio that Silas truly established himself as one of the ABA's best players. He made 50.9 percent of his shots, averaging 19.3 points per game, and began to show his ability to take over games in the fourth quarter.

With Bass coaching the team from Game 1 in 1975–76, Silas enjoyed his best season in silver and black. He scored an even 2,000 points, an average of 23.8 points per game that bested even Gervin, who averaged 21.8. Silas also led the team in assists, at 5.4 per game. He was one of four Spurs to make the ABA All-Star lineup, joined by Gervin, Larry Kenon, and Billy Paultz, and was

A Call to the Hall?

When Hall of Fame chairman Jerry Colangelo convened the special committee to consider direct election of players, coaches, and contributors from the ABA, his decision was hailed by many from the old red-white-and-blue league. Among those most pleased was Doug Moe, the former Spurs coach who was an original member of the ABA (and its leading scorer in the inaugural season.) Moe hopes that recognition finds James Silas, the great Spurs guard whose knee injury days before his NBA regular-season debut robbed him of a chance to prove his greatness after the merger with the older pro league.

"I'm very happy about this new committee," Moe, who still resides in San Antonio, told the *San Antonio Express-News*. "I don't know who decides these things, but I know there were a lot of players in the ABA who were every bit as good as any of the players in the NBA. You take a guy like James Silas, he never got a chance to prove how good he was because he got hurt his very first year in the NBA. But if this new committee is able to recognize him, well, that would be very nice."

As of the 2016 Hall of Fame inductions, Silas was still waiting.

a first-team All-ABA selection, recognition as one of the five best players in what turned out to be the final season of that league.

The dream season came to a crashing halt in Game 1 of the Spurs' first-round playoff series against Julius Erving and the New York Nets when Silas broke his right ankle. He missed the rest of the series, and without him the Spurs fell to the eventual league champions in seven games.

It was the beginning of a sad end to a career that should have made Silas a star in the NBA, as well as one of the greatest players in the short history of the ABA. A preseason knee injury limited him to 22 games at the end of the Spurs' first season in the NBA. Another knee problem early in the 1977–78 season cost him 45 games and made him a spot player after he did return.

"At first we didn't think the knee injury was anything serious," said Doug Moe, who took over as head coach when the team entered the NBA in the 1976–77 season. "The truth is that he was never the same after that injury. He was very good, but he wasn't the truly great player he was in his ABA years."

The "very good" Silas had a stellar 1978–79 season. His scoring average jumped from 3.9 points per game to 16 and he resumed being "Captain Late," taking over in crunch time. It was Silas for whom the final play of Game 7 of the Eastern Conference Finals was drawn up when the Spurs needed a basket to tie the score and send the game to overtime. His shot was blocked by Washington center Elvin Hayes.

Silas played two more seasons for the Spurs before the club traded him to Cleveland after the 1980–81 season.

"He was one of the best guards ever to play in the NBA," Moe said. "It's a shame the NBA never got to see the real 'Jimmy Si.'"

On February 28, 1984, Silas became the first Spurs player to have his number retired, his No. 13 jersey raised to the rafters at HemisFair Arena. It continues to hang at AT&T Center, along with six more numbers subsequently retired. But in this instance, Captain Late was first.

21 Salute the Little General

To say that Avery Johnson had to overachieve to forge a career in the NBA is an understatement. Undrafted out of Southern University, he played only 43 games as a rookie with the Seattle SuperSonics and 53 games in his second season. A deep bench player, Johnson played only 866 minutes in two seasons in Seattle and scored only 208 points. He was an emergency starter for 10 games when Nate McMillan was injured.

The Denver Nuggets signed Johnson to a non-guaranteed contract that brought him to training camp in 1990. He played 21 games, starting four, before being waived on Christmas Eve, a cruel blow he accepted with rare equanimity and even rarer optimism.

"I'll be fine," he told a *Denver Post* reporter as he walked out of McNichols Arena with his gear in a plastic trash bag. "I know I can play in this league."

Little more than three weeks later he was signed by the Spurs, where he played the remainder of the season for Larry Brown and an assistant coach named Gregg Popovich. Popovich saw something special in the 5-foot-10 point guard: a rare understanding of the game and innate leadership skills.

Johnson was back on the Spurs roster with another non-guaranteed contract the next season but again fell through the cracks when it came time for his deal to be fully guaranteed. Waived on December 17 this time, he landed with the Houston Rockets for the remainder of the season.

The Spurs called again seven games into the next season when it became apparent they needed on-court leadership in Jerry Tarkanian's ill-fated first season as an NBA coach. This time he signed for the remainder of the season, which he finished under coach John Lucas after the Spurs fired Tarkanian after only 20 games. He ended up starting 49 games and averaged career highs in scoring (8.7 points per game) and assists (7.5 per game). This set him up for a fully guaranteed deal the next season from the Golden State Warriors, where he played for head coach Don Nelson. Popovich was on Nelson's coaching staff by then and was convinced that Johnson could be a solid starting point guard in the NBA.

When Spurs chairman Gen. Robert McDermott brought Popovich back to San Antonio as general manager in the summer of 1994, Johnson found a home for the next six-plus seasons and a path to an NBA championship and a future career.

Johnson recalls getting a phone call moments after the free agent market opened in July.

"(Pop) was on my doorstep; I was one of the first guys he contacted," Johnson told the *San Antonio Express-News* in 2014. "The conversation was just all about doing something big in San Antonio and trying to get the team to its first NBA Finals. He said, 'If you want to be part of something big and special, come back to San Antonio.'"

Popovich didn't have to ask twice. Johnson signed the first long-term contract of his career, a three-year deal for $2.5 million. He appreciated the loyalty Popovich showed and would repay it two years later, when Popovich fired coach Bob Hill little more than a month into the 1996–97 season and took over on the bench himself. Johnson was one of Popovich's strongest advocates during the public controversy that ensued after Hill's dismissal. The player who came to be called the Little General calls it good fortune the digital age had not yet arrived in San Antonio, or anywhere else.

"Who knows what would have happened had we lived then in the microwave society I call social media," Johnson said in 2014. "It was perfect timing for Pop."

Johnson started every game he would play from 1994–95 through the 1999–2000 seasons. It was a mostly glorious run—the injury-plagued 20–62 season in 1996–97 was the exception—that produced one of the signature moments in Spurs history: the team's first NBA championship, in 1999.

That championship season also produced the biggest shot of Johnson's career, an 18-foot jumper at Madison Square Garden that provided the winning 78–77 margin in Game 5 of the 1999 NBA Finals against the New York Knicks.

A challenged perimeter shooter through his entire career, Johnson had worked hard on intermediate shots. The Game 5 winner, which went through the net with 47 seconds left, was the payoff. The Spurs' stifling defense made it hold up for the win and the title.

To Johnson, hitting the shot meant even more than winning a championship. It seemed like a validation of his entire life, from his days coming up in challenged circumstances in New Orleans to his struggle to prove he belonged in the NBA.

His story, he said, was about perseverance.

"My whole life, not just on the basketball court but off the court, is a big example to people out there, a lot of kids especially," he told reporters after Game 5. "It's really been an example of not giving up."

Johnson never averaged more than 13.4 points per game. He never made an All-NBA team. He never played in an All-Star Game. But his leadership earned him a nickname from his teammates—the Little General—and on December 7, 2007, the Spurs accorded him their highest honor, retiring his No. 6 jersey.

22 R.C. Buford

If you want to know what makes R.C. Buford so effective as a basketball executive for the Spurs, look up his biography on Wikipedia.

The online encyclopedia has two sentences summing up his career in basketball; three sentences describing his early career; eight sentences summing his NBA executive career; and two sentences on his personal life. There's a listing of notable trades, draft picks, and a listing of his coaching/GM "tree." That's it.

You learn next to nothing about Buford from the online biography and that is exactly the way he wants it. In Buford's world, the less you know about him and, more importantly, the less you know about how he operates as head of the Spurs' basketball operations department, the better.

In fact, the man whose official title with the Spurs is president of sports franchises (as well as Spurs general manager) is regarded as one of the smartest team executives in all of professional sports. He was named NBA Executive of the Year in both 2013–14 and 2015–16 and some of his NBA contemporaries have joked that the trophy that goes to the winner each season should be re-named the R.C. Buford Trophy.

Buford is inextricably linked to former Spurs coach Larry Brown because it was Brown who brought him to San Antonio when he was hired as Spurs coach in 1988. More importantly, it was while Buford was on Brown's coaching staff at the University of Kansas that he met Gregg Popovich.

Buford grew up in Wichita, Kansas, where he played high school basketball. A self-described "terrible player," he played at Texas A&M before transferring to Oklahoma State, then received a college degree from Friends University, in his hometown.

In 1983, Buford became a graduate assistant coach on Brown's staff at Kansas, and was eventually hired as a full-time assistant coach. He remained at Kansas with Brown for five years, culminating with the Jayhawks' run to the 1988 NCAA championship.

It was as a Kansas assistant that Buford first encountered Popovich, who was an unpaid assistant on Brown's staff during the 1986–87 season, when Popovich was on sabbatical from his job as head coach at Pomona-Pitzer Colleges. Popovich returned to the Division III schools the next season and Buford did his part to help Brown lead the Jayhawks to the national championship.

The Spurs hired Brown away from Kansas not long after the 1987–88 NBA season ended and he brought his entire Kansas staff with him: Ed Manning, Alvin Gentry, and Buford. Then he added a fourth assistant, luring Popovich away from Pomona-Pitzer.

Brown departed the Spurs midway through his fourth season. When he took over as Los Angeles Clippers coach a month later, he took Buford with him.

The four years Brown's assistants spent together in San Antonio formed life-long bonds. The connection between Buford and Popovich was especially close.

Buford reunited with Brown for the 1992–93 season in Los Angeles but moved to the University of Florida as an assistant under Lon Krueger for the 1993–94 college season. His stay there was brief because Popovich, named Spurs general manager on May 31, 1994, offered him a job as a Spurs scout a few days after he began running basketball operations.

Buford's rise in the team's front office was rapid. In less than five years he went from scout to director of scouting to vice president of basketball operations/assistant general manager. In 2002, Popovich named him general manager.

Popovich recognized something in Buford that he truly valued: his ability to judge some of the intangible attributes that make very good players great. In a *USA Today* article that ran during the 2007 playoffs, Popovich discussed Buford's unique vision: "A lot of guys can't judge competitiveness but R.C. can. He knows who is going to take a hit and who is going to stick their nose in there; who can be criticized and who can't; and who can handle adversity and those kinds of things."

The ability to see traits that other scouts overlook produced Buford's reputation as one of the NBA's best judges of talent. He also was a pioneer in scouting overseas. He is credited with discovering Manu Ginobili and Tony Parker, as well as Luis Scola, Ian Mahinmi, Beno Udrih, Fabricio Oberto, and Aron Baynes.

Buford also has been able to identify other basketball operatives who have the same eye for talent. Among those who served as understudies in his basketball operations department before getting their own jobs as general managers of other teams include Danny

Ferry, Sam Presti, Kevin Pritchard, Dennis Lindsey, Lance Blanks, and Rob Hennigan.

A master manipulator of the salary rules in the league's collective bargaining agreement, Buford has managed to keep the Spurs in championship contention through the entirety of his tenure as GM while exceeding the league's luxury tax threshold for overspenders only three times. He was named Executive of the Year for the 2013–14 season, when the Spurs went 62–20 and avenged their heartbreaking loss in the 2013 NBA Finals by beating the Miami Heat in the 2014 Finals for the franchise's fifth championship.

Buford's shrewd manipulation of Spurs contracts in the summer of 2015 allowed the team to restructure for a future without Tim Duncan while remaining a championship contender.

An early adapter to advanced analytics, Buford's lectures at MIT's annual Sloan Sports Analytics Conference are standing-room-only events and he is considered an analytics "superstar."

Don't tell Wikipedia.

23 Larry Brown

Though Larry Brown had a relatively mediocre 153–131 record (53.8 winning percentage) and coached the Spurs for only three and a half seasons, his impact on the franchise is indelible. Not only did he oversee one of the greatest turnarounds in club history— from 21 wins in his first season to 56 wins in his second year on the bench—he also was responsible for bringing both Gregg Popovich and R.C. Buford to the Alamo City.

Now that's a legacy!

Brown began his pro playing career as a member of the New Orleans Buccaneers in the American Basketball Association's inaugural season, 1967–68. He played for five different ABA teams in six seasons before retiring as a player after his 1971–72 season with the Denver Rockets.

Brown stopped playing so he could become head coach of the ABA's Carolina Cougars in 1972–73, at age 32. It was the start of a nomadic coaching career that has subsequently taken him to the Denver Nuggets (1974–79), UCLA (1979–81), New Jersey Nets (1981–83), University of Kansas (1983–88), the Spurs (1988–92), Los Angeles Clippers (1992–93), Indiana Pacers (1993–97), Philadelphia 76ers (1997–2003), Detroit Pistons (2003–05), New York Knicks (2005–06), Charlotte Bobcats (2008–11), and SMU (2012–2016).

Though his coaching record with the Spurs left much to be desired, Larry Brown (left) will forever be remembered as the man who brought Gregg Popovich to San Antonio.

In 1988, Red McCombs had just bought out all other Spurs investors and purchased the club, outright. The team had just suffered through a 31–51 season under coach Bob Weiss and been eliminated in the first round of the playoffs. McCombs wanted to make a publicity splash and Brown's Kansas Jayhawks had just completed a dramatic run to the 1988 NCAA title.

Why not bring in a onetime ABA star and successful ABA head coach to coach a one-time ABA team in need of a change?

A deal was struck but not before Brown exacted a pledge from McCombs that he could bring his three Kansas assistants—Alvin Gentry, Ed Manning, and Buford. He also asked for one more assistant, a Division III head coach who had been an unpaid assistant at Kansas in 1986–87. His name: Gregg Popovich.

Brown's first season taught all the coaches about patience. Waiting for David Robinson's pending release from military duty, the 1988–89 Spurs went 21–61. Upon the arrival of Robinson and Sean Elliott, the third pick in the 1989 draft, the Spurs' turnaround to 56 wins set an NBA record for improvement from one season to the next.

Brown's third season produced a 55–27 record but also a first-round playoff elimination that frustrated McCombs. The owner's patience ran out on January 19, 1992, after a loss at Boston Garden. When the team returned to San Antonio, general manager Bob Bass informed Brown he was being fired.

Bass took over on the Spurs bench himself and Brown quickly moved on to another job, finishing out the season for the Los Angeles Clippers, his sixth team in just 10 years in a career that would take him to 13 different teams, college and pro, in 33 years.

Of all Brown's many coaching stops, the one that ultimately had the most impact on the Spurs was his tenure at Kansas. In his first season there he hired a 23-year-old assistant coach named R.C. Buford. Then, when Gregg Popovich took a sabbatical from his coaching and teaching roles at the Claremont Colleges

(Pomona-Pitzer) in 1986, he landed at Kansas after first spending a few months at North Carolina immersing himself in an exploration of the coaching methods that had made Dean Smith one of college basketball's most successful coaches. He ended it by spending a season as an unpaid assistant on Brown's coaching staff at Kansas.

Brown first encountered Popovich when Popovich tried out for the 1972 U.S. Olympic team in Colorado Springs. Brown came to the tryouts at the request of head coach Henry Iba. After playing for an Armed Forces All-Star team following his 1970 graduation from the Air Force Academy, Popovich was invited to try out.

"The relationship between Pop and me dates back to Coach (Bob) Spear and Coach (Dean) Smith," Brown said. "I was involved with the Olympic team from a number of times Coach Iba was coaching. One, I played for him in 1964, and in 1968 and 1972 he asked me to help him, so I saw Pop try out for the Olympic team in Colorado Springs.

"Also, I actually cut Pop when he tried out for the Nuggets."

Brown, who played at North Carolina when Smith was an assistant under Frank McGuire, visited his alma mater while Popovich was there on his sabbatical and found he had not been fully engaged with the coaching staff in Chapel Hill.

"I went down to Chapel Hill and initially he wasn't doing a lot down there so I told him to come stay with me at Kansas. So he spent the year with me at Kansas. He sat on the bench and was a big part of our program," Brown said.

There was an immediate connection between the two related to what both had learned from Bob Spear, the Air Force Academy coach for whom Popovich had played and who had been a mentor for Dean Smith.

"Our backgrounds are so similar, with (Air Force) Coach Spear and Coach Smith being so connected," said Brown. "I just loved Pop as a person. I respected his knowledge, obviously, but he's also one of the most decent, loyal guys I've ever been around and I just wanted to be connected."

Brown and Popovich, who remain the best of friends (Popovich was best man at Brown's wedding in 1993), squared off in the 2005 NBA Finals, Popovich getting the better of the matchup when the Spurs won a hard-fought Game 7 against Brown's Detroit Pistons at AT&T Center.

24 The Beautiful Game

Just as the Spurs sacrifice financial gain for the good of the team, individual players sacrifice gaudy statistics for the sake of winning. On their way to their fifth championship in 2014, they showed the basketball-loving world the most thrilling passing game ever seen.

Forget the 1980s Showtime Lakers, who relied mostly on Magic Johnson to keep the ball moving on the fast break.

The 1980s Celtics? Sure, they had Larry Bird, the best passing big man of all time, but they also had Robert Parish and Kevin McHale, post players who focused on shooting once they got the ball in the painted area.

Coach Red Holzman's 1969 "find-the-open-man" Knicks of Walt Frazier, Earl Monroe, Bill Bradley, Dave DeBusschere, and Willis Reed came close to moving the ball as the Spurs did in 2013–14, but Reed, a classic, back-to-the-basket pivot man, was, unquestionably, a ball stopper.

The Spurs played every game of the 2013–14 season with one firm directive from Popovich: go from good to great, an admonition to pass up a good shot if a teammate were open for a great shot. They quickly discovered the value of ball sharing and, with it, the joy of a free-flowing, motion-based offense. As defenses clamped down during the playoffs, when the play typically becomes much more physical, they soon discovered that defenses couldn't bully an offense they couldn't catch up to.

One of the best examples came during Game 6 of the Western Conference Finals against the Oklahoma City Thunder. On one play, the ball, in the space of five seconds on the clock, moved from Ginobili to Mills to Duncan to Boris Diaw, who was wide open for a three-point basket that helped the Spurs win the game that sent them to the 2014 NBA Finals. Watching the replay revealed Thunder players, their heads on swivels, trying to keep up with the flight of the ball, entirely unclear about what to do or where to go. Ultimately, three of them converged on Duncan a split-second after he had passed to Diaw in the corner, nary a defender within 10 feet.

Former New York Knicks and Houston Rockets head coach Jeff Van Gundy was working as color analyst for the TNT Network's broadcast of Game 6. After witnessing the never-touch-the-floor ball movement that resulted in Diaw's uncontested three-pointer, he called on youth coaches everywhere to videotape the play and use it to demonstrate how basketball should be played.

"That play should be an NBA commercial," Van Gundy told the millions watching the game on TNT. "Like, 'This is NBA basketball.' That's beautiful offense and I hope the kids at home and their youth coaches just take that possession and show it on an endless loop."

By the time the Spurs had won four of five games against Miami in the 2014 NBA Finals by at least 15 points, including twice on Miami's home court, their selfless style suddenly had made them America's Team, even casual observers enamored of their stylish play and team-first ethic.

Bob Huggins, head coach of the University of West Virginia Mountaineers and one of college basketball's most successful coaches, took hope from the Spurs' success with such selfless play.

"I think it's the hope of all of us to get back to playing the game the right way," Huggins said. "It's more fun to play and coach and, frankly, more fun to watch when playing together the right way like the Spurs."

It was an online video montage of Spurs plays titled "The Beautiful Game," put together by Colin Stanton, a 26-year-old Spurs fan in San Diego, that brought the team's selfless play to the attention of the digital sports world. After it went online just before the start of the 2014 Western Conference Finals, it went viral, racking up 1.5 million views in one week before an NBA representative called Stanton and made him take it down because of a copyright issue. When Spurs chairman Peter Holt found out the video had been removed from YouTube, he interceded and it went back online.

Stanton told *San Antonio Express-News* reporter Lorne Chan that he wanted to make certain sports fans appreciate the Spurs for how they played and what they had accomplished.

"I just want people to appreciate the Spurs in full," Stanton told Chan, who now works for the Spurs. "If I helped in some way that's great but all the inspiration comes from the Spurs. I guess that mentality is kind of like the Spurs. (Coach) Pop would like that."

Popovich may have shrugged off those who wanted to make something artistic of what he believed was his simple share-the-basketball philosophy but the "The Beautiful Game" had become a "thing" by the time the Spurs finished off the Heat in the most lopsided NBA Finals in league history. Adam Silver, presenting the Larry O'Brien Trophy for the first time since taking over from David Stern on February 14, 2014, picked up on the theme. Congratulating the Spurs, he told them, their adoring fans, and the millions watching the telecast, "You showed the world how beautiful this game can be."

25 The 1987 NBA Draft Lottery

If you're wondering how a draft lottery drawing could appear so high on this list, consider: where would the Spurs be had not David Robinson joined the team for the 1989–90 season?

The answer is unclear but in all likelihood it would be: somewhere other than San Antonio.

The Spurs were a team on the rocks at the conclusion of the 1986–87 season. They had not had a winning season for four years and the team's finances were in shambles. There were rumors of dissension among the owners and more rumors that the team might be headed out of town, and no wonder: the season had just produced the worst record in franchise history, 28–54, and attendance at HemisFair Arena was spotty and that's being charitable. They ranked last in the league in putting people in the stands.

The team was coached by Bob Weiss, an accomplished magician except when it came to pulling wins out of a hat. The team's best player was big guard Alvin Robertson, a defensive menace who had been named Defensive Player of the Year in 1985–86, when he averaged a league-best 3.7 steals per game and made the All-NBA second team. Somehow, the Spurs still managed to give up 113.4 points per game, 16th in a 23-team league, while scoring only 108.3, 14th in the league.

Worse, the future looked even bleaker. Center Artis Gilmore was 37 years old and clearly at the end of his Hall of Fame career. Scoring star Mike Mitchell was only 31 but had a terrible season, his scoring average dipping from 23.4 points per game in 1985–86 to 12.7. By season's end he had checked himself into a drug treatment center in California.

The "consolation" for all this failure was the fourth-worst record in the NBA, better than only the 24–58 New York Knicks and New Jersey Nets, and the 12–80 Los Angeles Clippers, whose mark was, at the time, the second-worst in league history.

The fourth-worst record gave the Spurs a puncher's chance at winning the first pick in the upcoming draft. The pool of available players included one can't-miss franchise player: Robinson, the 7-foot-1 U.S. Naval Academy center.

Every team in the drawing knew that Robinson would not be available for at least two seasons because of an obligation to serve in the Navy after his graduation from Annapolis.

Every team also knew the wait would be worth it. As a senior, Robinson averaged 28 points, 11.8 rebounds, and a nation-leading 4.5 blocks for a mediocre Navy team. The previous season he led the Midshipmen into the NCAA Tournament's round of 16, the one and only time the school would advance so far.

How high was his potential?

Cleveland Cavaliers general manager Wayne Embry, a five-time All-Star center himself, believed it was unlimited.

"David Robinson," Embry told the Associated Press before the draft, "can be another Bill Russell."

The rest of the draft was not considered special, though the experts had grossly underestimated the potential of a small forward from tiny University of Central Arkansas named Scottie Pippen.

Robinson, though, was the prize.

Spurs general manager Bob Bass represented the club at the lottery drawing at the Equitable Center, in New York City. It was the third year of the NBA's draft lottery, which had been ordered by the league's Board of Governors after it became clear that some teams had "tanked" games to get the No. 1 pick in 1984, when the University of Houston's Hakeem Olajuwon was the consensus No. 1 overall pick. (North Carolina's Michael Jordan went No. 3, after Olajuwon and the University of Kentucky's Sam Bowie.)

One Lucky Spur

In addition to Bob Bass, also at the Equitable Center for the 1987 draft lottery was a Spurs fan named Roberto Pachecano, who had won a contest to be the team's "lucky charm" at the drawing. To enhance his lucky charm ability, he brought along a family lucky charm, a cattle spur that had belonged to his late father-in-law. He also wore a red chameleon pendant, a nod to Robinson's Naval service. According to Navy legend, he told reporters at the lottery, shipwrecked sailors believed they would be safe if they saw a red chameleon.

Watching the proceedings in the audience on lottery night, Pachecano beamed and clutched at his lucky cattle spur and red chameleon pendant.

"The Spurs will be safe now that they have Robinson," he would tell reporters who covered the drawing.

By 1987 the league had tweaked the process of having NBA commissioner David Stern pulling the envelopes containing team logos out of a clear drum. For one thing, the team with the worst record—in this case, the Clippers—was guaranteed no worse than the fourth overall position. Further, each team representative at the lottery, rather than Stern, got to pick one envelope from the drum for placement on the draft order board, the first envelope pulled put in the No. 7 position, then on to No. 1 for the seventh, and final, envelope pulled. The order for pulling envelopes was determined beforehand by a drawing of numbers by the team reps.

Bass went fifth in the envelope pull, his envelope placed in the No. 3 position. Sacramento Kings owner Frank McCormick went next, when there were only two envelopes remaining. When he pulled his envelope, to go in the No. 2 spot, nobody knew he was deciding between envelopes containing the logos of the Spurs and the Suns.

Seattle's Harry Weltman went last, without a choice to make: the envelope that contained the Spurs logo.

One by one, Stern then opened the envelopes. Each time he did so, Bass looked away. Afterward, he explained why to a reporter from the *Washington Post*.

"I used the same theory I use in golf," he said. "If a guy is trying to make a putt and I'm down four or five bets, I always look away. And today, I looked away all six times."

Indeed, videotape of the CBS-TV telecast of the 1987 lottery proceeding reveals that when Stern was opening the envelope containing the logo of the team that would get the No. 2 pick, the images of Bass and Phoenix Suns president and GM Jerry Colangelo are on a split screen. Colangelo intently eyed Stern while Bass had his head turned away.

When Stern pulled the Suns logo out of the No. 2 envelope, assuring the Spurs of getting the No. 1 pick, Bass pounded his first on the table at which all the team reps were seated.

Bass shook hands with Stern, then did a quick interview with CBS-TV's James Brown, who asked if the Spurs would make Robinson the No. 1 pick despite having to wait two years to get him in a Spurs uniform.

"We've waited 14 years," Bass answered. "What's two more years?"

When Brown asked what the Spurs would do to get Robinson under contract, Bass assured Spurs fans not to worry.

"Whatever it takes," he said. "We'll get Angelo (owner Angelo Drossos) after him. That's all."

As it turned out, it would take two years and an ownership change—Red McCombs bought out Drossos and the other Spurs partners on May 27, 1988—before the Spurs would get Robinson signed to a five-year deal that guaranteed that at its conclusion he always would be paid no less than the average of the two highest-paid players in the league.

26 50 Wins

The Spurs began the 2015–16 season after a successful rebuilding summer that made them one of a handful of legitimate championship contenders.

Adding two All-Star big men, LaMarcus Aldridge and David West, and retaining Tim Duncan, Manu Ginobili, and Danny Green made another season with at least 50 wins seem like a given, and why not? They had produced at least 50 wins in an NBA-record 16 consecutive seasons. Indeed, they went a franchise-best 67–15 in 2015–16.

The next-longest streaks of consecutive 50-win seasons: 12, by the 1980–91 Los Angeles Lakers of Kareem Abdul-Jabbar and Magic Johnson; 11, by the Dirk Nowitzki–led Dallas Mavericks, from 2000–11; 10, by the Bill Russell Celtics of 1959–68; and nine, by the Larry Bird-Kevin McHale-Robert Parish Celtics.

How amazing is such an accomplishment?

Consider that it took the Toronto Raptors 20 years to win more than 50 games in a season. The Nets, who entered the NBA from the ABA at the same time as the Spurs, have had only one 50-win season.

"I just don't know that we're ever going to see something like this happening again," former Dallas Mavericks All-Star guard and longtime broadcaster Derek Harper told Fran Blinebury, the great columnist for NBA.com who has been covering the league since 1980.

Former New York Knicks and Houston Rockets coach Jeff Van Gundy went a step further in Blinebury's excellent analysis of the streak.

"I used to say the 33-game winning streak of the Lakers (in 1971–72) was the most unbreakable record in the game," Van

Gundy said. "But, hey, the Heat got to 27. Now I'm convinced this one by the Spurs will never be touched."

Two things make the streak even more remarkable than it seems on first inspection: It included 50 wins in a lockout-shortened 2011–12 season, when it took the second-best winning percentage in franchise history (75.8 percent) to keep the streak alive. Further, it began in the 1999–2000 season that followed the team's first championship run in the lockout-shortened 50-game 1998–99 season, when it would have taken an unbeaten season to get to 50 wins.

The Spurs went 37–13 in 1998–99, winning 74 percent of their games. That extrapolates to 60 wins in a full season.

Aside from the 66-game 2011–12 season, the Spurs have had only one other season during the 50-win run that came down to the final week of the season with the streak in doubt. It took a 133–111 win over the Minnesota Timberwolves in the penultimate game of the 2009–10 season to get win No. 50. In no other season did they have to go past the 78th game to secure the streak.

"What they've done is sustain greatness," Van Gundy said in the NBA.com piece. "I think that's much more telling than five championships. First of all, it's something that nobody's done before. Winning 50 and having a plus-.500 road record all that time, to me that's incredible."

The common factors during the streak are two-time MVP big man Tim Duncan, head coach Gregg Popovich, vice president of basketball operations/general manager R.C. Buford, and the ownership group chaired by Peter Holt. Tony Parker has been on 15 of the 50-win teams; Manu Ginobili has been on 14; and Matt Bonner has been on 10, matching Bill Russell.

"I am totally against the whole mindset that everything is about championships when it comes to evaluating players, evaluating teams," Van Gundy continued.

"'Did they win a championship?' Really, is that all you've got?

"I'm telling you, sustaining greatness is much harder than a one-, two- or three-year greatness."

For the Tim Duncan Spurs, sustaining greatness has been a 50-win habit.

27 Kawhi Leonard

After the 2010–11 season produced a 61–21 record that gave them the No. 1 seed in the Western Conference, the Spurs went into the 2011 draft with the No. 29 overall selection.

They also entered the draft with a clear understanding they needed to make a move to position themselves for a brighter future after the No. 8 seeded Memphis Grizzlies eliminated them from the playoffs in six games.

The move that did the trick was a draft night trade that put Kawhi Leonard in a silver-and-black uniform.

A 6-foot-7 small forward who led the San Diego State Aztecs to the Sweet 16 in the 2011 NCAA Tournament, Leonard entered the draft as a candidate to sneak into the lottery. He did not quite make it but the Indiana Pacers made him the first non-lottery pick, selecting him with the No. 15 overall selection.

In fact, the Pacers had made the pick at the behest of the Spurs, who had negotiated a trade with them that now ranks as the best draft night deal in franchise history.

Sending two-way guard George Hill, an Indianapolis native and hard-nosed defender that Gregg Popovich called his favorite player, to the Pacers, the Spurs acquired the draft rights to Leonard and two second-round draft picks, Europeans Davis Bertans and Erazem Lorbek.

Leonard's impact was immediate and profound. Before the season ended he had supplanted Richard Jefferson as the starter at small forward and become, in the words of none other than Gregg Popovich, "the future face of the franchise."

Leonard has a 7-foot-3 wingspan and the second-largest hands ever measured at the NBA's pre-draft camp, 9.8 inches from the base of his hand to the tip of his index finger. Those freakish dimensions helped make him one of the NBA's best perimeter players.

The unsung heroes in Leonard's draft night acquisition were George Felton and Chip Engelland. After watching Leonard play numerous games, Felton was convinced he had the potential to be a star, if only he could improve his shooting. Engelland, the shooting coach who helped Tony Parker remake his jumper into a reliable weapon, watched film of Leonard's shooting stroke and asserted strongly that he could fix it.

Engelland's work began immediately after the draft. With the possibility of an ownership lockout of players looming—collective bargaining talks for a new contract between the league and its players association had gone nowhere leading up to the expiration of the collective bargaining agreement—Engelland spent the eight days between the draft and the lockout, which began on July 1, 2011, reshaping Leonard's shot and giving him a program to perfect it in the months before the lockout was ended, on December 8.

A tireless worker, Leonard arrived at his first training camp with a much improved jumper. When his rookie season finally got underway he was a regular in Popovich's playing rotation and was in the starting lineup for the first time in the 11th game of the season, sharing the starting spot with Richard Jefferson. When the Spurs sent Jefferson to the Golden State Warriors in a draft deadline deal, he moved into the starting lineup for good.

Leonard finished the season with averages of 7.9 points, 5.1 rebounds, and 1.3 steals and was named to the All-Rookie first team. When the season ended, USA Basketball, which oversees the

Men's Senior National Team (Team USA), invited Leonard to be on a select team of young stars to compete against Team USA as it prepared for the 2012 Olympics.

It was at training camp for the 2012–13 season that Popovich declared Leonard the future face of the Spurs franchise, putting a bit more pressure on the second-year player than he deserved. Leonard did not disappoint. His scoring average jumped by four points per game, to 11.9, and he averaged 1.7 steals per game. He was even better in the playoffs, averaging 13.5 points per game, plus 9.0 rebounds and 1.8 steals.

Then, in the 2013 NBA Finals, Popovich asked Leonard to defend Miami's LeBron James, with minimal double-team help. James made only 21-of-54 shots, 38.9 percent, in the first three games, as the Spurs took a 2–1 lead.

James and the Heat recovered to win their second straight NBA title in 2013 but Leonard had established himself as one of the few defenders in the league able to take on the four-time MVP, head-to-head, and when the Spurs returned to the Finals in 2014 it was Leonard, not James, who walked away with both a championship and the Bill Russell Trophy that goes to the NBA Finals MVP, and at just 22 years of age.

With Popovich encouraging Leonard to be more assertive at the offensive end, Leonard's scoring average continued its upward surge in 2014–15, to 16.5 points per game. It was his continued progression as a defensive ace that made him one of the Spurs' key players. Leading the league in steals, at 2.3 per game, Leonard became the first Spur since David Robinson to win the league's Defensive Player of the Year Award.

A restricted free agent after the 2014–15 season, Leonard re-signed with the team in July 2015, a five-year maximum deal worth $94.4 million. His play during the 2015–16 season proved he was, indeed, a maximum-value player. He was voted to the starting lineup for the All-Star Game, won his second consecutive DPOY

Award, was a unanimous choice for first-team All-NBA Defense, and was named to the All-NBA first team. He also led the Spurs in scoring, at 21.2 points per game, and in steals (1.8 per game), and was third in rebounds (6.8 per game).

Popovich's "future face of the franchise" assertion, uttered before the start of the 2012–13 season, became reality.

28 Bruce Bowen

When Bruce Bowen announced his retirement before the start of the 2009–10 season, a post on SBNation.com suggested the NBA re-name flagrant fouls in his honor.

It was meant to be what Bowen calls a "jokey joke," but it was based on a caricature of Bowen's defensive skill that was utterly erroneous. In 13 NBA seasons with four teams, Bowen was whistled for a grand total of seven flagrant fouls. In his eight seasons with the Spurs, he received only three.

Compare that to all-time flagrant leader Shaquille O'Neal, who received 37 flagrant foul penalties. And if you want to compare Bowen to another great perimeter defender with a well-earned reputation for physical play, try Metta World Peace (*nee* Ron Artest), who received 23 flagrants in 14 seasons.

In some ways, the website's suggestion was validation of Bowen's status as one of the most effective defenders of perimeter players in NBA history. Certainly, his defensive skill accounts for his high position on this list, because it is what made him a starter for the Spurs in every game he played through his first seven seasons in silver and black, three of which resulted in NBA titles.

That Bowen became a starter for any NBA team was a bit of a miracle. Undrafted out of Cal-Fullerton in 1993, where he had averaged 16.3 points per game as a senior while shooting just 28 percent from the college three-point line, Bowen had to work his way into the NBA by playing professional ball in France and in the now-defunct Continental Basketball Association.

Miami Heat coach Pat Riley brought him to training camp in 1995 but cut him after a week, with instructions to work on his shot and focus on his obvious defensive skills. Riley gave him a 10-day contract in mid-March of the 1996–97 season and he lasted to the end of that season.

After playing for the Celtics and 76ers he landed back in Miami for the 2000–01 season, starting 72 games and being named to the NBA's All-Defensive second team.

It was great timing for Bowen, a free agent at the conclusion of the 2000–01 season. Looking for a solid perimeter defender, Spurs coach and general manager Gregg Popovich signed Bowen and immediately put him in his starting lineup.

"He gave us an edge," Popovich would say years later. "He set a tone for our team that they followed."

Popovich told Bowen he would have to work hard on improving his shooting if he wanted to stay in the starting lineup and Bowen did just that. Working with Brett Brown, then the Spurs development coach, he developed a reliable corner three-point-shooting stroke that made him a valuable weapon. In his second season with the Spurs he led the league in three-point percentage, 44.1 percent, a big factor in a 60-win season that preceded a run to the team's second championship.

Still, it was Bowen's defense that made him one of the Spurs' signature players in the first eight years of the 21st century. He was a first-team All-Defensive selection five straight seasons (2003–04 through 2007–08).

Along the way he developed a reputation for aggressive play that some, including Ray Allen, called dirty. Some players and coaches suggested he went beyond dirty. Vince Carter and Amar'e Stoudemire accused him of intentionally trying to injure them by occupying landing space after they went up for jump shots. Former New York Knicks coach Isaiah Thomas also accused him of intentionally putting his feet in Knicks players' landing spots and threatened him physically.

"He used to get into opponents' heads," teammate Manu Ginobili told the *San Antonio Express-News*. "He was amazing at that."

Bowen's finest moments as an elite defender probably came during the 2007 NBA Finals, when he held Cleveland Cavaliers superstar LeBron James to 35-of-101 shooting in the Spurs' four-game sweep. For that he received at least one vote as Finals MVP.

Spurs captain Tim Duncan knew how important Bowen was to the Spurs in their 2003, 2005, and 2007 championship runs. On the eve of the ceremony at which Bowen's No. 12 was retired and raised to the rafters at AT&T Center on March 21, 2012, Duncan paid him the ultimate compliment by noting how different the Spurs became after he retired following the 2008–09 season.

"We've been trying to replace him ever since," Duncan said.

Bowen was overwhelmed by the team's decision to retire his number.

"I think it really shows how you might be a role player but there's a place for role players, as well," he said. "It's the by-product of staying the course, and look what happens."

Bowen's number was the seventh retired by the franchise and the first for a player who never once averaged double-figure scoring.

Still a San Antonio resident, Bowen moved on to a career as an NBA analyst for ESPN-TV after retiring from the game.

29 Big Shot Rob

By the time he arrived in San Antonio, Robert Horry already had played in 165 NBA playoff games and won five championships—two with the Houston Rockets and three with the Los Angeles Lakers.

He also had earned a reputation for clutch shooting that gave him a nickname for the ages: Big Shot Rob.

Indeed, Horry had a knack for hitting big shots—usually three-pointers—at the most critical moments of playoff games. His most famous last-second shot remains the three-pointer that left his hand with just three-tenths of a second remaining when he was playing for the Lakers in Game 4 of the 2002 Western Conference Finals against the Sacramento Kings. The Kings would have had a nearly insurmountable 3–1 series lead with a victory, but Horry's unlikely three-pointer—Sacramento's Vlade Divac tipped a missed shot by Shaquille O'Neal straight into Horry's hands at the three-point line—saved the day for Los Angeles.

The Lakers went on to eliminate the Kings and beat the New Jersey Nets in the 2002 NBA Finals, giving Horry his fifth championship ring.

Horry would play one more season for the Lakers but when he became a free agent after the 2002–03 season that produced the Spurs' second NBA championship, Gregg Popovich and R.C. Buford convinced him to come to San Antonio. Horry had averaged just under 30 minutes per game for the Lakers in 2002–03 and part of their pitch was a chance to become a true role player, his playing time reduced to help him extend his career.

Ironically, a clutch three-point shot Horry missed helped the Spurs win the 2003 NBA title. The Spurs and Lakers were tied in a

Robert Horry reveled in the moment after hitting one of the biggest shots in Spurs history, a three-pointer with 5.8 seconds left in Game 5 of the 2005 NBA Finals against the Detroit Pistons.

Western Conference semifinals series, 2–2, with Game 5 at AT&T Center. With 15 seconds left, Spurs guard Stephen Jackson made the first of two free throws to give the Spurs a 96–94 lead. When he missed the second free throw, L.A.'s Shaquille O'Neal grabbed the rebound and called timeout with 14.7 seconds left. That gave Lakers coach Phil Jackson time to draw up a play and he opted for a late three-point attempt for Horry.

This time Horry's shot went in and out and the Spurs came away with a win and a 3–2 series lead. Tim Duncan dominated Game 6 in Los Angeles, ending the Lakers' three-year reign as champs and setting up San Antonio's third championship.

When the Spurs advanced to the 2005 NBA Finals against the Detroit Pistons, the free-agent deal that put Horry in silver and black became one of the best deals the club ever made. It was Horry's three-pointer with 5.8 seconds left in overtime in Game 5 that gave the Spurs a 3–2 edge in a series that would go to seven games before the Spurs secured their third NBA title, the sixth of Horry's career.

Horry would add a seventh championship ring to his collection as a solid contributor on the 2006–07 Spurs who swept the Cleveland Cavaliers in the 2007 NBA Finals.

Horry retired after the 2007–08 season. He was 37 and, at the time, had played in more playoff games than any player in NBA history. His seven championships are more than all but six players (Bill Russell, Sam Jones, Tom Heinsohn, John Havlicek, K.C. Jones, and Tom Sanders) from the Boston Celtics dynasty of the 1950s and 1960s.

Perhaps the most amazing fact from Horry's career is this: through his 16 seasons he never failed to advance to at least the second round of the playoffs. He ranks No. 2 in playoff games played, 244, trailing only Derek Fisher.

Horry attributes his amazing playoff success to simply being on great teams but it has much more to do with his unique ability, including his uncanny shooting when games were on the line.

30 1,000 Wins

On February 9, 2015, Gregg Popovich became just the ninth coach in NBA history to record 1,000 wins, after the Spurs beat the Indiana Pacers at Bankers Life Fieldhouse in Indianapolis.

Though he did all he could to downplay the significance of the milestone, his players understood it was something special.

The fact it took a comeback from a 14-point deficit in the fourth quarter epitomized the "pounding the rock" philosophy that has guided Popovich and his team for more than 18 seasons.

Popovich went with a lineup of bench players to open the fourth. Aron Baynes, Boris Diaw, Marco Belinelli, Patty Mills, and Cory Joseph got the Spurs back in striking range in the first five minutes. Tim Duncan, Kawhi Leonard, and Tony Parker returned to grind the game to the finish.

And at the finish, Popovich drew up a play that worked to perfection.

After Duncan grabbed an offensive rebound with 21 seconds left, Popovich called for a timeout, during which he subbed Belinelli into the game for big man Baynes. When the Pacers didn't match the small lineup, things set up perfectly for the play Popovich designed: Leonard, isolated above the top of the key, with Belinelli stationed in the left corner.

Indiana left both its big men, center Roy Hibbert and power forward David West, on the floor, so when Duncan inbounded to

Leonard above the top of the key, the advantage was with the Spurs small forward.

Sure enough, when Leonard dribbled past West the Pacers had to rotate, Hibbert coming at him to double team. Belinelli's defender, Rodney Stuckey, rotated toward Hibbert's man.

"Have to give a lot of credit to Kawhi," Duncan told the *San Antonio Express-News* after the game. "He recognized the mismatch of having a big on him so he was able to penetrate, draw the defense, and make a great pass."

When Hibbert closed on him, Leonard side-armed a perfect pass to the corner to Belinelli, who pump-faked Stuckey into the air as he scrambled back to defend.

Unmolested, Belinelli drained a perfect 18-foot pull-up jumper with 2.1 seconds left to give the Spurs the 95–93 lead that held up for the milestone win.

"It was the definition of a pounding-the-rock win," Parker told the *Express-News.* "It was a great win for us. When we were down 14 at the start of the fourth quarter it didn't look good. We stayed together; we put some stops together, even though we couldn't hit a shot. We were 6-of-25 from three but we got a big shot from Marco at the end."

There was no on-court celebration for Popovich. Players trudged to the locker room. Assistant Ettore Messina gave Popovich a quick hug but that was it.

"I don't do too much celebrating," Popovich told the gaggle of reporters who asked him what it meant to finally reach the exclusive club. "I've been here a long time and I've got good players. Getting the players is difficult but I've been fortunate to have good ones and the time is the most important element. You've got to be around for a while. It's more a tribute to them than any coaches."

The most impactful of the good players who have worn silver and black under Popovich also shrugged off the significance of Popovich's milestone in the immediate aftermath.

"I think he probably downplays this as much as I will," said Tim Duncan, who scored 15 points and blocked five Indiana shots. "It's another win. It will look great when we look back on it but at this point just getting this win tonight is huge for us in this season and this point."

In truth, Duncan and his "Big Three" teammates—Parker and Manu Ginobili—understood that the win deserved to be honored.

"I'm happy for Pop," said Parker. "I feel lucky to have been with him for a lot of those wins. We've experienced so much together, the Big Three and Pop, we've had a lot of fun. I'm so happy for him."

Popovich knew there was something different about the game, too. A gourmand and wine connoisseur, he hosted the team at a postgame dinner and picked up the tab.

Ginobili, who came up limping late in a loss in Toronto and sat out the game for precautionary reasons, wondered why the NBA does not recognize playoff wins as well as regular-season wins.

"For me it's not 1,000," Ginobili told the *Express-News*. "It's 1,149. I just checked. I have no idea why they don't count the playoffs, which are more valuable. They should count double.

"Regardless, it's incredible. A thousand games is such an incredible milestone. I am happy for him."

Popovich joined two of his mentors—all-time wins leader Don Nelson (1,335 wins) and Larry Brown (1,098)—in the exclusive club that also includes Lenny Wilkens (1,332), Jerry Sloan (1,221), Pat Riley (1,210), Phil Jackson (1,155), George Karl (1,175), and Rick Adelman (1,042).

Only Jackson (1,423 games) and Pat Riley (1,434) got to 1,000 wins in fewer games than Popovich, who did it in his 1,462nd game.

Of those in the 1,000-win club, only Jackson has a better winning percentage, 70.4, than Popovich's 69.2.

31 Red McCombs

Should it be a surprise that someone born and raised in the tiny town of Spur, Texas, ranks as one of the most important individuals in Spurs history?

B.J. "Red" McCombs is a classic Texas business success story. A self-made billionaire, he always was willing to make bold decisions. One of his boldest moves: helping to bring pro basketball to San Antonio in 1973, when he was the biggest investor among the group that leased the Dallas Chaparrals for $1, with an option to buy the team that both sides of the deal understood as a de facto transfer of ownership.

Subsequent to his role as the main money man bringing the Spurs to San Antonio, McCombs remained a key figure in the organization's first two decades. In 1978, two years after the Spurs entered the NBA, he sold his interest in the team. In 1983, he bought back into the NBA when he gained sole ownership of the Denver Nuggets for roughly $2 million by assuming the team's debt and paying about $225,000 to the team's owners. In 1985, he sold the Nuggets to Houston businessman Sidney Shlenker for $28 million. In 1988, he regained controlling ownership of the Spurs when he paid $47 million to Angelo Drossos and his ownership partners for an 80 percent stake in the team. Finally, in 1993 he sold the Spurs to an investment group that included Gen. Robert McDermott, in all likelihood taking less money than he could have gotten had he been willing to sell to out-of-state investors who would have relocated the team.

Owner of some of Texas' most successful automobile dealerships, McCombs' decision to take full control of the Spurs in 1988 was vital to the team's future. The team had suffered through a dreary 31–51 season, and ranked last in the league in both attendance and per-game gate revenue.

"This is a very, very big step for my family," McCombs told the Associated Press after his purchase was announced. "To a boy from Spur, Texas, who was raised during the Depression era, it is a very serious investment. I feel it is a very good investment and our goal is to make the Spurs the absolute very best."

McCombs' strategy cut to the source of the team's problems.

"We will be doing everything that we know how to do to see those fans fill the rafters," McCombs told the Associated Press at the time. "We understand that we have to put a product out that people will want to come and see and that is our responsibility."

He delivered on the promise in short order, firing head coach Bob Weiss and replacing him with Larry Brown, whose Kansas Jayhawks had just won the NCAA title. He made Brown the league's highest-paid coach, signing him to an $800,000-per-year contract that angered his fellow NBA owners.

He made no apology for the decision, explaining that it was what he had to do to bring such a high-powered coach to such a small market.

Hiring Brown had collateral consequences because Brown brought with him assistant coaches R.C. Buford and Gregg Popovich, the eventual architects of the Spurs' two-decade run as the best franchise in all of professional sports.

Brown clashed with McCombs during his fourth season on the bench and asked to be fired after 38 games. GM Bob Bass, who had coached the team on three prior occasions, finished out the season on the bench.

Always looking to make a splash, McCombs then hired highly successful UNLV coach Jerry Tarkanian to coach the Spurs for the 1992–93 season. It was an experiment—Tarkanian never had coached at the pro level—and it was a disaster. "Tark the Shark" was fired after 20 games, his team 9–11, and replaced by John Lucas.

Lucas, who hired George Gervin as an assistant, guided the Spurs to a record of 39–22 and a spot in the playoffs. They fell to the Phoenix Suns in the Western Conference semifinals.

Having four coaches in two seasons was enough for McCombs. He put the team up for sale, eventually getting $76 million from Gen. Robert McDermott and his group.

Peter Holt, who would join the McDermott group in 1996 and become its chairman, appreciates the fact McCombs was so committed to seeing the team stay in San Antonio he was willing to make a financial sacrifice.

"He took less money than he could have gotten from somebody who wanted to take the team away," Holt said in an interview with the *San Antonio Express-News* in 2014. "Everybody cooperated to keep the Spurs in town."

32 Gen. Robert McDermott

Brigadier General Robert McDermott would still have a lasting legacy in San Antonio even if he'd never had a role with the Spurs. After retiring from a distinguished 25-year career in the United States Air Force, McDermott came to the Alamo City as chief executive officer of USAA, the insurance company that serves the military community and has become one of the largest insurers of automobiles and homes in the country. He certainly had the chops: he was a decorated combat pilot during World War II (Bronze Star and three Air Medals) and concluded his military career as permanent dean of faculty at the Air Force Academy.

Always active in community affairs, McDermott also served as chairman of the Greater San Antonio Chamber of Commerce. In a profile in *The New York Times* in 1987, then Mayor Henry Cisneros (who later served as Secretary of Housing and Urban Development in the administration of President Bill Clinton) called McDermott the city's most important non-elected leader.

"I suspect that every city has one businessperson who sets the tone for a particular area," Cisneros told the paper. "For the 1970s and 1980s, that person in San Antonio has been General McDermott."

It was in that capacity that, in 1993, McDermott was asked to join a group of local business leaders who were seeking to buy the Spurs from Red McCombs. Investors from out of town were willing to buy the team if they could move it, and McDermott's willingness to join the group was critical to McCombs' decision to sell to the group for the below-market price of $76 million.

Peter J. Holt, who now serves as chairman of San Antonio Spurs, LLC, understands that the team likely would have left the city had it not been for McDermott's involvement.

"That group is the group that really should be given the credit for keeping the team in town, starting with Gen. McDermott, God rest his soul," Holt told The *San Antonio Express-News* after the Spurs won their fifth title in 2014. "He put the group together. I don't know if anyone else could have pulled it off."

As if merely keeping the team in San Antonio were not enough to merit a place on this list, it is what McDermott did soon after taking over as the team's CEO in 1994 that secures his place. It was he who brought Gregg Popovich back into the Spurs fold as general manager and executive vice president/head of basketball operations.

At the time, Popovich's hiring stunned Spurs fans and puzzled most of the NBA. The former head coach of Division III Pomona-Pitzer had been an assistant on Larry Brown's Spurs staff for four seasons and just two more on Don Nelson's Golden State Warriors coaching staff. But Popovich had entered the Air Force Academy in 1966, when McDermott was still dean of faculty, and the Spurs chairman also knew him from his time at the Academy as an assistant coach. He got a strong recommendation from Nelson, who doubled as GM of the Warriors. But it was Popovich's background that mattered most to McDermott.

In a profile of McDermott in 2014, his daughter, Betsy Gwinn, told *Express-News* staff writer Tom Orsborn that her father, who died in 2006, had been sold on Popovich's "background as an Academy grad and just his commitment to discipline and excellence."

McDermott admitted he did not know a lot about basketball when he hired Popovich but he knew about character and exacted a promise from him: sooner or later, he expected Popovich to find a way to rid the team of Dennis Rodman. The controversial power forward was gone after the conclusion of Popovich's first season, traded to the Chicago Bulls for Will Perdue.

After paying about $35 million to join the ownership group in 1996, Holt replaced McDermott as CEO in 1996, fully aware of his predecessor's legacy.

33 Angelo Drossos

Perhaps it was his experience as a successful car salesman that endowed Angelo Drossos with the proverbial golden tongue. Then again, he had been a boxing promoter, so he was practiced in the art of hyperbole. He also had been a dance instructor, so he knew how to deliver a sweet line or two.

Whatever the explanation, there was no executive in basketball more entertaining than Drossos, part of the original ownership group that brought the Dallas Chaparrals to San Antonio in 1973 and renamed them the Spurs.

Consider:

- When ABA commissioner Mike Storen refused to approve the trade bringing George Gervin to San Antonio in exchange for cash, Drossos responded in a letter: "[Bleep] you. A stronger letter will follow."

- When describing the impact Gervin had with the Spurs years later, Drossos said: "George Gervin was to San Antonio what Babe Ruth was to New York. Babe Ruth was baseball in New York City. He was the Yankees. Gervin was the San Antonio Spurs. He was the symbol of basketball in this town."

- When the Spurs used the No. 1 pick in the 1987 draft to select David Robinson despite a Navy commitment that would prevent Robinson from playing in San Antonio for two years, Drossos—perhaps inspired by a recent visit of Pope John Paul II to San Antonio—declared Robinson's importance to the franchise by saying, "David Robinson may not be able to walk on water, but he can at least walk on the San Antonio River."

Although the colorful Drossos had a diverse background that included success as a stockbroker on Wall Street, he did not have basketball experience. Red McCombs, who hired Drossos to work at his car dealership, was the primary financial force behind the franchise relocating from Dallas, but it was Drossos who not only recognized the importance of adding star power to the team, but who also did much of the negotiating to bring accomplished players to the team.

The Spurs were not warmly greeted in San Antonio. After they began the 1973–74 season 10–12, crowds were dipping into the low four figures, so Drossos sent $300,000 to cash-strapped Virginia owner Earl Foreman for the rights to 6-foot-11, 240-pound center Swen Nater. At that point, Storen saw the talent drain in Virginia, which had already traded Julius Erving to the New York Nets, and announced no more deals could be made. But Drossos made the Gervin deal anyway and later won a federal court case for the right to keep Gervin in San Antonio.

That was only the beginning for Drossos. When the ABA folded, Drossos was a key figure on the committee that led to four ABA teams joining the NBA. Fellow owners obviously recognized the value of having a former boxing promoter, car salesman, etc., represent them.

More importantly for San Antonio, however, was that Drossos' presence on the committee ensured the Spurs would be one of the teams to move to the NBA, which charged the incoming ABA teams $300,000 each to enter the league. The Spurs were never a healthy franchise financially in the ABA—none of the teams were. So Drossos did what he did the best, selling new investors on the bright future of the Spurs in the NBA and charging them $300,000 for the right to join the fun.

During the first two decades of the team, Drossos was part of every major decision—from player acquisition to hiring coaches and front office personnel including Bob Bass, Doug Moe, Stan Albeck, and Larry Brown. Even though he left the franchise in 1988, his legacy is profound. Drossos established a big league attitude in a small market city. He connected the team and players with the fans and created a family atmosphere. And he brought elite players to the city, creating a tradition of winning and excellence that later would grow into championships.

Unfortunately, Drossos died in 1997 at age 68, never seeing the Spurs win a title. He was the foundation, the man who began the building of the Spurs Nation.

34 All-Time Awards

Using the NBA's official award categories as a guide, let's pick the Spurs' all-time Most Valuable Player, Teams (First, Second, and Third), Defensive Player, Most Improved Player, Sixth Man, and Coach.

Most Valuable Player: Tim Duncan

An easier pick than it should be considering the number of great players who have played for the Spurs. However, in franchise history only Duncan and David Robinson have won regular-season MVPs, and Duncan won in back-to-back seasons, 2001–02 and 2002–03. His second MVP season was the best single season for any player in club history. He averaged 23.3 points, 12.9 rebounds, 3.9 assists, and 2.9 blocks per game. More importantly, he led the Spurs to their second NBA championship and punctuated his amazing season with a near quadruple-double (21 points, 20 rebounds, 10 assists, and eight blocks) as the Spurs won Game 6 of the Finals to claim the title and send Robinson off to retirement with another championship ring. The fact Duncan was MVP of the first three NBA Finals in Spurs history puts the exclamation point on the declarative sentence "Tim Duncan is the San Antonio Spurs' All-Time Most Valuable Player!"

All-Time First Team: Tony Parker, George Gervin, David Robinson, Tim Duncan, Kawhi Leonard

Put them on the court together in each player's prime and they would challenge any All-Time First Team from any NBA franchise, including the Lakers, Celtics, and Bulls, the only franchises that have won more NBA titles.

All-Time Second Team: James Silas, Manu Ginobili, Artis Gilmore, Larry Kenon, Sean Elliott

All-Time Third Team: Avery Johnson, Alvin Robertson, Billy Paultz, Robert Horry, Mike Mitchell

(Note: Since Duncan played plenty at the center position during his career, any Spurs fan who prefers to put him at center on either the second team or third team may do so. But Robinson clearly is the greatest pure center in franchise history.)

Defensive Player: Tim Duncan

No Spurs player made more All-Defensive teams (15) than Duncan, who was first team eight times, including his selection for the 2014–15 season, during which he turned 39. During the 2015–16 season, he passed David Robinson as the franchise leader in career blocks. He has been the anchor of one of the NBA's all-time best defenses from his first game in silver and black.

Most Improved Player: Bruce Bowen

Start with the fact Bowen was both undrafted and unsigned after his college career at Cal-Fullerton. He spent three seasons playing professionally in France, where he was a scoring star despite the fact his perimeter jump shot was entirely unreliable. Miami coach Pat Riley gave him his first shot in the NBA and convinced him he could stick in the league if he focused on his defense. His response was to become an All-Defensive Team selection eight times, including seven times as a Spur.

Bowen never shot better than 40.9 percent in the five seasons he spent with three different teams before he arrived in San Antonio. Once he joined the Spurs, he went to work with the team's development coaches, starting with Brett Brown, and turned himself into a decent perimeter shooter and, amazingly, a reliable corner three-point shooter. In the Spurs' 2002–03 championship season, he led the league in three-point percentage, making 101-of-229 long-range shots, 44.1 percent. By the time he retired after the 2008–09 season, he had made 661-of-1,632 three-point shots for the Spurs, 40.5 percent.

Sixth Man: Manu Ginobili

Ginobili should have been in the starting lineup through the bulk of his career but Gregg Popovich discovered during the Spurs' playoff run to the 2005 championship that he could change a game's dynamics by bringing him off the bench. After starting all 74 games he played in the 2004–05 regular season, Ginobili came off the bench in nine of 65 games in 2005–06 and then, in 2006–07, he came off the bench in 36 of 75 games.

Finally, Popovich started him in only 23 of the 74 games he played in 2007–08 and he produced a career-high scoring average of 19.5 points per game and won the NBA's Sixth Man Award.

In subsequent seasons, Ginobili started more games than those in which he came off the bench only once, 2010–11, when he started all but one of the 80 games he played.

Coach: Gregg Popovich

The "no brainer" selection. The coach of all five of the Spurs championship teams, Popovich ranks ninth all-time in NBA wins (1,089) and has the third-highest winning percentage (69.2 percent) among those who have coached at least 500 games.

35 The 1997 NBA Draft Lottery

If you ask Gregg Popovich, he became a brilliant basketball man on June 25, 1997. Prior to that point, he didn't look too gifted. He was 64 games into a coaching career that has now surpassed 1,700 games and his team had won 17 times, just 27 percent of its games.

Since June 25, 1997, however, his teams have won 65 percent of their games. Brilliance, of course, came in the form of Tim Duncan, whose rights were secured by the Spurs that magical day in late June.

And they did need a pinch of magic—entering the lottery, they had only a 21.6 percent chance of winning the No. 1 pick and two teams had better odds. Peter Holt, who was part of a group that purchased the Spurs in 1993 and later bought controlling interest, represented the Spurs at the lottery in New Jersey and brought a couple of simple good luck items with him—a Spurs tie and a horseshoe lapel pin.

Popovich was so convinced that the Spurs had no chance to get Duncan that instead of sitting in the studio where the lottery order was being revealed, he stayed in the holding area.

"We were in a big tent that was next to the studios and they called us to go sit in the stands," Popovich said. "I didn't go in because there was no way we had a chance to get the No. 1 pick. I just stayed in the tent where the food and the beer were. I'm the only guy in the tent. Everybody vacated. So I'm watching this little TV, eating a burger and drinking a beer, and they get to the pick that was supposed to be us, but it was somebody else. I couldn't believe it. I was so shocked that I literally dropped my hamburger on the ground."

The fact that the Spurs and Philadelphia 76ers were the final two teams added to the shock. Sixers head coach Larry Brown had been Popovich's mentor; now, either the teacher or the student was going to become brilliant—in Popovich's case—or more brilliant, since Brown was already recognized as one of the premier coaches in the league.

This time, the student prevailed.

"All these people come rushing in the tent, just rushing at me," Popovich said. "They were congratulating me like I had done something. And I didn't do anything but eat a burger and they were rushing me telling me what a good job I had done."

Five championships later, Popovich is still amused by the events of that day.

That night, he and his wife, Erin, dined at a restaurant in New York and were still giddy about their good fortune.

The Scott Pollard Era?

Can any Spurs fan imagine a Scott Pollard Spurs dynasty?

For those who just asked "Who is Scott Pollard?" he was a 7-foot center from the University of Kansas who played for five different teams over 11 NBA seasons, averaging 4.4. points and 4.6 rebounds in 506 games.

But in the days before the 1997 draft, Gregg Popovich toyed with the notion of making him the No. 1 overall pick instead of Tim Duncan.

"It's true," Popovich said about an hour before his Spurs beat the Indiana Pacers to give him his 1,000th career win. "I loved the way Scotty played. Timmy was really smooth and all that and I was, 'Is that going to translate? Is he going to be tough?' He's long and lanky and thin and Scott Pollard was out there kicking you-know-what and taking names."

Popovich said the Duncan vs. Pollard "debate" didn't last long.

"It was actually a conversation," he said. "It did come up."

"You get the urge to want to stand and tell everybody what happened," Popovich told the *Boston Globe*. "It was like we had this secret and no one else knew it. We wanted everyone to know how lucky we were.

"You look at each other and you shake your head and say, 'Why did we deserve this? This means that for the rest of our lives, everything is going to go wrong.' You don't deserve another good thing to happen in your life after this. So we were scared to death. For the first couple of days, it was like you didn't believe that it happened. Where do we start with this guy? My god, this is such a good player, we can't screw this up."

If ever there was a one-man draft, it was 1997. After the Spurs selected Duncan, these players were chosen: Keith Van Horn, Chauncey Billups, Antonio Daniels, Tony Battie, Ron Mercer, Tim Thomas, Adonal Foyle, Tracy McGrady, Danny Fortson, and Tariq Abdul-Wahad.

Billups developed into an excellent player but he struggled his first five years in the league when he played for five teams. McGrady became a star player but never won a title, and in 1997, he was only 18 years old.

The Spurs were in the lottery only because they had lost David Robinson, who missed 76 games with a back injury. The previous season they had won 59 games, but with Robinson out, they won only 20. So they had a team, but no superstar.

The next year, they had two. Robinson was healthy and Duncan obviously made them even better. It took only two seasons for them to win the first championship in team history and, of course, along the way, Popovich became a great coach, although he has an explanation for his "brilliance."

"If you drafted Duncan after Robinson, your system would work, too," Popovich said, smiling at the memory. "We thought long and hard before we drafted Timmy. We deserve a lot of credit for that."

36 Duncan's Rookie Season

Eighteen years later it seems impossible to comprehend the self-doubt that plagued Tim Duncan during his rookie season. But in an interview for *NBA Rookie Experience*, the book about rookies I wrote for NBA Publications in 1998, Duncan made a remarkable revelation:

"I used to wake up at 4:00 in the morning going, 'Oh, my god, am I good enough to play with these guys?'"

In fact, it didn't take long for the basketball-loving world to understand that Duncan was plenty good enough to hang with NBA players. By the end of his first preseason anyone who knew anything about basketball also understood the impact he was going to make on the Spurs and on the rest of the league. Still learning Popovich's offense, figuring out how to make the most of the low post dynamics with his All-NBA teammate David Robinson, and trying to sift through the hundreds of plays in Popovich's offense and the complicated defensive scheme, Duncan finished the exhibition schedule having established himself as the team's starter at power forward by averaging 18 points and 10.6 rebounds per game.

He made his NBA debut at Denver's McNichols Sports Arena on Halloween Night, October 31, 1997, against a rebuilding Nuggets team that played four rookies, including starting point guard Bobby Jackson, who had been the 23rd selection in a 28-player first round.

Admitting to a major case of stage fright when the game began, Duncan soon showed everyone why he had been the top pick. He logged 35 minutes, scored 15 points on 6-of-9 shooting, grabbed 10 rebounds, blocked two shots, and came away with a 107–96 win.

Afterward, though, there was talk he had been "outplayed" by Jackson, who scored 27 points for the Nuggets.

It was in his third game as a pro that Duncan really opened eyes. Facing former Spur Dennis Rodman, the NBA's reigning rebound king, Duncan pulled down 22 rebounds, matching Rodman and impressing Bulls superstar Michael Jordan.

"I can see why he went No. 1," Jordan said after that game. "He has a lot of talent. He's matured. He's blossomed. He stayed those four years in college and his dividend is starting to show."

The Spurs won six of their first seven games with Duncan—the Bulls beat them in overtime in his 22-rebound gem—but when they lost six of nine games in late November, some experts tried to put the brakes on speculation he was destined for greatness.

Popovich rolled his eyes and shook his head.

"I think people's expectations for new people coming into the league are always a little ridiculous," the Spurs coach said, in *NBA Rookie Experience*. "They get overly excited about everybody and expect them to be either Magic Johnson or Kareem. With Tim Duncan I think you have those kinds of expectations because you see the amazing skill level he has. He can play outside; he can play inside; he can pass, catch, shoot, dribble…everything. He's got it all so it's going to make those expectations high.

"At the start of the season he lived up to them. Then it got difficult for him because, basically, our perimeter game went on vacation."

Duncan's response to the early struggle: a stretch of 14 games that began in mid-December in which he averaged 20 points and 11.9 rebounds. Those are All-Star numbers, and on January 22 Popovich summoned the rookie to his office.

Duncan got the word and felt like a junior high student called to the principal's office. When he got there Popovich informed him he would be playing in the All-Star Game at Madison Square Garden.

All-Star rookies rarely make major impact in the midseason game and Duncan logged only 14 minutes. He made the most of them by grabbing 11 rebounds.

After the All-Star break Duncan seemed more assertive on the offensive end, in part because Robinson was ailing with a sore knee. When the veteran center missed six games with "jumper's knee," Duncan took up the scoring slack. He led the team in scoring in all six games Robinson missed and in the six after the Admiral returned.

Near the end of the season Robinson suffered a concussion when Utah's Karl Malone elbowed him in the head in a game in Salt Lake City, an injury that required overnight hospitalization. The timing was awful for a team trying to optimize its playoff seeding, but Duncan helped the Spurs win two of the three games they would play without Robinson and four of their final five. In a key matchup against Western power Seattle, he scored 28 points and grabbed 17 rebounds. In the final five games he averaged 28.4 points and 11.6 rebounds.

By season's end there was zero doubt he would be Rookie of the Year and most NBA experts predicted the decision would be unanimous. When the results were announced, however, Duncan got only 116 of 119 first-place votes. New Jersey's Keith Van Horn, the No. 2 overall pick the previous June, got the other three. This was something of a scandal in San Antonio and many national NBA media experts called out the three unknown voters who did not put Duncan in the No. 1 spot on their ballots.

Duncan, though, was magnanimous. He noted that Van Horn had averaged nearly 20 points per game and didn't get to play alongside an All-Star center.

"Keith had a great year," he said at the ceremony where he was presented the Rookie of the Year trophy. "He played through a lot of injuries. It might have been different if he had been healthy."

Duncan also thanked his teammates, especially Robinson.

"I was fortunate," he said, "because I didn't have to come in and save the team. There were great players who were already here. All I had to do was come in and learn my way."

37 The A-Train

When the Spurs kept running up against—and losing to—the Kareem Abdul-Jabbar–led Los Angeles Lakers in the early 1980s, San Antonio general manager Bob Bass engineered a trade in the summer before the 1982–83 season that he believed would make it possible for the Spurs to get past Abdul-Jabbar and Co.

Bass sent center Dave Corzine, power forward Mark Olberding, and cash to the Chicago Bulls for 7-foot-2 All-Star center Artis Gilmore, considered the strongest man in the league.

When Gilmore scored 27 points and grabbed 20 rebounds to lead the Spurs to a road win in Game 2 of the 1983 Western Conference Finals, it seemed the deal might have been a stroke of genius. Instead, the Lakers won three of the next four games and eliminated the Spurs in six.

Nevertheless, the trade made Gilmore one of the team's most prominent players for five seasons in the early and mid-1980s.

Later, Gilmore would become just the third player with deep Spurs ties to be elected to the Naismith Memorial Basketball Hall of Fame.

Fellow Spurs Hall of Famer George Gervin remembers Gilmore from his first game against the Kentucky Colonels during his rookie season in the American Basketball Association. The 20-year-old Gervin had joined the ABA's Virginia Squires for the final half of the 1972–73 season after leaving Eastern Michigan University.

Early in that first game against the Colonels, one of the ABA's best teams, Gervin found himself sprinting out on a fast break. Two strides past midcourt, he wheeled toward the basket, took a pass, and then took one long, loping stride. He rose and extended his right arm to roll the ball off his fingertips with just the right spin, certain it would settle softly into the net.

Before the ball had gotten more than a few inches from his fingers, Gervin watched a huge hand appear, as if from nowhere, to smack the ball into the stands.

Gervin's signature shot, the finger roll, had run smack into the A-Train, rejected by Gilmore, who had caught up with Gervin from behind.

"We'd all heard Artis could block a lot of shots," Gervin said, "but I didn't know the cat could run the floor like that. I could put that finger roll up and over just about anybody, but Artis, well, he was something else. Man, Artis even blocked one of Dr. J's dunks in that game. He really made his presence known."

Gilmore entered the Hall of Fame as the first player voted in by a special committee tasked with honoring one player from the ABA each year, a fitting tribute to a great league that had long been overlooked by the Hall. His selection was long overdue for a player who scored 24,941 points and grabbed 16,330 rebounds in 17 ABA-NBA seasons. Gilmore's entire body of work is Hall worthy, including his two seasons at Jacksonville University. There, he averaged 22.7 rebounds, an NCAA record that still stands, and led the Dolphins to the NCAA championship game in 1970.

Gilmore was 33 by the time he arrived in the Alamo City in 1982, the best days of his career behind him. Nevertheless, Gervin recalls the excitement that surrounded his arrival.

"The big fellow coming to San Antonio really lifted our spirits," Gervin said. "He was still a dominant force when we got him. With him, we always felt we had a chance to defeat the Lakers.

Before David Robinson and Tim Duncan arrived in San Antonio, Artis Gilmore manned the paint for the Spurs for five seasons and was a two-time All-Star.

We felt that matchup with him and Kareem gave us a competitive center in the middle."

"After we made that deal, we were able to stay with Jabbar," said Bass, the GM who made the deal to acquire Gilmore. "Defensively, he could do a job on Jabbar. I will tell you this: after he joined the team I felt like when you walked out of the building after a game against the Lakers you didn't feel like Jabbar had just dominated, like he had in past years."

Gilmore believes he did what the team expected of him in that matchup.

"Yeah, Kareem and I matched up pretty well," he said. "But Magic Johnson and James Worthy, well, that was kind of overpowering in those particular areas."

Gilmore knew he could have been a dominant center in the NBA but passed on the established league in favor of the fledgling ABA when the Kentucky Colonels promised him a six-figure salary. Growing up with eight siblings in a three-room house in tiny Chipley, Florida, Gilmore had picked cotton and watermelons from a young age to help feed the family. When the Colonels came calling, the choice was easy.

"Back then," he said, "nobody in Chipley dreamed of being in any Hall of Fame some day. Back then, the dream was to get out of the cotton fields and be able to put food on the table."

Gilmore was both Rookie of the Year and ABA MVP in 1971–72, when the Colonels won 68 games. But not until Hubie Brown was hired to coach the team in 1974 did the Colonels realize their full potential.

An assistant to Larry Costello on the 1971 NBA champion Milwaukee Bucks team that featured Abdul-Jabbar, Brown brought with him the inside-out half-court offense that had optimized Abdul-Jabbar's dominant skills.

"We had a rule, as with Kareem," Brown said. "Every third time down the floor he had to get the ball in the post with a play, and he backed that up because in the ABA he shot over 60 percent, and in the NBA he still has the record, No. 1 (59.9). And he never tried to do things just to get up shots. He did what he did best, and the fact he could be a team player defensively, with the rebounding and shot blocking and stay within the offense and shoot such a high percentage, that's a staggering stat."

In their first season under Brown, the Colonels romped to the 1975 ABA title, losing only one of 13 playoff games. They beat the Pacers in five games in the ABA Finals, Gilmore scoring 28 and grabbing 33 rebounds in the clincher.

When the Colonels folded in 1976, Gilmore became the No. 1 pick in the ABA dispersal draft, going to the Bulls. Chicago went from 24 victories to 44 in Gilmore's first season, but had only one more winning season during his six years in Chicago. As it turned out, his first season with the Spurs, 1982–83, would be his only season with a winning record in San Antonio, but it was a good one, 53–29, with averages of 18.0 points per game and 12 rebounds.

38 The End of an Era

The end of the Tim Duncan era came as those who know him best always had predicted: quietly, without fanfare, and with nary a word from the greatest player in franchise history.

At 9:00 AM CDT, on the morning of July 11, 2016, the Spurs issued a 543-word press release announcing Duncan's retirement. Most of the release was a boilerplate recounting of Duncan's accomplishments in his 19 seasons with San Antonio.

There were no quotes.

It was the perfect farewell from the NBA's most reticent super-star, who eventually posted his own good-bye letter on the team's official website, Spurs.com.

Though it had been anticipated for weeks following elimination from the playoffs that marred the most successful regular season in franchise history, Duncan's departure was nonetheless jarring. Even his longest-standing teammates had difficulty wrapping their heads around the news.

"Even though I knew it was coming, I'm still moved by the news," guard Manu Ginobili posted on his Twitter account. "What a HUGE honor to have played with him for 14 seasons!"

It was left to others, primarily Gregg Popovich, to put the Duncan era, one of the most dominant in NBA history, in perspective.

"He's irreplaceable; it can't happen," Popovich said. "We're all unique but he's been so important to so many people it's just mind boggling. To think that he's going to be gone makes it really difficult to imagine walking into practice; going to a game; getting on the bus; taking him a piece of carrot cake; whatever it might be.

"He's been true to himself."

Numbers alone don't define the Duncan era but they inform any discussion of its impact.

Since Duncan joined the Spurs as the No. 1 overall selection of the 1997 draft, the Spurs won five championships and posted a 1,072–438 regular-season record. That .710 winning percentage is the best 19-year stretch in NBA history and was the best in all of the NBA, NFL, NHL, and MLB over its course. Only once during the Duncan era did the Spurs fail to win 50 games, and that was during the lockout-shortened 1998–99 season that produced the team's first NBA title. It would have taken a perfect regular season for the Spurs to get to 50 wins that season. As it was, they went

37–13, a .740 winning percentage that extrapolates to 61 wins. Over the next 17 seasons of the Duncan era, the Spurs won at least 50 games, including a 50–16 record in another shortened season, 2011–12.

Viewed through another statistical prism, the Duncan-era Spurs posted a winning percentage of at least .600 in each of Duncan's 19 seasons, an all-time record for most consecutive seasons with a winning percentage of at least .600 in the four major U.S. sports.

Much Love Always, Tim

Tim Duncan retired on his own terms and that included his very own way of saying good-bye to the fans who had supported him through his 19 seasons with the Spurs. He posted this letter on the Spurs' official website, Spurs.com, a little more than 48 hours after his retirement was announced:

If asked to write a script for my career 19 years ago there is no way I would've been able to dream up this journey.

I stand here at the end of this ride and look back in awe of what I've experienced.

The wins and losses will be remembered, but what I'll remember most are the people.

The fans inside the arena and out, the staff and coaches who pushed me and held me together, the teammates (and even opponents) who will be lifelong friends, sharing my ups and downs with family and close friends, and, most importantly, the snapshots of my kids growing up and reveling in watching Dad work. That is what I will cherish the most.

Thank you to the city of San Antonio for the love and the support over these years. Thank you to the fans all over the world.

Much love always,
Tim

Duncan, Ginobili, and point guard Tony Parker teamed up in 2002 and quickly became the Spurs' "Big Three" stars. Together, they won 575 regular-season games and 126 playoff games, more than any trio in NBA history. They also shared in four of Duncan's five NBA titles, the first of which Duncan won in just his second season, 1998–99. Duncan and Gregg Popovich have the most wins by a player-coach duo in NBA history (1,001) and the Spurs forward finished his career in San Antonio as one of just three players in NBA history, along with John Stockton and Kobe Bryant, to spend at least 19 seasons with one franchise.

Duncan's impact on his teammates and his quiet leadership also defined his era.

"The aura that he creates, the iconic figure that he established for us all those years, the security, the safety net, the home plate, the hub of the wheel…all that sort of thing is who he was as a player," said Popovich.

NBA commissioner Adam Silver acknowledged Duncan's place in NBA annals in a press release issued by the league.

"Tim Duncan is one of the most dominant players in NBA history," Silver said. "His devotion to excellence and mastery of the game led to five NBA championships, two regular-season MVP Awards, and a place among the all-time greats, while his understated selflessness made him the ultimate teammate."

Popovich long had maintained that his own career, also certain to land him in the Hall of Fame, owed its success to Duncan. So did a lot of other coaches, basketball executives, and teammates, a reality Popovich reiterated after Duncan's quiet departure.

"I would not be standing here if it wasn't for Tim Duncan," Popovich said. "I'd be in the Budweiser League someplace in America, fat and still trying to play basketball or coach basketball. But he's why I'm standing. He's made livings for hundreds of us, staff and coaches, over the years and never said a word. Just came to work every day. Came early. Stayed late. Was there for every single person, from the top of the roster to the bottom of the roster, because that's who he was, in all those respects."

Where will basketball history judge the Spurs' Tim Duncan era?

Does it compare to the Celtics' Bill Russell era, which produced 11 championships in 13 seasons, but in a league that had no more than 12 teams during Russell's career?

Does it rank with the Bulls' Michael Jordan era, which produced six titles but was interrupted by Jordan's brief retirement?

The entirety of the Tim Duncan era now is there for the basketball-loving world to judge.

Spurs fans should defend it as one of the greatest of all time.

39 Global Outreach

While basketball is considered the most American of sports—baseball, the so-called American pastime, was a variation of an Irish-English game called rounders—its inventor actually was a naturalized American born in Canada. Dr. James Naismith, who introduced the game at the Springfield, Massachusetts, YMCA in 1891, never could have imagined that in 2014 the Spurs would win the NBA championship with a roster of players born in seven countries outside the United States, with more international players (nine) than Americans (six).

The Spurs weren't the first NBA team to look outside the U.S. for talent. Indeed, Hank Biasatti, a Canadian citizen who was born in Italy, played for the Toronto Huskies of the Basketball

Association of America, which is what the NBA was called when it began in 1946–47.

When the 2014–15 season began, a record 101 international players were on NBA rosters, nearly a quarter of the league. The Spurs continued as the league leader in international players, with nine.

The globalization of the NBA generally is attributed to the worldwide popularity of the game erupting after the 1992 Olympics in Barcelona, Spain. In those games, the first American team with NBA players mesmerized the entire sports-loving world. The "Dream Team," including Michael Jordan, Magic Johnson, Larry Bird, Charles Barkley, and Spurs center David Robinson, romped through the games to gold and its members became international celebrities of the highest order. (The 1992 Dream Team was the Admiral's second appearance in the Olympics but not his last.)

Suddenly, athletes all around the world wanted to "be like Mike," emulating Jordan and his Dream Team pals.

The Spurs had been ahead of most NBA teams in realizing there were talented players to be found outside North America. Most of this early adaptation stemmed from Gregg Popovich's first tour of duty as a Second Lieutenant in the United States Air Force. It was 1970 and he had just graduated from the U.S. Air Force Academy, where he earned a degree in Soviet Studies and learned to speak fluent Russian. After graduating and receiving his commission, he played on an Armed Forces All-Star team that toured in Europe, including the Soviet Union.

Popovich's outstanding play on the Armed Forces All-Stars not only earned him an invitation to the 1972 U.S. Olympic Trials but also proved to him that the top players from Yugoslavia, Turkey, Germany, Italy, and Russia were on a par with NBA-caliber American players.

As an assistant under Spurs head coach Larry Brown in the summer of 1989, Popovich convinced general manager Bob Bass to let him scout a tournament in Dortmund, Germany, a prelude to the European championships. He already knew that the best player in the tournament was Lithuanian guard-forward Sarunas Marciulionis but he quickly discovered that Marciulionis was committed to signing with the Golden State Warriors.

Besides the Spurs and Warriors, only the Portland Trail Blazers, Atlanta Hawks, and Los Angeles Lakers scouted the 1989 European tournament. Popovich returned with a recommendation that the Spurs sign Yugoslavian Zarko Paspalj, a pure shooter despite an unorthodox, left-handed stroke. Paspalj flew to San Antonio in early July and signed a contract, thus becoming the first European-born Spur who had not played at least one season at an American college. (Sven Nater, born in The Netherlands and later a naturalized American citizen, was the first European to play for the Spurs but he had played collegiately at UCLA). He was one of five Europeans signed by NBA teams that summer, along with Marciulionis (Warriors), Russian Alexander Volkov (Hawks), and two more Yugoslavs, Drazen Petrovic (Trail Blazers) and Vlade Divac, who had been drafted by the Lakers.

Paspalj had little chance of getting much playing time because the Spurs had just made Sean Elliott the third overall selection of the 1989 draft. He was popular among his teammates but played a grand total of just 181 minutes, scoring only 72 points the entire season. He was waived a few days before the playoffs began so the Spurs could sign Mike Mitchell, a former Spurs scoring leader who had been playing in Italy.

Nevertheless, Paspalj was the player who paved the way to the team's influx of international players.

The Spurs bowed out of the international marketplace after the Paspalj experiment and Brown was fired midway through the 1991–92 season, Popovich moving on to Golden State at its conclusion. When Popovich returned as general manager in 1994 he brought with him two others who shared his international vision: Warriors director of player personnel Sam Schuler, given the same job with the Spurs; and Clippers assistant coach R.C. Buford, named the Spurs' head scout. The three were committed to bringing players from Europe to the Spurs but it would take five years before they could act on their plan.

Less than a month after winning the 1999 NBA title, Popovich, Schuler, and Buford had their sights on Russian forward Andrei Kirilenko but he was snatched before they had a chance to make him the final pick of the first round of the 1999 draft. Instead, they drafted a Chicago high schooler, Leon Smith. A few minutes later they traded his draft rights to the Dallas Mavericks for the draft rights to Yugoslav Gordan Giricek, the 40th overall selection.

With the next-to-last pick of the entire draft, the Spurs then chose a guard from Argentina who had completed his first season in the Italian professional league: Manu Ginobili.

Buford had seen Ginobili in the 1999 FIBA Under-22 championships in Australia and, while unimpressed with his defense and shooting, loved his ultra-competitive nature.

Giricek never played for the Spurs, who traded him in 2003 to the Memphis Grizzlies for a future second-rounder. But Ginobili, signed by the Spurs in 2002, would become part of the vaunted Big Three that would lead the Spurs to four championships.

Buford, who made numerous scouting trips to Europe after Popovich hired him back as head scout, locked on to a point guard from Paris ahead of the 2001 draft. It took two private workouts and a heap of convincing to change Popovich's mind about a player he initially wrote off as too soft for the NBA, but Tony Parker eventually became the first European to be selected by the Spurs in the first round (No. 28 overall).

A starter at point guard just five games into his rookie season, Parker joined Ginobili and Tim Duncan to form the Spurs Big

Three. A six-time All-Star and four-time All-NBA selection, he was MVP of the 2007 NBA Finals.

Since drafting Ginobili and Parker, the Spurs have drafted 16 international players from 12 different countries. They also have traded for or signed as free agents players from Australia, China, Great Britain, Italy, The Netherlands, Nigeria, Slovenia, Serbia, Turkey, and Venezuela.

40 Manu Goes Batty

One of the most amazing things ever seen at any basketball game at any level occurred during a game between the Spurs and the Sacramento Kings at AT&T Center on Halloween Night in 2009, and it had nothing to do with a basketball.

What happened was so spooky it defied belief on many levels.

Midway through the first quarter of the game, fans in various sections of the arena began mumbling and pointing when a bat—the flying kind—was spotted soaring around the arena.

South Texas is home to millions of Mexican freetail bats. Many of them live in caves and under highway overpasses. During spring and summer in San Antonio, hundreds of residents and tourists alike come out in the evening hours to watch the bats emerge from under overpasses along the Museum Reach of the famed San Antonio Riverwalk.

Some bats have made homes under the roof of AT&T Center. On rare occasions the noise and commotion of a game will arouse one of the winged creatures into taking flight, which is precisely what happened during the Spurs-Kings game.

Play continued as fans ducked and shrieked when the bat swooped above their heads. Finally, it began circling the court and lead referee Joe DeRosa called a halt to play.

DeRosa and fellow referees Courtney Kirkland and Ed Malloy used towels to swat at the bat but to no avail. Finally, the bat seemed to retreat into the upper reaches of the arena and play was resumed.

In the final minute of the first quarter the bat reappeared. With Sacramento's Kevin Martin gliding in for an uncontested layup after a Kings steal, the bat flew right past his head, causing him to miss the shot.

Play was immediately stopped and frustrated players and officials watched as the bat continued to circle the arena.

Spurs guard Manu Ginobili, however, was intent on action.

Watching as the bat circled, Ginobili sized up its flight and when it passed near him he struck, swinging his left arm and knocking it out of the air and onto the court, seemingly dead.

Calmly and quickly, Ginobili picked up the bat, walked past the baseline, and handed the poor creature to an usher, who took what he believed was a bat carcass outside, depositing it in a dumpster.

Spurs head athletic trainer Will Sevening, aware that bats often carry rabies and other diseases, thoroughly cleansed Ginobili's hands.

Eventually play continued but the drama of the bat incident was far from over for Ginobili. Members of the Spurs medical staff quickly dispatched a search party to try to find the bat in the dumpster so it could be tested for rabies.

The search was fruitless, the conclusion being that the bat had been stunned, rather than killed, and had flown away.

As a result, Ginobili had to endure a painful series of rabies shots, vowing never again to go near a bat.

Video of Ginobili's amazing bat-swatting feat was featured on ESPN's *Sports Center*'s Top 10 Plays and video of the incident went viral on YouTube, getting millions of views.

41 The Los Angeles Lakers

Any team that has had as much success as the Spurs collects rivals simply because others regard them with envy and a base desire to conquer. They entered the NBA with natural rivals from the ABA—the Nuggets, Pacers, and Nets—but those were foes with whom they shared a bond after the rough and tumble play and struggle to survive the final, financially challenged seasons of the ABA. They were denied natural regional rivalries when they got into the NBA because they were placed in the Eastern Conference. It was hard for San Antonians to relate to fans of the Knicks, Celtics, 76ers, Bullets, and Pistons.

Finally, when the league moved them into the Western Conference for the 1980–81 season, the Spurs and their fans discovered a rival that would last.

With their new conference affiliation making for four games nearly every season against Western teams, the Spurs and their fans immediately discovered that the path to an NBA Finals most often was going to run through Los Angeles, home to Kareem Abdul-Jabbar, Magic Johnson, and the Showtime Lakers.

There was a lot of jealousy involved in the rivalry but the Lakers, with their celebrity fans and a worldwide following, made despising them easy for San Antonio's blue-collar, street-smart fans, epitomized by the Baseline Bums.

The rivalry took off in the Spurs' second season in the West when they landed in a playoff matchup with the Lakers. After "The Bruise Brothers" bullied their way to a 48–34 record and a Midwest Division title they ran smack into Abdul-Jabbar in the semifinals. Kareem would not be bullied and the Lakers scored a 4–0 sweep.

The next season the Spurs traded for 7-foot-2 center Artis Gilmore. Advancing to the conference finals, they fared a little better against the Lakers. Gilmore had his moments and the Spurs managed two wins, but the end result was the same: no Finals for San Antonio and yet another trip for the Lakers.

The rivalry really began to simmer after Phil Jackson, who coached Michael Jordan and the Bulls to six championships in the 1990s, was lured out of retirement in 2000 by Lakers owner Jerry Buss. The Lakers had acquired All-NBA center Shaquille O'Neal after he became a free agent in 1996, teaming him with All-NBA guard Kobe Bryant. But that team had failed to make it to an NBA Finals, its path blocked first by the Utah Jazz, then by the Spurs, in 1998–99. Buss hired Jackson to satisfy O'Neal and he coached the Lakers to a championship in his first season. The Spurs had been eliminated in the first round by the Phoenix Suns after Tim Duncan was sidelined with a knee injury suffered late in the season. But that didn't stop Jackson from denigrating the Spurs' 1999 title because it had come after a lockout-shortened 50-game season.

Then, in Jackson's second season on the Lakers bench in 2000–01, his team handed the Spurs what was arguably their most embarrassing playoff ouster in franchise history: a 4–0 sweep in which their margins of victory in Games 3 and 4 were 39 points and 29 points.

Ouch!

The Lakers prevailed in the Western Conference semifinals in 2002, as well, so when the two teams met in the semifinals in 2003 the series had the feel of a medieval quest for the Spurs. Once again, Tim Duncan rose to the occasion. On May 15, 2003, the Spurs captain made 16-of-25 shots, scored 37 points, and grabbed 16 rebounds in a decisive, 110–82 victory that eliminated L.A.

That win was nearly as satisfying as the Game 6 NBA Finals victory over the New Jersey Nets that made the Spurs NBA champions for the second time.

There would be many more playoff matchups against the Lakers. One of the most gruesome was the infamous Game 5 of the 2004 semifinals, in which Derek Fisher nailed a buzzer-beating three-point shot on a play triggered with just four-tenths of a second remaining on the AT&T Center clock.

Through the last dozen seasons the matchups between guards Manu Ginobili and Kobe Bryant have been some of the most compelling in the NBA, and Bryant has called Ginobili his favorite opponent to play against. Despite that show of respect for a player Spurs fans idolize, Bryant was lustily booed each time he played at AT&T Center.

Of such emotions are the best rivalries made, and for Spurs fans there is nothing quite as satisfying as beating the Lakers—and nothing worse than losing to them.

42 The Spurs' Best Finals Game

After the Miami Heat stole Game 2 of the 2014 NBA Finals—beating the Spurs on their AT&T Center home court, 98–96, gaining home-court advantage in the best-of-seven series in the process—fans in San Antonio were in a deep funk. They wondered if their team was in for another disappointment at the hands of the Heat.

Tied at one game apiece, the series was about to shift to Miami's American Airlines Arena, where the Heat had not lost a game in the postseason and where Miami had handed the Spurs the toughest loss in franchise history the previous June.

Gregg Popovich responded with a subtle lineup change that turned the dynamics of the 2014 NBA finals on its head and an exhortation to Kawhi Leonard to assert himself at the offensive end.

The result was the best single NBA Finals performance in franchise history.

Popovich started veteran big man Boris Diaw at center instead of Tiago Splitter, who had started every playoff game up to that point.

Popovich reasoned that Diaw, one of the smartest players in basketball, could get the Spurs back to playing the freewheeling style that had gotten them to the Finals. He would be credited with only three assists but his effect on the game superseded the official box score. His ability to keep the ball moving and break down the Miami defense was profound.

Miami's LeBron James, the four-time Most Valuable Player and two-time Finals MVP, had scored 35 points in Miami's Game 2 win. Leonard, who had been asked to defend James with minimal double-team help, had totaled only 18 in Games 1 and 2. Popovich wanted more but mostly he wanted Leonard to be more aggressive at the offensive end, to look for his own shot and get to the basket.

Leonard was plenty aggressive, right from the opening tip. He took five shots in the first period and made them all, scoring 16 in the period and sparking the Spurs to a 22–11 lead in the first six minutes. But that was just the beginning of the most efficient quarter in NBA Finals history. By the time it had ended the Spurs had made 12 of 14 shots, 85.7 percent, an all-time Finals record that was good enough for a 41–25 lead.

Tim Duncan's Best Finals Game

The Spurs have played 34 NBA Finals games and won 23 of them, a remarkable winning percentage of 67.6 percent when you consider that, by definition, the Finals matches the two best teams in the NBA.

While the team's performance in Game 3 of the 2014 NBA Finals clearly surpasses all others—Popovich's assertion that the Spurs, as likely as not, never again will shoot 76 percent for one half of any game pretty much says it all—one individual Finals performance by a Spur ranks as one of the greatest in NBA history.

In fact, no player ever came closer to putting up a Finals quadruple-double than Tim Duncan did in Game 6 of the Spurs' 2003 NBA Finals victory over the New Jersey Nets.

At age 26, Duncan was in his physical prime and he played all but two minutes of Game 6. Guarded by one of the league's premier defensive players, Nets power forward Kenyon Martin, he made 9-of-19 shots and 3-of-5 free throws, for 21 points. He dominated the backboards, grabbing 20 rebounds. With the Nets double-teaming him on nearly every catch of the ball, he found open teammates for 10 assists. He was just as dominant at the defensive end, blocking eight shots.

It was Duncan's second triple-double of the playoff run. He had 15 points, 20 rebounds, and 10 assists in another close-out game, Game 6 of the Spurs' first-round series against the Phoenix Suns. In the Spurs' 24-game run to their second championship, Duncan missed a points-rebounds double-double only twice.

Clearly one of the greatest Finals games in league history, Duncan's Game 6 lacked only the drama of a Game 7 showdown that would have elevated it to NBA legend. It stands up nicely against the game that is generally considered the greatest Finials Game 7: Walt Frazier's 36-point, 19-assist game (with five steals) for the New York Knicks in their Game 7 win over the Los Angeles Lakers in 1970.

Curiously, both Duncan and Frazier have summer homes on St. Croix in the U.S. Virgin Islands. Duncan, of course, grew up there.

They cooled off in the second quarter but only by comparison to their record-setting first. By halftime they had made 75.8 percent of their shots to forge a 71–50 lead.

Urged by their coach, Eric Spoelstra, to slice into the Spurs' halftime lead by half in the third quarter, the Heat responded with a rally late in the third that drew them within seven, 81–74.

With momentum and a partisan crowd roaring it seemed the tide had shifted. Then Spurs reserve guard Marco Belinelli made the biggest shot of his two seasons in silver and black. The only Italian ever to play for the NBA's most global of teams took a pass from—who else?—Diaw and drained a three-pointer that silenced the crowd and pushed the Spurs' lead back to double digits.

Leonard heated up again in the fourth quarter, and by the time he made the second of two free throws with 3:35 left in the game, he had 29 points and the Spurs were back up by 16 points.

It was a performance for the ages and seemed to take more than just one game from the Heat, who seemed utterly dispirited.

Popovich tried to toss it off as just a result of hot shooting. "I don't think we'll shoot 76 percent in a half ever again," he said afterward. "That's crazy."

Maybe so, but it's the primary reason Game 3 is the greatest Spurs Finals game.

The Spurs' Best Regular Season

Some Spurs fans may want to forget the 2015–16 season altogether because it ended in such disappointing fashion after a second-round ouster in the playoffs. But there is no denying the excellence that produced the best regular-season record in franchise history: 67–15.

Only six teams in NBA history—the 2015–16 Warriors (73–9), 1995–96 Bulls (72–10), 1971–72 Lakers and 1996–97 Bulls (69–13), 1966–67 Philadelphia 76ers (68–13), and 1972–73 Boston Celtics (68–14)—won more games in a season. And for a franchise that had won five NBA titles, the best record in team history is no small achievement. That it was accomplished after significant roster change made it all the more remarkable.

After an off-season that brought six new players to the roster, including All-NBA big man LaMarcus Aldridge and All-Star forward David West, players and coaches alike cautioned fans against expecting too much too soon from a group that had to learn to play together. But by the midpoint of the season it was clear the new group was headed for something special. At the 41-game halfway point, the Spurs had won 35 games and were unbeaten on their AT&T Center home court (23–0).

The retooled roster produced win streaks of 13, eight, and seven games, and three more of six in a row. Had they not locked up no worse than the No. 2 record in the league with two weeks left in the regular season, it seems reasonable to assert they could have challenged the 70-win threshold. As it was, Gregg Popovich was able to begin resting veteran players sooner rather than later, and the team's one and only losing streak of the season came in games 78, 79, and 80.

Small forward Kawhi Leonard, who signed a five-year, $94 million contract in July, wasted no time establishing that he was now the team's top player. On opening night he scored a career-high 32 points (he would extend that mark to 33 points by season's end) and re-asserted his Defensive Player of the Year bona fides by holding Oklahoma City's four-time NBA scoring leader, Kevin Durant, to 22 points on 6-for-19 shooting.

Leonard's emergence as the team's scoring leader also made him a legitimate Most Valuable Player candidate and he finished second in MVP voting—a distant second, to be sure—to Golden State's Stephen Curry, the first unanimous MVP in league history.

Leonard had his own unanimous postseason selection, getting all the first-place votes in balloting for Defensive Player of the Year, the first Spurs player ever to win back-to-back DPOY Awards.

Leonard was voted to the Western Conference starting lineup for the All-Star Game and LaMarcus Aldridge was named a reserve for the February 14 game in Toronto. Gregg Popovich coached the victorious Western Conference lineup.

The season also signified a transition from the team's Big Three era. Tim Duncan, the 39-year-old team captain, played fewer minutes than any season of his 19-year career, even the lockout-shortened, 50-game 1998–99 season. Duncan's scoring average dipped below double figures, to 8.6 points per game, for the first time. In fact, he recorded career lows in every major statistical category, no surprise when you consider the truncation of his playing time and the toll that age and injury had taken through one of the greatest careers in league history.

Shooting guard Manu Ginobili, 38, also had a difficult season, missing 13 games in February and March after a testicular injury that required surgery to repair.

Point guard Tony Parker, the third leg of the Big Three triangle, had to adjust his game to an offense that was oriented much more to an inside-out attack than to the perimeter game that had made him one of the NBA's most dangerous point guards. His scoring dipped to 11.9 points per game, his lowest output since his rookie season in 2001–02, as he became more facilitator than scorer.

Leonard (21.2 points per game) and Aldridge (18.0) finished one-two in scoring but the best record in franchise history was forged primarily at the defensive end of the court. Led by Leonard's ability to shut down many of the league's best scorers, the Spurs allowed only 92.9 points per game, second to Indiana in fewest points allowed.

When the playoffs began most NBA experts looked ahead to what they anticipated would be a dramatic Western Conference Finals matchup between the Spurs and Warriors, but the Spurs never made it to the anticipated confrontation. They were derailed by the Oklahoma City Thunder in a second-round series marked by drama and controversy.

Spurs fans will point to the official NBA acknowledgment that the referees made five incorrect calls in the final 13.5 seconds of the Thunder's 98–97 win in Game 2. (Most will ignore the fact three of the five incorrect calls were in the Spurs' favor.) It was another admittedly incorrect call in Oklahoma City's Game 5 win—a foul given to Danny Green that sent Thunder star Kevin Durant to the foul line for two free throws that changed the dynamics of the final 55 seconds of a game that was tied, 90–90, when the incorrect call was made—that will haunt the Spurs and their fans. Playing from behind after Durant made both foul shots, the Spurs suffered their second home-court loss of the series, 95–91.

The playoff run ended in Oklahoma City when the Thunder dominated Game 6.

Popovich focused on the positives of the season.

"(The players) made it enjoyable to come to work every day and they gave everything they could and went as far as they could," he told reporters in a day-after press conference. "I'm really pleased with their effort and their ability to just persevere all year long and keep their eye on what we were trying to do. It's just a group that was very special."

44 Peter Holt and San Antonio Spurs, LLC

A decorated Vietnam War vet (Silver Star for valor, three Bronze Stars, and a Purple Heart) and the owner of heavy equipment dealership Holt Cat (the largest Caterpillar heavy equipment dealership in North America), Peter Holt became chairman of the Spurs ownership group in 1996 and has guided the franchise through its most successful phase.

In 1996, Holt joined other investors who had been assembled by Gen. Robert McDermott when the group bought the team in 1993 from B.J. "Red" McCombs for $76 million. Holt's buy-in was estimated at 35 percent, the largest single share. That made him CEO and managing partner.

Holt had modest expectations for his new venture and soon discovered how difficult the business of the NBA could be. Injuries to key players, including Hall of Fame center David Robinson, led to the worst record in franchise history, 20–62, in their first season of controlling interest.

"The kids (son, Peter John, and daughter, Corinne) that summer, my wife and I told them we were buying into the Spurs and they were all excited because we all loved the Spurs and had season tickets and went all the time. By the end of the season, they said, 'Dad, can we sell the Spurs? Everybody on the playground at school thinks you're an idiot.'

"That's a true story. Everybody thought I'd screwed it up."

Holt had not screwed up but that first season was a graduate level education in the business of pro sports.

"I've only had one losing year and that was my first year, 1996–97, which now I'm glad happened, and not just because we got Tim (Duncan)," Holt told the *San Antonio Express-News* in a

2014 interview. "I didn't know we were going to get Tim. We were third (worst record), not first. But it helped me understand how difficult this business is. It really did. I mean, the year before we had been in the Western Conference semifinals and we had David (Robinson). I thought everything was going to be peachy keen and we went 20–62."

Since that tough "rookie" year the Spurs chairman has seen his team win five NBA championships and has watched the value of the franchise skyrocket to $1 billion, according to a 2015 estimate of NBA team values by *Forbes* magazine.

Nineteen years after he joined the ownership group and became CEO, Holt is one of the most successful and influential owners in all of professional sports. He has served as chairman of the NBA owners executive board and its labor relations committee. He gained the respect of his fellow owners right from the start of his ownership by listening and learning.

"When Peter came into the league, he was the quiet guy who listened, who absorbed everything, who did it the right way," former Phoenix Suns owner Jerry Colangelo told the *Express-News* in a 2015 interview. "He took the quiet path and people respected him, and I believe that has continued."

Holt was an early believer in Gregg Popovich, who had been hired as general manager by McDermott in 1994. He supported his decision to dismiss head coach Bob Hill and take over as head coach early in the 1996 season. Then, when the Spurs got off to a slow start when the lockout-shortened 1998–99 season finally began, he resisted the urgings of many fans and sports pundits to make a coaching change. On top of that was pressure to build a new arena that would make it easier for the team to survive financially in a small pro sports market.

Backing Popovich paid off when the Spurs won their first NBA championship a short while before voters were asked to approve some tax measures dedicated to funding a new arena, now known as the AT&T Center.

"Very frankly, I wouldn't be here if he operated like some other (owners) have operated in the past in our league, in a short-sighted sort of way," Popovich said of Holt in 2014. "Peter Holt had faith in me way back in the beginning. He believed in us, believed in me, and allowed me to step out and do it the way I thought it should be done. So I owe him a great deal."

R.C. Buford, president of sports franchises for Spurs Sports & Entertainment, LLC, says it is unfair to call Holt a "hands-off" owner. He prefers to call him an owner who empowers those he has put in decision-making positions.

"He has been a leader for our organization, for our ownership group, in several important initiatives, including the initiative to keep the team here, the initiative to get the arena built, the initiative to put together an organization that (franchise player) Tim Duncan would want to stay for," Buford said in a 2015 interview

The Ultimate Franchise

When *ESPN The Magazine* created the Ultimate Franchise rankings in 2003, the goal was to develop criteria to accurately reflect what fans "want most in return for the emotion, money, and time" from the 122 North American pro sports franchises (NBA, NFL, MLB, and NHL). The network then hired an opinion research firm to survey more than 100,000 fans in order to rank the teams based on the selected criteria. For example, fans were asked to rank teams based on championships won or expected and the effort of players on the field and likeability off the field, but also on venue experience (fan-friendly environment, frequency of game-day promotions) and ownership (honesty and loyalty to fan base).

The Spurs are the only franchise to rank in the Top 10 every year since the ranking was developed and have finished first three times (2004, 2006, and 2014) and second three times (2005, 2007, and 2008).

conducted by the *Express-News*. "And culturally and value-wise, he fits with the San Antonio community."

Sylvan Stephen Lang, one of the 1993 investors and still a member of the ownership group, put it this way in a profile of Holt that ran in the *Express-News* in 2015:

"He lets the professionals do the managing. Peter doesn't step much into the basketball operations. Now, we wouldn't enter into a $10 million player contract or a major television deal without him being involved. But on a day-to-day basis, he leaves it all up to R.C. and Pop, and that is why we are successful."

Holt believes the entire ownership group—it includes some corporate entities, in addition to individual investors, such as Hall of Famer David Robinson—deserves the credit for keeping the team in San Antonio when there was pressure on McCombs to sell it to others who would have relocated it.

"Start with 1993, before I ever showed," Holt told the *Express-News* in a 2014 interview a few days after the team won its fifth NBA title. "That group is the group that really should be given the credit for keeping the team in town. Starting with Gen. McDermott, God rest his soul. He put the group together. I don't know if anyone else could have pulled it off.

"Luckily, AT&T had just come to town, (AT&T CEO) Ed Whitacre, and he had seen the football team in St. Louis leave town and he hadn't been here but about six months when Gen. McDermott got with him and then everybody else jumped aboard in 1993 and put the deal together in 30 days. Credit Red McCombs, because he took less money than he could have gotten from somebody who wanted to take the team away. Everybody cooperated to keep the Spurs in town and they're the ones who really kept it here because I think it really had a chance to go."

Including Holt and his wife, Juliana Hawn Holt, the ownership group numbers 20 investors in a limited liability company known as San Antonio Spurs, LLC. The investors are: ARAMARK Sports and Entertainment Group; Raymond Joseph Barshick; Cassandra Carr; Clear Channel Communications, Inc.; George C. Hixon; H.H. Sports, Ltd.; IBC Capitol Corporation; Sylvan Stephen Lang; James R. Leininger; R&B Partnership (Russell and Bruce Hill); David M. Robinson; AT&T Media Holdings, Inc.; Markey Family Partnership; Sierra Sports and Entertainment Family Limited Partnership; SWBC; Sunrise Sports and Entertainment; Valero Energy Corporation; Zachry Hospitality Corp.; and Estate of Jeanne Lang Matthews.

On March 9, 2016, the 67-year-old Holt turned his position as chairperson and CEO of Spurs Sports and Entertainment over to Julianna, who then named Spurs president of business operations Rick Pych as co-CEO. Peter Holt continues on the Spurs' board of managers and participates in team affairs as part of the ownership group.

45 Reloading

The Spurs entered the summer of 2015 prepared for change. With Tim Duncan having turned 39 and Manu Ginobili about to turn 37, the club did not know if one or both of them would retire or return.

What Gregg Popovich did understand was that the 2015–16 Spurs roster would be considerably different than the 2014–15 roster. Two days after the Los Angeles Clippers scored a 111–109 win over the Spurs in Game 7 of one of the most competitive first-round series in franchise history, he addressed the media and confirmed what most Spurs fans already suspected.

"The makeup of the team...will probably look considerably different than it looks this year because we have so many free agents and we want to retool a little bit," he said. "We want to try to start—not exactly over again—but these last four seasons have been a grind and we put the team together with that in mind, that this year we'd have all the free agents so we can decide what we want to do moving forward, as far as the makeup of the team."

Popovich and general manager R.C. Buford for several years had planned for the summer, during which they knew several impact free agents would be available, including All-NBA center Marc Gasol and All-Star big man LaMarcus Aldridge. The contracts of numerous Spurs players had been structured to give the club an opportunity to dip below the NBA's collectively bargained salary cap for the first time in more than a decade.

Only seven players were under contract for the 2015–16 season when free agency began on July 1. The Spurs had a game plan for restocking the roster that covered all contingencies.

"R.C. and his group have always done a great job of doing things, both frugally and with class," Popovich said. "If money needs to be spent, it's spent. But it's never done unwisely. We've never put the organization in a situation where they're paying a ridiculous amount of money for no value.

"My complete faith and trust in R.C. is never going to change, because of the track record he has, thinking not just for the next year and the next two years, but the next three years, the next seven years, that type of thing."

It's unlikely either Popovich or Buford foresaw that things would play out as positively as they did. Not only did the Spurs land Aldridge, a 6-foot-11, 240-pound post man out of the University of Texas who was coming off the best of his nine seasons with the Portland Trail Blazers, they also re-signed 2014–15 Defensive Player of the Year Kawhi Leonard to a maximum contract and returned their starting shooting guard, Danny Green, at a relative bargain price.

None of those deals would have been possible had not Duncan and Ginobili agreed to return for another season at dramatically lower salaries that cleared enough room under the NBA's $70 million salary cap to make a maximum contract offer to Aldridge that made him the team's highest-paid player.

Duncan signed a two-year deal worth a total of $10.9 million, the 2015–16 season at just $5.25 million, a drop of $5.1 million from his 2014–15 salary.

Ginobili agreed to a two-year deal for a total of $5.75 million, starting at $2.8 million for 2015–16.

Trading starting center Tiago Splitter to the Atlanta Hawks for a future second-round draft pick—the Hawks were able to absorb Splitter's salary into available cap space—cost the Spurs a solid interior defender but freed up another $9.25 million in cap space. They also lost free agents to other teams—Marco Belinelli to the Sacramento Kings; backup point guard Cory Joseph to his hometown Toronto Raptors; and backup big man Aron Baynes to the Detroit Pistons—but cleared another $12.8 million off their salary cap.

When Indiana's two-time All-Star big man David West, who had opted out of the final season of his contract with the Indiana Pacers that was to have paid him $12.2 million, signed on with the Spurs for the veteran minimum salary of $1.5 million, the Spurs' free-agent summer became so good that *Sports Illustrated* gave the club an A+ in its assessment of the summers of all 30 NBA teams, the only team to get such a high mark.

Once the Aldridge, Leonard, Green, and West deals were complete, the Spurs re-signed Matt Bonner to a one-year minimum veteran deal at $1.5 million that actually cost them only $947,276, league rules requiring the NBA to reimburse them for the amount of Bonner's salary above the minimum for a two-year veteran.

Finally, the team traded a future second-round pick to the Sacramento Kings for backup point guard Ray McCallum.

The effect of all the wheeling and dealing is profound, putting the Spurs in position to do something unprecedented in NBA history: transition from a dominant era—the Tim Duncan years—to a roster that figures to be a championship contender once Duncan and Ginobili retire and without having to drop out of the playoff picture in order to rebuild through the draft lottery.

Aldridge's decision to join the Spurs was the key, as he figures to eventually fit into the spot that will be vacated by Duncan's eventual retirement. He is a four-time All-Star who had just averaged 23.4 points per game and 10.2 rebounds in Portland and was at the top of the free-agent wish list of several high-profile NBA teams, including the Dallas Mavericks (Aldridge is a Dallas native), Miami Heat, New York Knicks, and Los Angeles Lakers.

Looking to the future, the Spurs' core players will be Aldridge, Leonard, Green, and All-NBA point guard Tony Parker, with solid depth that should keep the Spurs among the NBA's best for many more years.

46 Danny Green

When Manu Ginobili suffered a fractured fifth metacarpal on his left hand during a loss to the Minnesota Timberwolves in the fifth game of the lockout-shortened 2011–12 season, an opportunity presented itself to James Anderson.

The 20th selection of the 2010 draft, the 6-foot-6 shooting guard from Oklahoma State got the first shot at becoming the Spurs starter at shooting guard, replacing Ginobili, who was the Spurs' top scorer through the first four games of the truncated season.

Instead, Ginobili's injury became a career-changing opportunity for Danny Green.

Anderson got his first start against the Golden State Warriors in a game at AT&T Center two days after Ginobili's disheartening injury.

It did not go well. He played 12 minutes of the first half and missed three of four shots.

By the next game Spurs coach Gregg Popovich had benched Anderson and put Gary Neal in the starting lineup. Neal scored 12 points in a win over Dallas. But it was Green who had the breakout game, when he scored a career-high 24 points in the third game without Ginobili.

"It's all about opportunity," Neal said after that one, understanding that Green had just seized the day, as well as Anderson's spot in Popovich's playing rotation.

By the 27th game of the season Green had moved into the starting lineup. It was the start of something very important for the Spurs and Green. He started all but a handful of games for which he suited up from that 2011–12 season on through 2014–15, establishing a role as one of the most reliable three-point shooters in the league and a solid perimeter defender often assigned to some of the NBA's best shooters.

After signing a four-year, $40 million contract with the club on July 13, 2015, Green began the 2015–16 season as one of the core players expected eventually to help the Spurs ease into the post–Tim Duncan era.

Signing an eight-figure contract looked improbable at the start of Green's career. Though he had been the winingest player in the history of North Carolina, one of the most successful programs in college basketball, he wasn't sure he would make an NBA roster. He had to wait until the second round of the 2009 draft to hear his name called, by the Cleveland Cavaliers. He played only 20 games for the Cavs in his 2009–10 rookie season and was waived before the start of the 2010–11 season. That led to his first stint with the Spurs. He signed a non-guaranteed contract with San Antonio on November 17, 2010, but was waived a week later. He went to the NBA's D-League and the Spurs re-signed him in March.

Green showed enough promise in the final two weeks of the season to know he had a good shot at making the team the next season. His chance at a full season with the Spurs had to wait on settlement of the 2011 NBA labor dispute. He played in Europe in the meantime.

Finally, he signed with the Spurs for the NBA minimum and began the 2011–12 season that changed his career and made him an NBA champion and Finals record holder.

In the 2013 NBA Finals, Green set a record for three-point baskets made in an NBA Finals.

In 2014–15, he broke the franchise record for three-pointers in a season when he made his 191st long-range basket in Game 81. The old mark, set by Chuck Person, had stood since the 1995–96 season.

Green's re-signing with the Spurs after hitting the free-agent market on July 1, 2015, was a surprise. Estimates of his value to other teams was estimated to be as high as $60 million over four seasons. But, like teammates Tim Duncan and Manu Ginobili, Green sacrificed financially to remain a Spur.

47 LaMarcus Aldridge

Through the first 18 years of the Popovich-Duncan dynasty the Spurs built and renewed their roster primarily through the draft. There were occasional signings of veteran free agents—Michael

Finley and Antonio McDyess, for example—but only to augment a roster that produced an NBA title in Duncan's second season.

But when LaMarcus Aldridge hit the free-agent market on July 1, 2015, the Spurs were in line to make their pitch to the 6-foot-11, 260-pound big man, a five-time All-Star and three-time All-NBA selection who had averaged no fewer than 21.1 points and 8.0 rebounds in his five previous seasons with the Portland Trail Blazers.

They weren't alone. After All-NBA center Marc Gasol, also an unrestricted free agent, made it clear he would remain with the Memphis Grizzlies, with whom he had played his first eight NBA seasons, Aldridge became the undisputed prize among available unrestricted players. Only teams able to approach a maximum contract for the then-29-year-old All-Star were serious bidders and the Spurs, who were far over the NBA's salary cap, found ways to create the cap space to put themselves among them. Among their strategic moves: a trade that sent big man Tiago Splitter to Atlanta for a non-roster player and a future draft pick; and restructured deals, for less money, for both Tim Duncan and Manu Ginobili.

Aldridge and his representatives from Wasserman Media Group, Arn Tellem and George David, dictated the terms of the recruiting process: the teams Aldridge would consider were invited to make their pitches to him in Los Angeles over three days, beginning at 9:00 PM on June 30, the very moment free agency began.

Aldridge narrowed the recruiting process to seven teams: the Trail Blazers, Lakers, Rockets, Heat, Mavericks, Suns, and Spurs. Eventually, he added the Raptors. The Spurs were among the last to make their pitch but their low-key, player-oriented approach resonated. It was a relatively simple appeal, presented by head coach Gregg Popovich, general manager R.C. Buford, and players Tim Duncan, Tony Parker, Kawhi Leonard, and Patty Mills.

Popovich's approach to recruiting free agents never has been about dogs, ponies, bells, or whistles. The Spurs head coach (and president of basketball) takes a simple, straightforward approach: make sure a potential signee understands the Spurs culture and let the chips fall where they may.

Aldridge liked what he heard and the Spurs went to the top of his list. However, when the Suns arrived for their presentation with a surprise "guest," All-Defensive Team center Tyson Chandler, with whom they had reached a verbal agreement to join their team, Aldridge put Phoenix at the top of his list, according to an interview with Aldridge conducted by Adrian Wojnarowski, of Yahoo! Sports.

As the recruiting process dragged into a fourth day, Popovich flew back to Los Angeles for a second face-to-face meeting that got the Spurs back on top. On July 4, Aldridge phoned Popovich to let

R.C. Buford and the Spurs signed LaMarcus Aldridge, the biggest free-agent prize on the market, to a four-year, $80 million contract in 2015.

him know he would be a Spur and the Independence Day fireworks seemed a little more spectacular in the Alamo City, for it was the first time the Spurs had landed the most sought-after free agent of the summer.

From the start of training camp Popovich and Aldridge's new teammates warned against expecting too much from a player who would have to adjust to a new system and new teammates, and Aldridge did struggle to find a comfort zone through the preseason. After one especially bad game (against the Suns, the team that was runner-up in the Aldridge sweepstakes), he returned to the court half an hour after the game and worked on his jump shot for nearly an hour.

Through his first 10 regular-season games he was shooting just 44.2 percent and averaging only 15.2 points per game, hardly the All-Star-caliber numbers he had produced in Portland.

Ironically, his defensive play had been much better than most had expected and he declared that it had been much simpler to pick up the Spurs' complex defensive scheme than it had been to adjust to the offense.

By midseason, however, his overall play had made him an All-Star for a fifth consecutive season and by season's end Popovich would assert that no new Spurs player ever had assimilated more smoothly than had Aldridge, who finished the season with a scoring average of 18.0 points per game and a team-best rebounding average of 8.5 per game. He was selected to the All-NBA third team, one of only three active players to have made All-NBA for a third consecutive season, along with LeBron James and Chris Paul.

Aldridge's production improved markedly in the playoffs, averaging 21.9 points per game on 52.1 percent shooting, making it clear he would be a pivotal player in the Spurs' transition to the post–Big Three era.

2011: The Big Hiccup

The Spurs were in rebuild-on-the-fly mode after they were bounced out of the 2009 playoffs in five first-round games by the Dallas Mavericks. Bruce Bowen, a defensive mainstay on three championship teams, clearly was at the end of his career. Veteran big man Kurt Thomas, 36, and starting center Fabricio Oberto, 33, seemed to have little left in their tanks. Two days before the 2009 draft the Spurs packaged them in a trade with Milwaukee for small forward Richard Jefferson, who twice had averaged more than 22 points per game for the New Jersey Nets.

Jefferson's first season in San Antonio, 2009–10, wasn't a total bust but it was definitely a disappointment. His scoring average dipped from 19.6 points per game to 12.3. Spurs fans blamed him for the team's troubles, especially after he underperformed in the playoffs, his scoring dropping even further to 9.4 points per game, in an embarrassing sweep thanks to the Phoenix Suns in the second round.

Plenty of NBA experts believed the team's long run of dominance with Tim Duncan had reached its end.

Lo and behold, a few small tweaks to the roster—finally signing 2007 draftee Tiago Splitter and adding free-agent shooting guard Gary Neal—and some adjustments to the team's style of play that made Tony Parker the focal point of the offense produced the best record in the Western Conference in 2010–11.

Jefferson managed to find a niche, shooting less but becoming one of the league's top three-point shooters, at 44.0 percent.

Manu Ginobili had a resurgent season, averaging 17.4 points per game and making the All-Star Game for the second time in his career. But his bounceback suffered a major setback in its final regular-season game when Ginobili suffered an elbow injury early in a 106–103 loss in Phoenix. Initially diagnosed as a hyperextension-sprain, it would eventually be revealed as a fracture.

Still, the Spurs went into the playoffs as the West's No. 1 seed, matched up in the first round against the No. 8 seed Memphis Grizzlies.

Memphis, though, was no ordinary No. 8 seed. The Grizzlies had one of the best centers in the NBA, Marc Gasol, one of the most relentless rebounders in basketball, Zach Randolph, and a disruptive perimeter defender, Tony Allen.

The Spurs were in trouble right from the tipoff of Game 1, which they played without Ginobili. The Grizzlies stole home-court advantage with a 101–98 win, then gained a 3–1 series lead by defending their home court in Memphis.

It took a miracle shot, Gary Neal's three-pointer that barely beat the fourth-quarter buzzer, to send Game 5 into overtime, which the Spurs dominated to send the series back to Memphis.

The Spurs had no answer for Randolph's physicality in Game 6. Though they led for a brief moment with 4:40 left in the fourth quarter, "Z-Bo" scored 17 of his 31 points in the period and the Grizzlies and their fans celebrated as if they had won the Finals.

For a second straight summer, the Spurs would hear suggestions that they had fallen from the ranks of the championship contenders; that age finally had caught up with them.

It was tough to take for everyone, including Popovich. The Spurs coach wondered what could have been had not Ginobili been hurt in the final regular-season game.

"The typical knee-jerk reaction of most talking heads is, 'Well, they're too old,'" Popovich told the *San Antonio Express-News* in an exclusive and candid assessment. "They've been telling us we're too old for six years or longer. It's always intrigued me, because who's old? Timmy's older. (Antonio McDyess) is older. But that's not the reason we lost the series. Timmy's not Timmy, like he used to be. But that's not why we lost the series. We didn't lose it because 'Dyess is old. Tony's not old, Manu's not old, Richard's not old. George Hill's not old, Matt Bonner's not old. It's overstated."

The Spurs lost the series, he said, because some players "didn't show up" for all the games.

It didn't help that Ginobili wasn't Ginobili.

"I don't care about the age, athletic thing. I care about performance," Popovich said. "That team won 61 games. I contend if Manu was healthy, we'd still be playing. I don't have any doubt we'd still be playing. That's frustrating."

Popovich and general manager R.C. Buford would make changes in the long off-season that followed—the start of the 2011–12 season would be delayed until late December by a labor dispute—and during the season, as well. McDyess retired; two-way guard George Hill was sent to the Indiana Pacers for the rights to the 15th selection of the 2011 draft, Kawhi Leonard; veteran point guard T.J. Ford was signed to a free-agent contract shortly after the labor dispute ended in December; Boris Diaw was signed to a free-agent contract in late March; free-agent point guard Patty Mills was signed a few days after Diaw's deal; and, on March 15, 2012, Jefferson, Ford (who had suffered a career-ending injury), and a future first-round draft pick were sent to the Golden State Warriors for swing man Stephen Jackson.

It was the beginnings of the next phase of the Tim Duncan dynasty, and it would produce another trip to the Western Conference Finals and hope for the future.

Out of the pain of an upset, the seeds of another championship were sewn.

49 Desert Fever

More than a few attendees at Spurs games have scanned the retired jerseys hanging from the rafters at AT&T Center and wondered, *Who is Moore, No. 00?*

They can be forgiven for not knowing about Johnny Moore, the University of Texas point guard who wore No. 00 for the Spurs for eight seasons.

Moore was on a path to become one of the best point guards in franchise history when he contracted a rare form of meningitis, coccioidmycosis, more commonly known as Desert Fever. It is caused by a fungus indigenous to the southwestern United States and it is estimated that 10 percent of the population of the area is exposed to the fungus. It typically is found in the soil and can be spread when the soil is disturbed and dust is strewn.

Only one in a thousand of those exposed contracts meningitis. That means Moore's case was literally a one-in-a-million occurrence.

It was during Moore's fifth season in silver and black that he suddenly began having unendurable headaches. Nothing helped, not even the strongest of over-the-counter pain medications.

After a game on December 20, 1985, against the Clippers at the Los Angeles Sports Arena, his headache was so bad he tossed and turned all night, sleeping only for brief stretches.

With a game the next night in Denver, the team's wake-up call at its hotel near Los Angeles International Airport came at 5:00 in the morning. As he awoke he felt like he had the worst hangover of his life.

He knew something was out of the ordinary.

Amazingly, in a 128–118 win over a very good Nuggets team that had gone to the Western Conference Finals the previous season, Moore made 11-of-17 shots, scored 22 points, and handed out 11 assists despite being guarded by one of the NBA's premier perimeter defenders, Lafayette "Fat" Lever.

It would be the final game of the season for a player who was the NBA's leader in assists at the time (9.0 APG).

When the Spurs got back to San Antonio the next day he visited a team doctor to see what could be done about his persistent headache.

Later, he would tell reporters he had figured he would get a prescription for a more powerful headache medication. Instead, he underwent tests for three days.

Results revealed the meningitis, inflammation of the membranes covering the brain and spinal cord.

Brain surgery was ordered.

Moore's season was over and his absence had a profound effect on the team. His teammates, devastated by the news of his illness and deprived of his All-Star caliber play, went 18–35 the rest of the season, finishing eighth in the Western Conference, 12 games under .500 and, worse, locked in a first-round playoff against the Lakers, the West's best team.

The Spurs were swept in the best-of-five series.

After two brain surgeries Moore would return for the 1986–87 season but he was a shell of his former self. He averaged only 8.6 points and 4.5 assists per game.

The following season he played only four games for the Spurs before the club waived him, reluctantly and sadly.

The Spurs re-signed Moore as a free agent on November 22, 1989, and he appeared in 53 games as a reserve behind Maurice Cheeks. In just under 10 minutes per game he averaged 2.2 points and 1.5 assists.

It would be his final season in the NBA and Spurs fans were left to wonder how good he might have been had he not contracted Desert Fever, and no wonder. Through the 2014–15 season, he remains the all-time Spurs leader in assists in one season, 816 in 1984–85, one of three seasons when he finished in the top three in the NBA. He is the only Spurs player ever to lead the league in assists (9.6 in 1981–82). Four times he finished in the NBA's top 10 in assists per game and he is the all-time franchise leader in assists per game, at 7.4. His career scoring average in his five-plus seasons before contracting Desert Fever was 10.5 points per game.

Recognizing Moore's courage in dealing with his misfortune and what he had done before he was stricken, the Spurs retired his No. 00 on March 20, 1998.

50 71 Points

Go to the list of the highest scoring games in NBA history and you will discover there have been only 10 games when a player scored 70 or more points. Wilt Chamberlain did it six times, including the only 100-point game.

On April 24, 1994, center David Robinson became just the fourth player to crack the 70-point barrier when he produced 71 points in the Spurs' regular-season finale against the Los Angeles Clippers, securing the league scoring title in the process.

By doing so the Admiral joined an exclusive list that included Chamberlain, Lakers great Elgin Baylor (71 on November 15, 1960), and Denver Nuggets phenomenon David "Skywalker" Thompson (73 on April 9, 1978).

Lakers guard Kobe Bryant was added to the 70+ club when he produced an 81-point game against the Toronto Raptors on January 22, 2006, the second-highest total in league history.

Circumstances for Robinson's career game were similar to those that produced George Gervin's 63-point game on April 9, 1978, when he knew he needed at least 59 to pass Thompson for the scoring title. Robinson went into the final day of the season trailing Orlando's Shaquille O'Neal, a former San Antonio prep star (Cole High School), by 0.06 points per game in the race for the league scoring title.

Unlike Gervin in 1978, it was Robinson who had to put up big scoring numbers in hopes that O'Neal would not be able to pass him in a game later the same day.

Just as in 1978, the Spurs were locked into playoff position, fourth in the ultra-competitive West. That made the outcome of the game immaterial, so pursuit of the scoring title by Robinson was the goal. Head coach John Lucas instructed his players to feed Robinson in the post right from the opening tip. Of course, this was the priority for nearly every game, but on this afternoon it was emphasized even more, especially by one of Lucas' assistant coaches, a former player named George Gervin.

Robinson's teammates went along and the Admiral scored the first 18 Spurs points of the game.

Understanding Robinson would have to put up as many points as possible because O'Neal would be playing later that night, Lucas played him 44 minutes. Though he was double-teamed on every catch and occasionally triple-teamed, Robinson produced an efficient offensive explosion. He made 26-of-41 shots (63.4 percent) and even made 1-of-2 three-pointers. He went to the foul line 25 times, making 18 free throws.

The Associated Press story about the game included this quote about his gratitude to his teammates.

"It was unbelievable," Robinson told the AP. "My team has been behind me the whole year. They always push me to do a lot of individual things. As a leader, I just try to win games, but tonight they really wanted me to shoot it. When the game started they were looking for me almost every time down the court."

There was a bit of controversy as the game neared its conclusion. After Robinson surpassed Gervin's club record when he made a free throw and got to 64 points with 1:33 to play, Lucas instructed his players to intentionally foul Clippers on each of their possessions to stop the clock and allow for more scoring opportunities for Robinson, who then added seven points in the next 59 seconds.

Lucas finally took Robinson out of the game with 34 seconds left, the Clippers crowd giving him a standing ovation.

Afterward, Robinson seemed stunned by what he had done.

"I looked up at the scoreboard and saw 71 points," he told reporters covering the game. "I said, 'Oh, my goodness.'"

His total was 19 points more than his previous career high of 52 points.

For his part, O'Neal scored 32 points to lead Orlando to its 50th win of the season. Magic head coach Brian Hill mocked Lucas' intentional fouling strategy in the final minutes of the Spurs' blowout win, telling the *St. Petersburg Times*, "We certainly wanted Shaquille to win the title but we didn't make a mockery of the game like (the Spurs) did in Los Angeles."

With his final scoring average of 29.8 points per game, Robinson became the second Spurs player to lead the league in scoring, and no Spur has been the league's top scorer since. Teammate Dennis Rodman led the league in rebounding for the season (17.3 per game), making the Spurs the first team in league history to have both the scoring leader and rebounding leader.

51 The Merger

When the NBA agreed to absorb four of the six remaining ABA teams after the 1975–76 season, it refused to call the move a merger. Rather, the older established league announced it had agreed to "expand" by four teams, those teams being the Spurs, the New York Nets, the Indiana Pacers, and the Denver Nuggets.

The ABA for years had hoped to merge with the NBA even as the league's leverage shrank, team by team, until only seven remained to play through to the end of the 1975–76 season. One of those, the Virginia Squires, folded a few weeks after the Nets beat the Nuggets on May 13, 1976, to win the final ABA title.

Spurs officials and their fans didn't care what the deal was called as long as the team hadn't been left out.

Angelo Drossos, one of the San Antonio businessmen who had brought the Spurs to town three years earlier, was chairman of a group of ABA representatives who attended the NBA League Meetings in Hyannis, Massachusetts, after the 1976 NBA Finals.

The Boston Celtics, led by Dave Cowens and JoJo White, had just beaten the Phoenix Suns to win the NBA title but anyone who knew anything about the game understood that both the Nets, with Julius Erving, Brian Taylor, and "Super John" Williams, and the Nuggets, with David Thompson, Dan Issel, and Bobby Jones, were a match for either the Celtics or the Western Conference representative in the NBA Finals, the Phoenix Suns. There had been exhibition play between ABA and NBA teams and the ABA had more than held its own.

Even the great Bill Russell recognized the parity between the leagues. In an interview with the *San Antonio Express-News* in 2015,

Spurs great George Gervin recalled Russell's advocacy of a merger that would bring the two leagues together.

"Bill Russell knew we had a lot of guys in the ABA that could play," Gervin said. "Every time I see Bill he tells me this story: he says, 'You know, when I was coaching Seattle the commissioner would ask, 'Who wants to play some ABA guys in the preseason?' And I would say I want to play those guys because I knew those guys could play and there would be some opportunities for some jobs.'

"He was a big advocate for us and he was the man in the NBA. Having that kind of respect for us and wanting us to be successful kind of calmed things down for guys, that we had somebody of his caliber saying, 'These guys can play and one day y'all are going to see.'

"And they did."

Against that backdrop Drossos led the small group of ABA team representatives to Hyannis with the goal of getting as many teams in the NBA as possible.

His greatest hope, of course, was that the Spurs might be among those allowed to enter the "established" league.

Drossos knew the financial reality of the ABA was dire. A 1976–77 season was unlikely. Before he left for Massachusetts he confided to Barry Robinson, then the sports editor of the *San Antonio Express-News*, that the future of pro basketball in San Antonio was at stake in Hyannis.

"This is it, one way or another," Drossos told Robinson. "If they turn us down it's over. There is no way the ABA can continue. Basketball in San Antonio will be dead."

ABA commissioner Dave DeBusschere and NBA commissioner Larry O'Brien had begun "merger" talks a few months before the end of their respective seasons, both men committed to the process. Drossos was joined by Nuggets president Carl Scheer, Nets owner Roy Boe, and Indiana Pacers owner Bill Eason as the core of the ABA's merger committee.

After a session with O'Brien on June 15 that stretched to 4:00 in the morning, the two sides were hung up on monetary details. The NBA had agreed to take the Spurs, Nuggets, Nets, and Pacers but wanted a $4.5 million entry fee from each. The ABA owners knew they had to make an accommodation for the two teams that weren't coming with them into the NBA. Bleary-eyed, Drossos made what he called a "final, final" offer, then went to bed.

About 9:00 in the morning he got a call from DeBusschere asking him to come to O'Brien's suite.

Drossos recounted the moment to the *Express-News*:

"I went upstairs in my stocking feet and Mike Burke, owner of the Knicks, said, 'Welcome to the NBA.'"

There had been a breakthrough, Boe agreeing to give the Knicks a $4 million "territorial invasion" fee that would have immediate consequences. To finance the fee he sold Erving's contract to the Philadelphia 76ers for $3 million.

It was a glorious moment for the Spurs that came with burdens. The four teams had to pay for the privilege of joining the 18 teams already comprising the NBA. Additionally they had to "buy" the agreement by the owners of the Spirits of St. Louis and the Kentucky Colonels to approve the "merger" that would disband their teams. Colonels owner John Y. Brown was paid $3.3 million. Dan and Ozzie Silna, owners of the Spirits, cut a deal for $2.2 million plus a piece of the TV money the Spurs, Nets, Nuggets, and Pacers would eventually receive.

The four new NBA teams would be locked out of the first round of the draft in their first year in the league and they would not receive any of the NBA's TV revenue for four years. Their deal with the Silnas called for each team to pay the Silnas one-seventh of their TV shares, in perpetuity.

Drossos flew back to San Antonio and held a press conference to discuss the deal.

"I think we now have basketball in San Antonio forever," he said. "I'm looking forward to sitting back like every other fan and watching us win world championships."

Before he could sit back he had to reach out to new investors to raise the entry fee and settlement costs that totaled about $4.5 million. He sold shares in the team and by the time the $4.5 million was raised the ownership group totaled 65 individuals and/or businesses.

Eventually, Drossos would get to sit back and watch games as a fan after he sold his interest in the team to Red McCombs in 1988. Sadly, he died in 1997 at age 68, two years before the Spurs won the Larry O'Brien Trophy for the first time.

52 The Rodeo Road Trip

When the Spurs moved into the SBC Center, their state-of-the-art new arena for the 2002–03 season, the change came with baggage.

The $186 million bond referendum for a new basketball arena specified a multi-use space in which to host the annual San Antonio Stock Show and Rodeo. This resulted in a drastic change to the Spurs schedule.

Previously housed in the Joe and Harry Freeman Coliseum, the San Antonio Stock Show and Rodeo was locked into an opening on the annual schedule on the Professional Rodeo Cowboys Association (PRCA) Tour over three weeks every February. The conversion of the facility from an indoor sports (basketball and ice hockey) and concert venue to a rodeo arena is no small feat, and the stock show takes over vast areas of the parking lots that surround the arena.

In effect, the Spurs are evicted from their home court for roughly three weeks. Other NBA teams undergo similar stretches of their 82-game schedules. The Chicago Bulls have an annual circus road trip while Ringling Brothers, Barnum and Bailey circus takes over United Center. The Lakers and Clippers annually hit the road while the Staples Center is taken over by the Grammy Awards for about two weeks.

Unlike any other team facing long stretches of life on the road, the Spurs have found a way to make the most of their trip, so much so it has become part of the lore of the Tim Duncan era. Since the Spurs began making their rodeo trek they have a combined record of 82–35 on the trip, a ridiculous winning percentage of 70.1 percent. And that includes the one and only losing rodeo trip since 2003, a 4–5 record in 2015. Over the same time frame no team that has made a road trip of at least seven consecutive games has won more than 62 percent of its games. The Golden State Warriors have gone 18–11 on four trips of seven or more games, a 62.1 winning percentage.

The Spurs' very first rodeo trip established a nearly mythological stature to the annual ordeal. When they departed San Antonio and their home court at what then was known as the SBC Center

Road Warriors

On April 7, 2015, the Spurs extended their streak of consecutive seasons with a winning road record to an all-time-best 18 with a 113–88 win at Oklahoma City. Since Tim Duncan was drafted prior to the 1997–98 season, the San Antonio Spurs have amassed the best road record in the NBA over the past 19 seasons and are one of only three teams to have a .500 or better record (457–294).

Only three teams in NBA history have had runs of at least 10 straight seasons with winning road records: the Spurs, from 1997–98 through 2015–16 (19 seasons); the Lakers, from 1979–80 through 1990–91 (12 seasons); and the Celtics, from 1959–60 through 1968–69 (10 seasons).

(headquartered in San Antonio, SBC Communications Co. signed a long-term naming rights agreement in 2002; when SBC changed its name to AT&T, Inc. in 2005, the venue became the AT&T Center) the Spurs were 28–15 and trailed the Western Conference–leading Dallas Mavericks by six games. When they dropped the first game of the trip, falling to the Minnesota Timberwolves at Target Center, they found themselves seven games back of Dallas. Two nights later they were to play against the 33–12 Indiana Pacers, led by All-Stars Reggie Miller and Jermaine O'Neal.

Tony Parker's best game of the season—28 points and seven assists—sparked the Spurs offense and their stifling defense did the rest. Bruce Bowen limited Reggie Miller to 6-of-15 shooting and the Pacers shot only 36.4 percent as a team. For the Spurs it was one of their biggest wins of the season, 106–97.

By the time they played again at SBC Center they had won their final eight on the trip and were on a steady climb that ultimately would put them in a tie with Dallas for best record in the NBA, 60–22.

On their return to San Antonio, players told of how they had bonded on the trip, complete with team dinners and excursions.

The lore of the rodeo trip had begun. When the inaugural rodeo trip was followed by a 7–1 tour in 2003–04, a 5–2 trip in 2004–05, and a 6–2 trip in 2005–06—an 81.3 winning percentage—it had become full-blown mythology.

By the time he made his 10th straight rodeo trip, Bill Schoening, the radio voice of the Spurs and a part-time singer-songwriter, had immortalized the trip in song. "Adios, Auf Wiedersehen, Au Revoir, Ciao; Nine straight road games, We'll get through somehow," Schoening crooned, and Spurs fans loved it.

Of course, Gregg Popovich does his best each year to minimize the significance of the trip and 2015's losing rodeo record took a bit of the luster off its near-legendary status. But as long as the Spurs share their arena with the Stock Show and Rodeo, the NBA schedule makers have no choice but to put them on the road for most of February.

53 Doug Moe

Every Spurs fan knows the franchise leader in wins by a coach. A member of the NBA's nine-member 1,000-win club, Gregg Popovich went into the 2016–17 season with 1,089 victories.

Only an avid Spurs fan knows which coach ranks No. 2 on the franchise list: Doug Moe.

In just three-plus seasons as Spurs coach from 1976 to 1980, Moe coached the Spurs to 177 victories and brought them within a few minutes of the team's first trip to the NBA Finals.

He did it all with a smile on his face that belied one of the most competitive spirits ever seen on a basketball court.

Hiring Moe was the first decision Bob Bass made when club owner Angelo Drossos moved Bass from the team's bench to the front office as general manager.

It was a good hire. Moe brought with him from Denver a fast-paced, pass-oriented offense that was perfect for the Spurs' personnel, especially guards George Gervin and James Silas. Plus, he brought a red-white-and-blue appreciation of what the ABA had brought to basketball and a chip on his shoulder to prove that the Spurs, Nets, Pacers, and Nuggets not only belonged in the NBA, but that they played a better brand of basketball.

Playing for the New Orleans Buccaneers, Moe had been the leading scorer (total points) in the inaugural ABA season. He won an ABA title as a member of the Oakland Oaks in the league's second season. He became an ABA assistant coach under Larry

Brown for both the Carolina Cougars and the Denver Nuggets, one of the two finalists in the final season of the ABA, 1975–76.

Moe's first season with the Spurs became a struggle when Silas, a player Moe considered co-equal with Gervin in importance in his offense, suffered a knee injury in a preseason game and missed 60 games. Additionally, Silas' backup, George Karl, was out after knee surgery. Still, Moe's team managed a 44–38 record but fell to the Boston Celtics in a best-of-three "mini-series."

With Silas back to run the show, Moe's second season produced a franchise record 52 wins and a regular-season scoring title for Gervin, who scored 63 in the season finale to pass Denver's David Thompson in the tightest scoring race in league history.

Gervin understood that Moe's approach was perfect for his free-flowing game and followed with a second straight scoring title in 1978–79, when the Spurs went 48–34 and then advanced to the Eastern Conference Finals after a hard-fought semifinals series against former ABA standout Julius Erving and the 76ers.

What followed was a heartbreak in the Eastern Conference Finals that was so profound Moe insists he remembers little else from his time on the Spurs bench.

Ahead by 10 points midway through the fourth quarter of Game 7 against the Washington Bullets, the Spurs missed 10 of their last 14 shots. With eight seconds left, Washington's Bobby Dandridge hit a jumper that held up for a win that sent the Bullets to the NBA Finals.

Incensed by the disparity of foul calls in the fourth quarter by referees Paul Mihalik and John Vanak—the Bullets shot 15 free throws in the period to four for the Spurs—Moe told reporters that the two refs had "stolen" the victory from his team. The two refs, he suggested, should be "set before a firing squad."

NBA commissioner Larry O'Brien fined Moe $5,000, a hefty sum in 1979.

Moe became a victim of his own success. With his team mired at 33–33 in the 1979–80 season that followed, he was fired by Drossos and replaced for the final 16 games by GM Bass, whom he had replaced on the bench four years earlier.

Aware of dissatisfaction among ownership and unhappy with how the season had unfolded, Moe was prepared for dismissal. He and his wife, whom he affectionately calls "Big Jane," celebrated with a bottle of champagne.

Eventually, Moe got a second chance to coach in the NBA. In nine-plus seasons with the Denver Nuggets, he went 432–357 and coached the Nuggets to the 1985 Western Conference Finals. He has the most wins in Nuggets franchise history, 432, and the team retired his "number" in 2002. In 1992 he signed a three-year contract to coach the Philadelphia 76ers but was fired 56 games into his first season when the team was 19–37.

His final tally as a head coach: 628–529. As of the start of the 2016–17 season he ranks 23rd on the list of most NBA coaching victories.

Moe and his family loved their time in San Antonio, retaining their home in the suburbs of the city even after he was hired by Denver and, later, Philadelphia. His humor, candor, and joy for life endeared him to Spurs fans and media, and earned him high praise from none other than Gregg Popovich.

"When you think about Doug Moe you think about one of the most genuine people on the planet," Popovich said. "Exactly what you get—on the court, off the court, on the golf course, out socially—is Doug Moe, every minute of every day. It is always fun, it is always honest, and not many of us can say that's the way we are."

54 0.4 Seconds

Type "0.4 seconds" into any search engine and the first result will be a YouTube video of the final moments of Game 5 of the 2004 Western Conference semifinals between the Spurs and the Lakers.

Watching the video might be one of the most painful things Spurs fans should do before they die.

Any true Spurs fan knows that 0.4 seconds is the amount of time remaining on the AT&T Center clock after Tim Duncan made an amazing shot that gave the Spurs a 73–72 lead in the pivotal game of a series that was tied, 2–2.

All the Spurs had to do to take a 3–2 series lead was defend against the play that Lakers coach Phil Jackson drew up during the timeout after Duncan's shot went through the net.

Instead, the Lakers took the 3–2 edge in the series back to the Staples Center when Derek Fisher took an in-bounds pass from Gary Payton and launched an 18-foot jumper over the out-stretched hand of Manu Ginobili that just beat the final buzzer.

The instant his shot swished through the net Fisher sprinted the length of the court and straight into the tunnel that led to the Lakers locker room. His teammates quickly followed suit and NBC-TV play-by-play broadcaster Al Michaels joked, on air, that "they will try to get on their plane before the officials can get over to the scorer's table."

Indeed, referees Danny Crawford, Joe Forte, and Ronnie Garretson had signaled that the shot had counted, then spent several minutes reviewing replays before finally declaring that the ball had been out of Fisher's hand before time expired.

Back on their home court for Game 6 the Lakers scored an 88–76 win that ended the Spurs' hopes of defending their 2003 NBA title.

But had they really won Game 5?

How had they managed to throw an in-bounds pass and get off a shot before time expired?

Many Spurs fans remain unconvinced that they did.

The Spurs weren't convinced, either. They filed an official protest of the call, claiming the referees made a correctable error in starting the game clock late.

The NBA denied the protest, ruling that the game clock "started appropriately."

The Greatest Clutch Shot Nobody Remembers

Call up the YouTube.com video of Derek Fisher's buzzer-beating shot from Game 5 of the Spurs-Lakers series in 2004 and the video will begin with Tim Duncan's shot that nearly everyone inside the AT&T Center thought had won the game for the Spurs.

It qualifies as one of the most difficult clutch shots of Duncan's career but is largely forgotten because it was rendered meaningless by Fisher's heroics.

With 5.4 seconds remaining the Spurs trailed by a point when Manu Ginobili inbounded to Duncan from the right sideline and cut past him for what was to have been a return pass. L.A.'s Kobe Bryant got between Duncan and Ginobili, forcing the Spurs captain to improvise. Spinning to his left he took two dribbles with his left hand and rose to put up a jumper over Lakers center Shaquille O'Neal. Leaning to his left as he released the ball over O'Neal's outstretched hand, Duncan crashed to the floor as the ball settled cleanly through the net, giving the Spurs a 73–72 lead.

Mobbed by his teammates—Ginobili leaped on his back as he arrived back at the team bench—Duncan was confident the lead would hold up.

It did not, and one of the greatest shots of his career became a sidebar to history.

San Antonio TV stations broke down video of Fisher's shot, frame by frame, and concluded that more than four-tenths of a second had elapsed from the time he first touched the ball to the time it left his hand. Their conclusions may have been correct but the game clock does not start until one of the three referees triggers it with a button each wears on his or her belt. All three are tasked with hitting the button as soon as the ball is touched, the clock automatically triggered by the first of the three.

Reaction to the outcome was as expected.

Fisher: "I was halfway into my shot even as I was catching the ball. As it got closer I knew the ball was going in."

Jackson: "That's the thing you love about basketball. You never know how it will end."

Spurs coach Gregg Popovich: "That's the cruelest loss I've ever been a part of."

Spurs guard Devin Brown, assigned to do everything he could to make sure Lakers star Kobe Bryant did not get open on the final play: "One stop. Point-four. You'd take that any day. All we needed was one stop…one stop."

The heartbreak of 0.4 seconds eventually was eclipsed in Spurs lore by the collapse in the final 28.2 seconds of Game 6 of the 2013 NBA Finals against the Miami Heat, which included Ray Allen's three-pointer that tied the score with 5.2 seconds left in regulation.

But no single shot ever hurt the Spurs and their fans more than Fisher's game winner.

55 Bones

Though he played only four seasons for the Spurs, Brent Barry helped them win two championships, including one in his very first season in silver and black.

A skinny (hence the nickname, "Bones"), athletic, 6-foot-7 guard-forward from Oregon State University, Barry played for the Clippers, Heat, and Bulls before settling in with the Seattle SuperSonics for five solid seasons, from 1999 through 2003–04. The Spurs signed him to a free-agent contract on July 15, 2004, and he settled into an important role as sixth man, playing behind Manu Ginobili and Bruce Bowen.

In the 23-game grind to the 2005 championship, Barry assumed a pivotal role after the Denver Nuggets stunned the Spurs in Game 1 of their first-round playoff series by winning 93–87. Coach Gregg Popovich responded with a lineup change, putting Barry in the starting lineup and bringing Manu Ginobili off the bench. Barry responded with 16 points, making all four of his shots from three-point range. Ginobili produced 17 points, on 5-of-7 shooting, and the Spurs won the game.

Popovich kept Barry in the starting lineup the rest of the series, the Spurs winning the next three to close out Denver.

Barry had another monster game in Game 1 of the Western Conference Finals against the Phoenix Suns, the No. 1 seed in the West. Making 5-of-8 from long range, he came off the bench to score 21 points, helping the Spurs steal home-court advantage on their way to a 4–1 series win that sent them to the NBA Finals against the Detroit Pistons

When Popovich cut his playing rotation to seven for NBA Finals Game 7 against the Pistons, Barry played 29 minutes and contributed five points, four rebounds, and two assists, earning his first NBA championship ring.

Barry was third in the NBA in three-point percentage in the Spurs' 2006–07 championship season (he led the league in 2000–01, while with Seattle) and was a solid contributor as the Spurs swept the Cleveland Cavaliers in the 2007 NBA Finals.

Injured during the 2007–08 season, Barry was traded to Seattle on February 20, 2008, which immediately waived him. The Spurs re-signed him as a free agent on March 24.

As valuable as Barry was as a contributing bench player, he also was a jokester and free spirit whose humor was appreciated by his teammates and the media covering the team. He became a star in the humorous TV commercials featuring Spurs players, created by one of the team's prime sponsors, the H-E-B Store chain.

When NBA commissioner David Stern presented the Spurs with their championship rings in a ceremony before the 2005–06 season opener at AT&T Center, Barry accepted his ring and planted a kiss on the embarrassed Stern's face.

Barry also had a career highlight at the Alamodome during his rookie season with the Los Angeles Clippers, winning the slam dunk contest before the 1996 All-Star Game. Barry reprised Julius Erving's free-throw line slam from the 1976 ABA All-Star event in Denver for the winning dunk.

56 Dr. K

After helping Memphis State get to the NCAA championship game as a junior, Larry Kenon began his pro career with the New York Nets, where he became a rookie star playing alongside Julius "Dr. J" Erving.

Kenon's outstanding play right out of the gate earned him a spot on the ABA All-Star team. Combined with a hairstyle similar to Erving's, it also earned him a nickname: "Dr. K." He earned an ABA championship ring when the Nets defeated the Utah Stars in the 1974 ABA Finals.

But there weren't enough shots to go around for two high-scoring small forwards. After the Spirits of St. Louis upset the defending champion Nets in the first round of the 1975 ABA play-offs, Nets owner Roy Boe approached Spurs coach Bob Bass with a trade proposal: Kenon and center Billy Paultz for Spurs center Swen Nater. Eventually, the deal became two trades that included defensive-minded Nets guard Mike Gale coming to San Antonio and four lesser Spurs players going to New York.

For Bass, it was a great deal that brought two starters, Kenon and Paultz, to San Antonio.

Kenon's impact with the Spurs was immediate. In his first season in silver and black, he was the team's No. 3 scorer (18.7 points per game) and its leading rebounder (11.1 per game).

Not only was Kenon named to the ABA All-Star team that played the league-leading Denver Nuggets in the famed 1976 ABA All-Star Game, but he was chosen to compete in the first-ever slam dunk contest. Though he received some high marks for his dunks, Erving stole that show by taking off from the foul line for one of the most iconic dunks of all time.

When Doug Moe took over as head coach for the Spurs' first season in the NBA, 1976–77, Kenon was a perfect fit in his run-and-gun offense. He averaged 21.9 points and 11.3 rebounds, helping to pick up the scoring slack after an injury sidelined scoring leader James Silas for all but 22 games.

A key contributor on the Spurs team that took the Washington Bullets to Game 7 of the 1979 Eastern Conference Finals, Kenon scored 23 points in the heartbreaking Game 7 loss.

A two-time NBA All-Star (1977–78 and 1978–79), Kenon set a franchise and NBA record when he was credited with 11 steals in a December 26, 1976, game against the Kansas City Kings. He also scored 29 points and grabbed 15 rebounds in that game.

Kenon left the Spurs after their disappointing 1979–80 season, signing a free-agent contract with the Chicago Bulls. Though he was in his prime after arriving in Chicago his scoring average dipped from 20.1 points per game in his final season with the Spurs to 14.1 points per game, and he played only two more seasons.

Memphis State (now University of Memphis) retired Kenon's No. 35 in 2014.

The Popovich Legacy

When Dwane Casey was named head coach of the Toronto Raptors in 2011, he had a 1,300-pound boulder placed just inside the front door of the team's dressing room.

Casey explained its meaning to his players and then told team reporters why he had the rock placed in the dressing room: "I knew we were going to be a work in progress. Every time we walked on the floor we were going to have to have something to get us to think about how we have to get better…we've got to work to get better. It's from a story about a stonecutter. Every time the stonecutter hits a rock it may not break. You may have to hit it 100 times but on that 101st time you hit it, now you crack the rock."

Imitation being the sincerest form of flattery, Gregg Popovich probably smiled. Casey, after all, had simply stolen the message he has preached to the Spurs from his first day as head coach in

1996, one he himself interpreted from 19ᵗʰ century journalist and reformer Jacob Riis: keep hammering at the rock.

Aside from his "pound the rock" admonition, Popovich's impact among NBA coaches has been immense. His legacy is—pardon the expression—set in stone. He has been an innovator and a model of consistency and has shared his knowledge and friendship with coaches across the globe. When he joined the NBA's 1,000-win club, the *San Antonio Express-News* asked other NBA head coaches about Popovich's legacy. Here are the best of their responses:

Glenn Rivers, Los Angeles Clippers: "Pop's had an amazing impact on the league but more on coaching, in general, because he's a coach's coach. He's proven again that guys do want to be coached. I think there was a feeling for a while that guys do not want to be coached but they do. They want to be coached; they want to be led. Pop has shown, once again, that that's how to do it. He's also been great for small markets. He's proven you can win anywhere if you do it the right way.

"His ability to adapt, that's what all great coaches do. You almost have to. Pop started out as a defensive guy and then he became an offensive guy. He's not married to anything. He's married to how his team can win and I think that's what makes him so brilliant."

Monty Williams, former New Orleans Hornets head coach: "It's hard to put in words for me because I was there when he first took over as a head coach. I remember what that program was like when he took over, to where it is now. I don't think I've ever seen anything like that in sports. To be able to win in one spot, Coach (Phil) Jackson has won in two spots, but Pop has been able to do it in one spot.

"He's been tremendous. And I think the thing that will go unnoticed is all the people that he's helped in coaching positions, GM positions, that have come through that program as well."

Stan Van Gundy, Detroit Pistons: "I think, No. 1, he's been at the top of our profession and set a model of consistency, year in and year out, but what I have more respect for more than anything is that he is really no different than he ever was. He's a great supporter of other coaches and he's a down-to-Earth guy. He cares about the game and his team. He's not wrapped up in a lot of crap. He's not a self-promoter at all. He lets his work speak for itself and he gives all of the credit to his players. If he only had 99 wins he'd be a class act but what he is now is one of the most successful coaches in history *and* a class act."

Erick Spoelstra, Miami Heat: "Probably the most significant and admirable thing he's done is build a real culture with this (Spurs) organization. It's consistent leadership and there's an absolute style of play that's enviable by everybody in the league—defensive-minded, sharing of the basketball, everybody being involved in a balanced attack. That's now the model every organization is trying to emulate.

"His legacy is bigger than just the banners. It's the culture and the style of play the league is now trying to emulate. That's the ultimate compliment."

Tom Thibodeau, Minnesota Timberwolves: "It's a mark of greatness to be in one place and to set a standard that he has. I happened to be in San Antonio prior to his arrival. I was actually there about three weeks as he was settling in as the general manger so I have a pretty good understanding of where it was and what he's taken it to.

"His strong leadership provides his order and he established that right from the beginning and he's maintained it right throughout and in every area: as a leader; as a teacher and coach; and as a communicator."

Brett Brown, Philadelphia 76ers: "What will be his lasting legacy? I think there's a level of accountability and discipline; the ability to coach superstars and demand from everybody; the ability to annually attain success; the ability to coach defense and fluctuate with players and adapt to the times.

"Then, to put your fingerprints on an entire city is so much more than just what you do in basketball."

Jason Kidd, Milwaukee Bucks: "He showed you don't always have to wear a tie. That's one of the coolest things, as you can relax a little bit and be yourself. Being able to have fun with it."

58 The Red Mamba

When the Spurs traded Rasho Nesterovic to the Toronto Raptors for backup forward Eric Williams and backup center Matt Bonner on July 16, 2006, hardly anyone expected Bonner would have a greater impact on the Spurs than Nesterovic, who had started 203 games at center after David Robinson retired in 2003.

An exception was Jeff Van Gundy, who had just completed his third season as head coach of the Houston Rockets when the trade came down.

Bonner, Van Gundy said, was a perfect fit for the Spurs because of his ability to stretch the floor as a big man with exceptional three-point shooting ability.

Van Gundy was right, and when the 2015–16 Spurs season began Bonner was still on the roster, beginning his 10th season in silver and black. He is one of only six players in franchise history to play at least 10 consecutive seasons with the club, a remarkable accomplishment for a player who never averaged more than 8.2 points per game.

Bonner's unique gift is uncanny accuracy from beyond the three-point line. The league leader in long-range accuracy in

Matt Bonner has become a beloved figure among both teammates and fans since arriving in San Antonio in 2006.

#Letbonnershoot

Despite his consistently superior three-point shooting, Matt Bonner never got an invitation to the NBA's All-Star Weekend three-point contest until 2013, when an online campaign brought his omission to the attention of NBA fans through a campaign launched on social media.

The Spurs sharpshooter was leading the league in three-point shooting percentage, 48.4, but he was averaging only 11 minutes per game and 3.8 points per game, largely overlooked by NBA officials who pick the contestants. Bonner's brother, Luke, created the Twitter hash tag, #letbonnershoot, and it took off on the online message service after it was promoted by the Canadian rock band Arcade Fire.

The movement worked and Bonner got his invitation to the three-point contest at Houston's Toyota Center. He justified the support from the thousands who supported #letbonnershoot when he advanced to the finals of the event.

Cleveland's Kyrie Irving made 17 of his first 18 shots in the finale and put up one of the best scores in the history of the contest to win, but Bonner had proved he belonged in the competition.

2010–11, when he made a career-high 45.7 percent of his three-point attempts, he entered the 2016–17 season with a career three-point percentage of 41.4 percent.

Of the 74 NBA players ever to shoot at least 45 percent from three-point range in a season, Bonner and Steve Novak (a former Spur) are the only two true "bigs," at 6-foot-10.

Bonner's quirky shot, a semi-push shot launched near his right ear, combined with his tenacity and attention to detail, made up for his slow foot speed and lack of athleticism and made him a contributing player during the post-Robinson-Duncan dynasty era. He has started 106 regular-season Spurs games and eight playoff games, including Game 6 of the 2014 Western Conference Finals against the Oklahoma City Thunder, when the Spurs closed out the series with an overtime win.

Heading into the 2016–17 season Bonner ranked eighth in franchise history in NBA games played, fourth in three-point baskets made (656), and fourth in three-point shots attempted (1,588).

The red-headed Bonner arrived in San Antonio with a nickname that bespeaks the quirkiness that has made him one of the team's most popular players. During the two seasons he spent with the Toronto Raptors he got around Canada's largest city via its "Red Rocket" streetcar system. When Raptors fans found out, via the media, Bonner instantly was dubbed "The Red Rocket."

Bonner was fine being the Red Rocket but Lakers star Kobe Bryant, who called himself "Black Mamba," referred to him as "Red Mamba" in a posting on Twitter looking back on when Bryant scored 81 points against the Raptors on January 22, 2006. Bryant's post on January 22, 2013, read, "The white mamba wasn't in the building but the red mamba was…Matt Bonner."

It took a while before Bonner went along with Bryant's moniker but he finally embraced it, even showing up in his home town of Concord, New Hampshire, for a fundraising event for his RockOn Foundation as DJ Red Mamba, complete with mask and cape.

59 Down Under

Here's a question that even the most avid of Spurs fans might have trouble answering: who was the first Spurs player from the southern hemisphere to earn a championship ring?

It is not Manu Ginobili.

In 1999 the Spurs signed swing man Andrew Gaze, the son of legendary Australian coach Lindsey Gaze. Andrew had played seven games with the Washington Bullets in the final month of the 1993–94 season before heading back to Australia to play in the National Basketball League for four more seasons. Before the lockout-shortened 1998–99 NBA season began, the Spurs signed the 33-year-old, 6-foot-7 guard-forward from Melbourne, who had played college ball at Seton Hall University.

Gaze played only 19 games in the 50-game season and was inactive throughout the playoff run. Nevertheless, he earned his championship ring. His single season in silver and black was the beginning of a relationship with players from Australia and New Zealand that continued through the bulk of the Duncan-Popovich era.

Sean Marks, a 6-foot-11 center-forward from Auckland, New Zealand, won a ring as a member of the 2004–05 Spurs, though he was inactive through that playoff run, just as Gaze was. Marks eventually joined the club's basketball operations department as an assistant general manager and spent one season on Popovich's coaching staff. In 2016, he was hired by the Brooklyn Nets to be their general manager.

It was the Spurs' signing of point guard Patty Mills in 2011 that eventually made the Spurs the most popular NBA team in Australia. One of the quickest players in the NBA, the 6-foot Mills is a shooting guard in a point guard's body. He struggled through his first full season, 2012–13, but showed potential as an explosive scorer and three-point marksman, hitting 40 percent of his shots from behind the line. (Later that season the Spurs signed New Zealand big man Aron Baynes, a raw-boned, 6-foot-10, 260-pound bull in a china shop.)

When Popovich challenged Mills to return for the 2013–14 season in better condition, he reported for camp having significantly lowered his percentage of body fat. He quickly earned the job as Tony Parker's backup and doubled his scoring average, going from 5.1 points per game to 10.2. He led the team in three-point field goal percentage, 42.5, seventh-best in the NBA.

Mills' play was even more dynamic in the playoff run that produced the team's fifth championship, especially in the five games of the NBA Finals against the Miami Heat. He made 13-of-23 three-pointers in the championship series, making 5-of-8 and scoring 17 points in Game 5. He averaged 10.0 points per game in the series, fifth-best on the team.

As remarkable as Mills' emergence had been during the season and through the playoff run, it became nearly miraculous when it was revealed that he had played through most of the season with a torn rotator cuff in his right shoulder. The injury was repaired about a week after the conclusion of the Finals and he missed 31 games of the 2014–15 season.

60 Solar Eclipse

Though no team serves the role of Spurs rival more completely than the Lakers (See No. 41), there was a stretch early in this century when it seemed the Phoenix Suns were the Spurs' most consistent obstacle on their road to an NBA title.

The competition between the two teams from 2004–05 through 2008–09 was intense and filled with remarkable moments that have become part of Spurs lore. They include an infamous playoff incident when "Big Shot Rob" Horry became "Cheap Shot" Rob, at least to Suns fans.

It was after Mike D'Antoni took over as head coach that the Suns coalesced around the NBA's fastest-paced offense under the direction of Steve Nash, so good at running D'Antoni's seven-seconds-or-less offense that he won back-to-back Most Valuable Player Awards. D'Antoni was an offensive genius whose approach to player movement, ball movement, pace, and the dictum that "the only bad shot is an open shot not taken" is largely responsible for the sea change in NBA style that ultimately became the Spurs' "beautiful game" offense in their run to the 2014 NBA title.

In 2004–05 the Suns raced to the NBA's best record, 62–20, behind Nash, Amar'e Stoudemire, Shawn Marion, and Quentin Richardson. Nash averaged 15.5 points per game and a league-best 11.5 assists for the NBA's highest-scoring team, winning the first of his two MVP trophies.

The Spurs, 59–23 in the regular season, met the Suns in the Western Conference Finals but it was not a fair fight. The Suns had lost high-scoring guard Joe Johnson in their semifinals matchup against the Dallas Mavericks when he suffered a fractured orbital bone near his left eye. The Spurs showed they could play at a fast pace themselves in rolling to a 4–1 series win that left Suns fans wondering what might have been had not Johnson been out.

It would be two more years before the Spurs and Suns would meet again in the playoffs, this time in the second round. Phoenix had the No. 2 seed, the Spurs the No. 3 seed, and both teams advanced easily to the semifinals.

It would be one of the most controversial playoff series in NBA history and stoke the fires of a searing rivalry that would linger for years.

The Spurs stole home-court advantage in Game 1 in Phoenix, but the Suns would regain it with a win in Game 4 that turned the series on its ear. With Phoenix ahead 100–97, with 22.9 seconds left and possession of the ball, Popovich ordered a quick foul. Horry took the foul on Nash, hip checking him hard into the scorer's table at AT&T Center. It was a flagrant foul, category II, that brought immediate ejection for Horry, meaning automatic

suspension from Game 5 in Phoenix. The Spurs were in trouble…
or were they?

Replays of the incident showed that both Suns star Amar'e
Stoudemire and backup forward (and future Spur) Boris Diaw rose
from the Suns bench and took a couple of steps in the direction
of the melee that erupted after the foul. An NBA review brought
Game 5 suspensions for both Stoudemire and Diaw for violating
the league's restriction on players leaving the bench during games.
The Game 5 advantage swung back to the Spurs and they took a
3–2 series lead behind Manu Ginobili's 26 points.

The Spurs advanced to the Western Conference Finals with a
114–106 win in Game 6, the Suns and their fans forever embit-
tered by what they perceived as cruel injustice.

D'Antoni's run in Phoenix lasted only one more season but it
produced yet another playoff matchup with the Spurs, this time in
the first round after a 55–27 Suns record produced only the No.
6 seed. The No. 3 seeded Spurs romped to a 4–1 series win and
D'Antoni would depart a few weeks later, hired to coach the New
York Knicks. Johnson would sign a free-agent contract with the
Atlanta Hawks and the Suns would not even make the playoff field
in 2008–09.

D'Antoni and Suns fans are left to wonder what might have
been had not the Spurs—and fate—stood in their way.

 **Mitch**

Mike Mitchell played in 488 games in seven seasons with the
Spurs. That he remains the seventh-highest scorer in franchise
history (ABA and NBA) in fewer than 500 games underscores the

melancholy associated with his departure from the club, for he was one of many NBA players in the 1980s whose careers were short-circuited by substance abuse.

A 6-foot-7, 215-pound small forward from Auburn, Mitchell became an All-Star with the Cleveland Cavaliers before joining the Spurs in 1981, part of a four-player trade. Once in San Antonio he immediately established himself as a scorer who could transition the team beyond the end of George Gervin's Spurs career. In his first five seasons he scored 8,271 points and averaged 21.8 points per game, and he finished his seven Spurs seasons with 9,799 points and a scoring average of 20.1 points per game, which remains the fourth-highest in franchise history (minimum of 330 games), behind only Gervin, David Robinson, and Larry Kenon.

But it was his play in the postseason that truly endeared him to Spurs fans, and if playoff performance is the ultimate test of a player's fortitude and competitive spirit, few Spurs have exceeded the postseason heart shown by Mitchell.

"Mitch" is best remembered for his standout play against the defending champion Lakers in the 1983 Western Conference Finals. With the Lakers focusing their perimeter defensive effort against Gervin, Mitchell stepped up his play and averaged 25.7 points and 10.3 rebounds in six games.

In only 35 playoff games for the Spurs, Mitchell's 646 postseason points rank 11th in franchise history. Danny Green, whose 86 points in the 2016 playoffs bumped Mitchell out of the top 10, has played 79 postseason games.

Mitchell's playoff scoring average of 18.5 points per game is third-highest in franchise history, trailing only George Gervin (27.9 points per game) and Tim Duncan (20.6).

Mitch was a favorite of fans and the reporters who covered the team, for he had a reputation as a "stand-up" player who believed in personal accountability, as well as a gregarious person who was generous with his time.

His personal accountability was never more evident than during his postgame assessment of what happened when he explained a missed 10-foot jump shot that could have given the Spurs a win over the Lakers in Game 6 of the 1983 Western Conference Finals in the most honest manner possible: "I had an open shot and I blew it," he told reporters.

Despite that miss, Mitchell's play in that six-game series cemented his reputation as a player who elevated his play in the postseason.

Spurs general manager Bob Bass had acquired center Artis Gilmore from the Bulls in the summer of 1982 for the express purpose of neutralizing Lakers center Kareem Abdul-Jabbar after the NBA's all-time scoring leader had dominated the Spurs in a 4–0 sweep of the 1982 Western Conference Finals. Mitchell had averaged 25.8 points and 9.5 rebounds per game and Gervin had averaged 32.3 points in that series, but Abdul-Jabbar had made the difference by controlling the interior play.

Gilmore did his part, scoring 52 points and grabbing 34 rebounds in Spurs victories at the L.A. Forum in Games 2 and 5, and Mitchell's 12-of-21 shooting in Game 5 made up for Gervin's 8-of-24 shooting.

Gervin and Mitchell continued their high-scoring ways for two more seasons. They combined for 49.2 points per game in 1983–84 and 43.4 points per game in 1984–85, when Mitchell ended Gervin's eight-season run as the team's top scorer. Gervin was traded to the Bulls a few days before the start of the 1985–86 season, when Mitchell repeated as the Spurs scoring leader, at 23.4 points per game.

Sadly, Mitchell's career began its downward spiral the following season, his scoring average dropping to 12.7 points per game before he entered a drug rehabilitation program. He returned to the Spurs the following season and averaged 13.5 points in 68 games but it would be his final season in the NBA.

He went on to play overseas for 10 years, mostly in Italy.

Mitchell died in 2011, at age 55, after a two-year battle with cancer.

62 Bob Bass

Although the Spurs began the 1974–75 season with a record of 18–10, management did not like head coach Tom Nissalke's direction of the team nor the style he employed. The Spurs had already contacted Bob Bass, who was serving as general manager of the Memphis Sounds, and told him a change was being made. After Nissalke was fired, Bass accepted the job, then looked at the schedule.

"They presented me with a nine-game road trip without a practice," Bass said. "It was quite an experience."

The Spurs managed only a 2–7 record on that road trip, but won 31 of their final 46 games and finished the season 51–33. They were upset in the Western Division semifinals by Indiana, but more importantly, a two-decade relationship began between Bass and the Spurs.

Bass coached full time only one more season before moving into the front office, where he was part of the management team that later hired Doug Moe, Stan Albeck, Cotton Fitzsimmons, and Larry Brown as head coaches. He also served as an interim coach three times when coaching changes were made during the season.

But the biggest contribution Bass made to the team involved the Iceman, George Gervin, who was listed as 6-foot-7, 180 pounds in the program, but was taller and lighter.

"He was extremely thin," Bass said. "I don't know if he even weighed 170 and we measured him at 6-foot-8¾. But he had all the talent in the world and we had to put him in a position where he could use it."

Gervin was only 22 years old at the time and playing forward, because that's traditionally where taller players played at the time. The era of the 6-foot-9 guard did not really catch on until Magic Johnson joined the Lakers in 1979, but Bass knew that Gervin simply could not compete defensively while giving up 30 or more pounds to opposing small forwards.

Gervin had already wrested the scoring leadership from guard James Silas, but often still deferred to his veteran teammate, who was 25 but perhaps the best guard in the ABA.

"Ice led the team in scoring every year except one when Silas was the leading scorer," Bass said. "In the playoffs, we played Indiana and they had a guard named Don Buse, who shut Silas down in two of the games and they took the first three games of the series. In the last game, Donnie Freeman, our starting two-guard got hurt, and so I moved Ice to guard and he just took off. He had like 37.

"We won the next two games, so Indiana made a switch. Slick Leonard, their coach, came back and moved a 6-foot-7 forward named Billy Knight to guard to try and stop Ice. He didn't stop Ice, but that let Buse guard Silas again and he did a good enough job for them to win the series. But we saw Ice was better suited for guard, so the next fall, I was coaching again and left him there. And he was the tallest guard in the NBA until Magic Johnson came along at 6-foot-9."

Bass was an integral part of everything the Spurs did during his two decades with the team. He was GM in 1987 and was a strong proponent of drafting David Robinson, even though Robinson had a two-year Navy commitment. Although drafting Robinson seems now to be a no-brainer, the 1987 draft had sensational talent— Scottie Pippen, Kevin Johnson, Horace Grant, Reggie Miller, Mark Jackson, and Reggie Lewis.

But Robinson was a once-in-a-generation talent and when he joined the team for the 1989–90 season, Bass surrounded him with an excellent supporting cast and the Spurs improved from 21 wins the previous season to 56. Robinson was voted Rookie of the Year and Bass was rewarded with the NBA Executive of the Year award.

Bass left the Spurs to join the Charlotte Hornets in 1995 and did such a good job in building that team that he again won the Executive of the Year award, in 1997. He retired in 2004 after spending 36 years in professional basketball including all or parts of 10 seasons as a head coach. He ended his coaching career with a 311–300 record, but more than records or executive decisions, Spurs fans need to remember him as the man who made George Gervin a guard.

63 Coach Bud

When Gregg Popovich returned to the franchise as general manager in 1994, one of his first moves was to hire a former star for Pomona-Pitzer named Mike Budenholzer to serve as the team's video coordinator.

It didn't take Budenholzer long to impress his boss. Popovich made him an assistant coach when he took over on the bench during the 1996–97 season. Their long relationship had begun in 1988 when Popovich recruited Budenholzer to play at Pomona-Pitzer. However, he never coached him there, leaving the Division III school to take a job as an assistant on Larry Brown's Spurs staff.

By the time the Atlanta Hawks hired him as their head coach in the summer of 2013, Budenholzer had served 17 years on Popovich's staff, longer than any other Popovich assistant coach. In 2007 he became Pop's No. 1 assistant after P.J. Carlesimo departed for Seattle to become the SuperSonics' head coach.

Budenholzer proved he had a remarkable feel for the game and absorbed Popovich's intricate offensive scheme so thoroughly that the head coach insisted Budenholzer knew it better than he did. Assuming head coaching duties on the rare occasions Popovich missed games for health reasons (and on more numerous occasions when the head coach was ejected from games), Budenholzer's name began to be mentioned when head coaching jobs came open. But he never seriously considered other teams because he enjoyed his situation with the Spurs and was regarded as Popovich's eventual successor.

Popovich convinced Budenholzer that he owed it to himself and his family to seriously consider becoming a head coach if the situation were right. He finally departed the Spurs when former Spurs player and assistant general manager Danny Ferry offered him the Atlanta job.

Budenholzer's injury-plagued Hawks went 38–44 in his first season on the bench but produced the best record in the Eastern Conference in 2014–15, earning him Coach of the Year honors. At the press conference at which he was presented the Red Auerbach Trophy, he choked up as he thanked Popovich for all that he taught him.

"I was very, very fortunate to be so close to a coach who's done so much for the league, done so much for so many coaches, and has shared so much with me," he said. "And I can't even begin to articulate how thankful I am and all the things I've learned."

64 Malik Rose

A second-round draft pick of the Charlotte Hornets in 1996, Malik Rose was cut loose by the Hornets after playing only 525 minutes in his rookie season. The Spurs snapped him off the free-agent market for a bargain price, just under $500,000 for two seasons.

The gregarious Philadelphian played less in his first season in silver and black than he had as a rookie, just 429 minutes, but endeared himself to his teammates through his work ethic, upbeat attitude, and sharp sense of humor.

By his second season with the Spurs he established a spot in Gregg Popovich's playing rotation, a solid contributor on the franchise's first championship team. He played behind Tim Duncan at power forward and occasionally backed up center David Robinson—never mind that he was just 6-foot-7.

In the Spurs' second run to an NBA title, in 2002–03, Rose averaged a career-high 24.5 minutes per game, started 13 games, and enjoyed his best season. He averaged 9.3 points per game and 5.8 rebounds in the playoffs and appeared in all 24 games. In Game 2 of the Western Conference Finals against Dallas he enjoyed a career highlight playoff game when he produced 25 points in 27 minutes off the bench. His aggressive play in the post resulted in 18 trips to the foul line and he made 15 free throws in a game the Spurs had to win after dropping the series opener on their AT&T Center home court.

Just before the 2004–05 trade deadline the Spurs shook up their rotation when they traded Rose and their 2005 first-round draft pick to the New York Knicks for center Nazr Mohammed and a 2006 first-round pick. The deal stunned and disappointed Spurs fans, who were sorry to see one of San Antonio's most popular players depart. Rose had been very active in community affairs and had opened a popular restaurant, Malik's Philly's Phamous, which specialized in Philly cheesesteak sandwiches.

Rose began the 2015–16 NBA season as manager of basketball operations for the Atlanta Hawks.

65 Take a Stroll on the Riverwalk

NBA tradition insists that every championship team share its triumph with some sort of public celebration. Typically, this means a parade through the heart of whichever city claims the champs, the players riding in cars or floats or atop double-decker buses.

The Spurs have their own unique championship parade venue: the San Antonio Riverwalk.

Winding through the heart of downtown San Antonio, the San Antonio River first was channeled in the 1930s when the Texas state legislature created the San Antonio River Authority to govern flood control projects and other aspects of managing the river. Originating about four miles north of downtown San Antonio, the river eventually covers about 240 miles and feeds into the Guadalupe River about 10 miles before the Guadalupe enters into San Antonio Bay at the Gulf of Mexico.

According to the official San Antonio Riverwalk website, the Riverwalk was completed around 1941, when the first walkways, stairways to street level, and rock walls along the banks were completed. The Riverwalk website also declares that it is the No. 1 tourist attraction in the state.

San Antonians have enjoyed parades on the river since 1936. The city's annual Fiesta celebration, which usually coincides with the first round of the NBA playoffs, includes a river parade with Fiesta royalty, rock bands, and others waving from the barges that carry tourists along the river daily. Thousands line the watery route and watch from the streets above.

But not even this popular annual parade matches the Spurs championship parades on the river. From the 1999 NBA championship river parade, which attracted an estimated 250,000 fans, some of them perched in the cypresses that line the river, to the 2014 parade with its stops at the Arneson River Theater for impromptu speeches, the championship parades have become a unique San Antonio tradition.

Visiting the Riverwalk is a must for any San Antonio Spurs fan, especially if it's the site of another NBA championship celebration.

BoBo

Boris Diaw has earned a special place in the hearts of Spurs fans for two reasons:

No. 1—his insertion into the starting lineup for Game 3 of the 2014 NBA Finals was instrumental in the Spurs' utter demolition of the Miami Heat in the most satisfying NBA championship run in franchise history.

No. 2—his halting couple of steps from the Phoenix Suns bench onto the AT&T Center court in the final moments of Game 4 of the 2007 Western Conference semifinals resulted in his suspension from Game 5, and likely contributed to the suspension of teammate Amar'e Stoudemire. Those suspensions were a major factor in the Spurs' return to Phoenix for Game 5 and scoring a pivotal victory. It put them in control of their toughest series on their way to the 2007 NBA title.

Diaw would much prefer that Spurs fans know more about the former than the latter, but there is no denying that both were big factors in two of the Spurs' five championship runs.

Versatile enough to play all five positions, Diaw came to the Spurs from the Charlotte Bobcats late in the 2011–12 season. Unhappy in Charlotte, where Bobcats fans were quick to boo his often-lackluster play, Diaw negotiated a buyout of his $9 million contract. By the time the ink was dry on his buyout papers the Spurs had a deal that put him in silver and black. The fact that Diaw had been a high school teammate and close friend of fellow Frenchman Tony Parker made his signing a natural fit for him and the team.

Once he had a chance to go through a Spurs training camp, Diaw's unique skill set—the ball-handling and passing skills of a point guard, a solid shooting stroke out to three-point range, the heft of a backboard-banging power forward-center, and a remarkable basketball IQ—made him one of the Spurs' most important reserves.

One rap on Diaw's game always had been that he was too unselfish; that he did not look often enough for his own shot. To Gregg Popovich, that made him a perfect fit for the "good to great" passing game offense he was employing more often. Diaw started 24 games in 2013–14 and averaged 9.1 points per game, 4.1 rebounds, and 2.8 assists. Popovich also knew he was a better athlete and defender than most believed and trusted him to make the right play in clutch situations.

After Diaw played all but three minutes of the fourth quarter and overtime in the Spurs' victory in Game 6 of the 2014 Western Conference Finals against Oklahoma City—and scored a career playoff high 26 points—Popovich also knew he could count on him when things got tight.

After the Miami Heat won Game 2 of the 2014 NBA Finals to steal home-court advantage, Popovich made a lineup change that turned the series on its ear. Diaw replaced Tiago Splitter as starting center and helped facilitate the "beautiful game" offense that produced three straight wins by an average of 19 points.

Diaw scored only 22 points in the three games but also had 23 rebounds and 18 assists.

Boris Babacar Diaw-Riffiod is the son of Issa Diaw, a former high jump champion from Senegal, and Elisabeth Riffiod, considered one of the greatest players in the history of women's basketball in France. He has played on the French men's national team since 2003 and was captain of the French team that won the 2013 Eurobasket tournament.

Diaw has established a nonprofit foundation to organize sports activities for Senegalese youth and aid education in Senegal.

67 Becky Hammon

All you need to know about Becky Hammon's appointment to the Spurs coaching staff on August 4, 2014, is this: nowhere in the press release announcing her hiring was there any mention of her gender.

Gregg Popovich and R.C. Buford gave Hammon a job as an assistant coach because they believed she had the potential to be a great coach. As far as they were concerned, the fact she was the first woman in any of the North American professional sports leagues—NBA, NFL, NHL, and Major League Baseball—hired as a full-time assistant was irrelevant.

Except it wasn't. Her hiring was big news all around the NBA and the entire basketball world. It was hailed by women's advocacy groups and by her fellow NBA coaches.

But it was no publicity stunt aimed at making the Spurs look like pioneers in gender equity.

Hammon's path to a spot on the Spurs bench began with a playing career as a high school star in Rapid City, South Dakota, and then being a three-time All-American at Colorado State University. Undrafted by any WNBA teams after college, she made the roster of the WNBA's New York Liberty after a standout training camp and soon established her credentials as one of the league's best players. She also played overseas (as did many WNBA stars) and in 2007 was traded to the San Antonio Silver Stars.

Her eight seasons with the Silver Stars brought her to the attention of Popovich and Buford, who recognized qualities they believed would someday make her a good coach. Occasionally, she could be seen at Spurs practice sessions, helping assistant coaches as

> **Stay Tuned**
> After Becky Hammon's first season as a full-time assistant, Gregg Popovich had her coach the Spurs team in the annual Las Vegas Summer League, where she underwent intense scrutiny as the first female head coach in summer league history.
> She did not disappoint. After her Summer Spurs lost their first game, they won their next seven, capturing the Summer League title.
> It was enough for some media outlets, including *Sports Illustrated*, to predict she would become the first female head coach in NBA history.

they worked with Spurs players on skill development and all aspects of game preparation.

By then, the Spurs felt she would one day be added to the staff. But Popovich told her the extra scrutiny made it important that they see how she handled a coaching internship. When she was sidelined by a knee injury for most of the 2013 season. Popovich and Buford made her an adjunct assistant coach and included her on some road trips.

"They've been observing me for the past eight years," she told the *San Antonio Express-News* on the eve of her first season as a full-time assistant. "How I play, how I communicate with my teammates, fans, and the community. They've been watching me from afar and then these last few years, knowing I'm coming to the end of my career.

"Pop told me, early on, 'As cool as it would be to hire you, you have to be qualified and I have to make sure you're qualified.'

"I think that's the best way to go about it. It could be catastrophic if I wasn't qualified and then it sets the whole thing back. To be perfectly honest it's never been about the woman thing. It's been about, 'Hey, she's got a great basketball mind and we'd love to have her and think she'd be a great addition to our program.'"

Dallas Mavericks coach Rick Carlisle, president of the NBA Coaches Association, hailed her hiring and stressed its legitimacy.

"It's important that people know this wasn't some whim," Carlisle told the *Express-News*. "She sat in meetings all last year and they all got to know her and she got to know them. Pop thought she could add something. It's important to note that she earned the position and she was qualified for it.

"Everybody is looking for the best people. Why should it matter whether they're male of female?"

Hammon didn't ask to be a pioneer in pro sports coaching but she understood the significance of her hire.

In 2014, Gregg Popovich and the Spurs made Becky Hammon the first full-time female assistant coach in American professional sports.

"Obviously, the (historic first) is great and it's a tremendous honor but I think the bigger point is I'm getting hired because I'm capable, because of my basketball IQ and stuff that they've seen in me personally," she said at a press conference at which her hiring was announced. "I know I'm just thrilled for the opportunity to coach these unbelievable athletes and, from what I've known, unbelievable people."

The very fact the Spurs held a press conference showed the organization understood the significance of the moment. The hiring of every other assistant coach in franchise history had been announced via press release.

Popovich skipped the Hammon announcement. His only comment was included in the press release handed out to the media.

"Having observed her working with our team this past season I'm confident her basketball IQ, work ethic, and interpersonal skills will be a great benefit to the Spurs," read his statement.

68 Ettore Messina

One of the most successful coaches in European basketball history—the Gregg Popovich of Europe, if you will—Ettore Messina was added to the Spurs coaching staff in 2014 and immediately became Popovich's lead assistant.

Popovich and Spurs general manager R.C. Buford had known and admired Messina for more than a decade when he resigned as head coach of Spanish League powerhouse Real Madrid on March 4, 2011. Buford invited Messina to spend the rest of the season with the Spurs and the coach accepted.

It was the first step in the road to becoming the first European-born lead assistant in NBA history.

With four Euroleague titles, four Italian League titles, five Russian League titles, and selection as one of the 50 greatest contributors in Euroleague history, Messina long had been considered a strong candidate for a job on an NBA bench. While a successful coach in the Italian League he had coached two Spurs starters, Manu Ginobili and Rasho Nesterovic, before they joined the Spurs.

During the final weeks of the 2010–11 season, Popovich determined he wanted him on his staff if the opportunity ever arose. When assistant coach Sean Marks opted to return to Buford's basketball operations staff as an assistant GM before the 2014–15 season, the opportunity arrived. At age 54, Messina joined the Spurs.

In November the 65-year-old Popovich missed a pair of games in November to undergo what the team called a minor medical procedure and Messina became the first European-born head coach in NBA history, albeit on an interim basis. (Former Cleveland Cavaliers head coach Dave Blatt has dual American and Israeli citizenship, but was born in Boston, Massachusetts.)

Messina's record as a Spurs head coach: 2–0. Under his guidance they defeated both the Indiana Pacers and Sacramento Kings at AT&T Center.

Manu Ginobili, who said he was having "Bologna flashbacks" after scoring 28 points for Messina in the win over the Pacers, has no doubt about the coach's future.

"For sure he has the potential, the experience, the knowledge to become a head coach one day," Ginobili told the *San Antonio Express-News*. "Here or somewhere else, I don't know. With European coaches, especially like him who have won everything and been around, it's just a matter of adapting to the league, the rules, the players, the environment. You need a little time to adjust to that."

69 Three Arenas

In their 43 years in San Antonio, the Spurs have had only three home courts: HemisFair Arena, the Alamodome, and the AT&T Center.

Spurs fans have meaningful memories from each of them.

One reason Red McCombs, Angelo Drossos, and the other original Spurs investors were easily able to bring the Dallas Chaparrals to San Antonio was the existence of HemisFair Arena, which had been built to present major indoor events associated with HemisFair '68, the 1968 World's Fair.

Seating capacity for the first Spurs season was 10,146. For the last few seasons of the ABA that was more than enough, though the team managed to bump it up by 300 seats for the final ABA season.

The intimate atmosphere was instrumental in developing the relationship between the team and its energetic fans, the rowdiest of whom became known as "The Baseline Bums."

When the Spurs entered the NBA in 1976, seating at HemisFair was expanded to 16,000 and it served the club through its first 17 NBA seasons.

Hoping to lure an NFL team, civic leaders, led by then mayor Henry Cisneros, managed to get a funding issue on the ballot in 1989 and San Antonians passed a measure that allowed for construction of a 60,000-seat domed arena that could host football and be converted to a smaller venue for basketball and ice hockey.

Its enormous seating capacity for basketball enabled the city to bid on NCAA tournament events, including the Final Four, which the arena hosted in both 2004 and 2008. In fact, the basketball version of the Alamodome was a disaster from an aesthetic standpoint, with a huge drapery separating it from a large, unused portion of the football field. Fans in the upper reaches often brought binoculars to follow the action. Players sometimes complained that the enormous dimensions affected their depth perception and hindered their shooting.

Alamodome seating capacity for Spurs games was around 36,000, though 39,554 were crammed in for Game 2 of the 1999 NBA Finals between the Spurs and the New York Knicks.

By the end of the 1990s, the Spurs had determined they needed a smaller, basketball-first facility. Threatening to re-locate unless such a venue were built, the Spurs got a bond issue on the ballot in 1999 that would fund a new arena, to be built in an industrial area on San Antonio's east side. The bonds would be paid off by a small increase in the tax on cars rented at San Antonio International Airport.

An Explosive Start

When it came time for the 1994–95 Spurs to play their first regular-season game at the Alamodome, on November 4, 1994, the team's game operations department was determined to start things off with a bang: an extensive fireworks display before the Spurs were introduced.

There was only one problem: the Alamodome was equipped with smoke-activated water cannons in case of fire. Smoke detecting sensors had been covered before the display but one of the covers had come loose and the pre-tipoff fireworks activated one of the cannons.

Hundreds of fans scrambled for cover, soaked on their way to shelter from the "storm." Worse, areas of the playing court also were drenched.

Tipoff was delayed for nearly an hour while the water was cleaned from the court.

The Spurs were on fire, so to speak, at the outset of the game, racing to a 38–23 first-quarter lead over the Golden State Warriors. However, the Warriors rained points on them in the second half, scoring a 123–118 victory.

Though the city's tourist industry vigorously fought for approval, good timing ruled the day for the Spurs. The vote took place less than a week after the Spurs defeated the Knicks at the Alamodome to win their first NBA title.

The bond issue won in a landslide.

The new arena was completed in time for the 2002–03 season and timing was again in the Spurs' favor. They won their second NBA title in their brand-new home, then known as the SBC Center.

70 Michael Finley

When the Mavericks used the "amnesty" clause in the 2005 collective bargaining agreement to remove Michael Finley's $16 million salary from their team payroll, the Spurs stepped in and convinced the high-scoring forward to sign with them for the mid-level cap exception.

Gregg Popovich flew to Chicago, Finley's off-season home, and made a no-nonsense pitch to the 32-year-old two-time All-Star who had averaged at least 20 points per game in five seasons. The Spurs coach told Finley he respected his game and thought he would be a great fit for a team that had just won its third NBA title in six seasons. He promised neither a starting spot nor guaranteed minutes.

Convinced the Spurs offered his best chance to finally win a championship ring, Finley passed on a richer offer from the Miami Heat and a similar mid-level offer from the Phoenix Suns.

The instant he signed his contract the Spurs became the favorites for the 2006 NBA title.

Though he had started every game he had played for the Mavericks in the previous eight seasons, Finley settled easily into a reserve role with the Spurs. His shooting percentage dipped to a career-low 41.2 percent, yet he teamed with Nick Van Exel, Brent Barry, and Robert Horry to give the Spurs the NBA's best bench unit. His 42.3 percent three-point shooting helped make him one of four Spurs to average double-figure scoring, at 10.1 points per game.

The Spurs cruised to a club-record 63 wins but Finley's championship dream ended when the Mavericks, the team that had waived him to get rid of a contract they deemed onerous, emerged from a dramatic, seven-game second-round series with an overtime win in Game 7.

If Finley feared he had made a mistake by choosing the Spurs over the Heat, who won the 2006 championship, the 2006–07 season justified his decision. After a 58-win season in which his scoring average fell below double figures for the first time in his career, Finley started every game of the Spurs' 20-game run to their fourth NBA title. After they won Game 4 in Cleveland to record just the eighth Finals sweep in NBA history, Finley had tears in his eyes as he hoisted the Larry O'Brien Trophy for the first time.

Finley's stay in San Antonio ended awkwardly. As his fifth season in silver and black reached the stretch run, he requested to be waived so he could sign on with another team. The Spurs were 33–24 when he made the request, to which the Spurs complied. After clearing waivers he signed with the Boston Celtics, who fell to the Los Angeles Lakers in the 2010 NBA Finals. He did not get off the bench in the final game of his career, Game 7 of that Finals series.

71 Give Thanks to Pomona-Pitzer

Before Larry Brown hired him as an assistant on his 1987–88 Spurs coaching staff, Gregg Popovich spent nine years as head coach of the Pomona-Pitzer Sagehens in Claremont, California.

Popovich always has insisted he could have been happy coaching at the Division III schools for the rest of his life and he remains close to many players he coached there.

Don't doubt his assertion. What Popovich discovered at Pomona-Pitzer was paradise for academics and free thinkers. Pomona College and Pitzer College are two of the five undergraduate schools that make up the Claremont Colleges, located on a one-square-mile campus between Los Angeles and San Bernardino in Claremont, California. The schools describe their approach as "reminiscent of the Oxford-Cambridge model."

Campus life within the Claremont square mile is unique. Students can walk from one campus to another without knowing the distinction. It is an environment that may not exist at any other institutions of higher learning in America: five liberal arts colleges that belong to one community but retain individual identities.

Intercollegiate athletics at the campus are kept in perspective. Players truly are student-athletes—no athletic scholarships are offered—and attendance at games is, to be kind, sparse.

"Nobody comes to the games," former Spurs assistant Mike Budenholzer, a 1992 graduate of Pomona College, told the *San Antonio Express-News* in a 2015 interview. "It's a little humbling. You put in all those hours because you love it. You're not getting the chicks or free meals. There's no training table. The league we play in, you get in a couple vans and you drive from Claremont to

Cal Lutheran or Occidental or wherever. We took these horrible sack lunches. I ate a lot of soggy sandwiches."

When Popovich arrived in 1979 the Sagehens were one of the worst college basketball teams in NCAA Division III. In his first season, 1979–80, they went 2–22. By the time he left, in 1988, his teams were among the best in the Southern California Intercollegiate Athletic Conference, having won the conference title in 1986.

"When Pop got there, Division III basketball was a half step up from intramurals and wasn't taken seriously on a lot of different

What's in a Vitae?

In 1979, Gregg Popovich, one of two assistants on head coach Hank Egan's Air Force Academy coaching staff, was on a recruiting trip in Los Angeles with fellow assistant Reggie Minton, an Air Force major who was older and more experienced as a coach. Minton got a call offering an opportunity to change his career path. A friend at Pomona College told him about an opening for a new basketball coach for Pomona-Pitzer and had recommended him for the job.

When Minton decided the job was not for him he suggested Popovich would be perfect.

The rest is history.

"(Popovich) and I were out on the road recruiting, staying at the Marriott on Century Boulevard in L.A. I got a call from a guy at Pomona-Pitzer. He and I had gone to College of Worcester, in Ohio, and he called to see if I was interested in the job. At that point in time I was committed to the military, beyond the point I could pick up and leave without making a sacrifice to my years in the service," said Minton, who eventually replaced Egan as Air Force Academy head coach and now serves as executive director of the National Association of Basketball Coaches. "I turned it down but recommended that Pop would be perfect for the job. He said to have Pop send him his vitae (curriculum vitae).

"I'm thinking, *What the heck is a vitae?* I knew right then and there I wasn't the right guy for that job.

"That was the beginning for Pop and it went from there."

levels," Budenholzer said. "I don't know if this happened other places earlier but he really took Pomona-Pitzer basketball from something that wasn't taken seriously and turned it into a program.

"He had to do everything and by the time I got there (in 1988) we were building a nice gym and recruited. He came there and took something and built it out of next to nothing. I had brothers who were there and played for him so I can tell you that is no exaggeration."

In addition to coaching the basketball team for the combined Pomona and Pitzer Colleges, Popovich also taught history. In 1987, after his seventh season, he was offered a chance to take an academic sabbatical, a paid one-year leave to pursue another sort of academic exercise he wanted.

The Sagehens of 1986–87 had just completed their best season in 68 years, winning the SCIAC title with a record of 16–12. Four starters were to return for the 1987–88 season but Popovich eagerly accepted the chance for the sabbatical. He turned his team over to assistant coach Charlie Katsiaficas, asking only that he stick with the man-to-man defensive scheme that Popovich preferred.

His sabbatical was a graduate level course in basketball coaching, taking him to the campus of University of North Carolina and, finally, to the University of Kansas, where Brown made him an unpaid assistant on his coaching staff.

Popovich returned to Pomona-Pitzer after his season with the Jayhawks, but Brown knew that if he ever returned to the NBA he wanted Popovich on his staff.

The Pomona-Pitzer sabbatical turned out to be a turning point in Spurs history.

72 Captain Jack

One of the most beloved Spurs of the Popovich-Duncan era also was the most enigmatic.

Stephen Jackson came to the club as a free agent before the 2001–02 season, when he played only 23 games in an injury-plagued first season in silver and black. He became a starter at shooting guard a third of the way through the 2002–03 season.

In the 2002–03 playoff run he averaged 12.8 points per game and 4.1 rebounds and had some heroic moments, especially during Game 6 of the Western Conference Finals against the Dallas Mavericks, when he made 5-of-7 three-point shots and scored 24 points in the game that sent the Spurs to their second NBA Finals. But he also committed 26 turnovers in the six Finals games.

When he became a free agent a few weeks after the championship parade on the San Antonio River, the player his teammates had dubbed "Captain Jack" expected a lucrative, long-term offer from the Spurs and was disappointed when he didn't get one. The Spurs were about to make Manu Ginobili their starter at shooting guard; when they refused to increase their offer, Jackson ended up signing with the Atlanta Hawks for just $1 million.

Jackson finally returned to the Spurs for the final month of the 2012–13 in a trade that sent Richard Jefferson and T.J. Ford to the Golden State Warriors. He helped San Antonio advance to the Western Conference Finals against the Oklahoma City Thunder, making 26-of-43 playoff three-pointers, leading all postseason long-range shooters at an astounding 60.5 percent.

With Kawhi Leonard securely established as the Spurs' starting small forward in 2012–13, Jackson's playing time diminished as the season neared conclusion and he made it clear he was unhappy. Gregg

Stephen Jackson wasn't always an easy player to manage, but fans appreciated his passion and he helped the Spurs win the NBA championship in 2003.

Popovich told him he would be playing behind both Danny Green and Manu Ginobili in the playoffs, and when Jackson acknowledged he could not accept such a role he was waived a few days before the end of the season. He told his followers on Twitter, "I would never say a player is better than me when I know they're not."

It was a sad end for an ultra-competitive Spurs player who delighted the team's fans.

73 Ginobili's Foul

When the Spurs signed two-time All-Star guard-forward Michael Finley to a free-agent contract on September 2, 2005, adding him to a roster that had just beaten the Detroit Pistons in the 2005 NBA Finals, they instantly became favorites to mount a successful defense of their championship.

After they roared through the most successful season in club history, winning an NBA-best 63 games, back-to-back NBA titles seemed even more likely.

Then they ran into the second-best team in the Western Conference in the second round of the playoffs. The Dallas Mavericks had won 60 games and should have been the No. 2 seed in the postseason tournament. Because the NBA guaranteed no worse than the No. 3 seed to division winners, the Mavericks, who played in the Southwest Division with the Spurs, were dropped to the No. 4 seed, putting both teams on the same side of the playoff bracket.

Predictably, the series was close, right from the start. Except for a 113–91 Mavericks blowout in Game 2, each game was decided by a few clutch plays. Games 1, 3, 4, 5, and 6 were decided by a combined 14 points.

The Spurs faced elimination in Game 6 in Dallas. Manu Ginobili (30 points), Tim Duncan (24), and Finley (16) combined for 70 points to keep the Spurs alive with a 91–86 win.

Game 7 at AT&T Center started disastrously for the Spurs, who trailed by as many as 19 points and were down 14 at halftime. But Duncan, Ginobili, and Tony Parker combined for 26 of the team's 28 points in the third quarter, cutting Dallas' lead to six, 84–78, going to the fourth period.

In the fourth, Duncan and Ginobili scored every Spurs point until Finley knocked down a three-pointer with 1:43 left to cut Dallas' lead to a single point, 101–100.

With 32.9 seconds remaining Ginobili nailed a three-pointer that gave the Spurs a 104–101 lead.

As long as the Spurs could keep the Mavericks from making a three-point shot, victory seemed imminent. They did their best to deny the three-point line, forcing Mavericks star Dirk Nowitzki to put up a two-point shot with 21.6 seconds left. Even a Nowitzki make would leave the Mavs trailing by a point, forced to foul on the Spurs' next possession.

Instead, the ultra-competitive Ginobili ran at Nowitzki and tried to block his fall-away jumper. Not only did Nowitzki make the shot, but he added the free throw, knotting the game at 104–104.

Popovich was furious with Ginobili but gave him a chance to atone on the final possession of regulation time. Ginobili's short shot just before the buzzer slid off the rim.

The game went to overtime, where the Mavericks emerged with a 119–111 victory.

The Mavs would go on to the NBA Finals, where they fell to the Miami Heat in six games.

The Spurs were left to bemoan the worst foul in franchise history.

74 The R.J. Deal

After they were humbled by the Dallas Mavericks in the first round of the 2009 playoffs—Dallas won its four games by an average of 12.75 points—the Spurs knew they needed to make a major off-season acquisition. They sent 37-year-old defensive star Bruce Bowen, center Fabricio Oberto, and power forward Kurt Thomas to the Milwaukee Bucks for Richard Jefferson, an athletic small forward who had averaged 19.6 points per game in his first season in Milwaukee after seven seasons with the Nets.

The deal was hailed as a solid response to the decline that seemed to follow the team's fourth title run in 2006–07. Jefferson was just 29 when the trade was made, considered a second-tier star and a player who twice had averaged more than 22 points per game in eight seasons with the New Jersey Nets. He had been on the 2004 U.S. Olympic team with Tim Duncan and was athletic enough to have been a contestant in the All-Star Weekend slam dunk competition.

It did not take long before Spurs fans decided the deal was a disappointment. Asked to fit into a system that did not emphasize his strengths—scoring on post-ups and isolations—Jefferson did not come close to the lofty expectations that in retrospect were unreasonable. His scoring average dropped from 19.6 points per game in his one season with the Bucks to 12.3 points per game.

After his disastrous first season with the Spurs, Jefferson worked all summer with coach Gregg Popovich, who wanted him to become a better spot-up shooter, especially from three-point range. He became a very good three-point shooter the next season—his 44.0 percent shooting ranked fifth in the league—and adapted his game accordingly, taking 307 of his 642 shots from beyond the arc.

Nevertheless, his scoring average fell even further, to 11.0 points per game, and he was even worse in the horrific first-round playoff loss to the Memphis Grizzlies. He made only 3-of-17 shots in the final four games of the series, after which Popovich said he had been "MIA," a military term meaning "missing in action."

At the trade deadline in the lockout-shortened 2011–12 season, the Spurs gave up on the Jefferson experiment. His scoring average down to 9.2 points per game, he was traded, along with guard T.J. Ford and a first-round draft pick, to the Warriors for swing man Stephen Jackson, a Popovich favorite who had helped the Spurs win their second title in 2003.

The Chaparrals

The Spurs were born in 1973 at a point when no team in any of the four major American sports considered San Antonio worthy of a franchise. Then again, when a team that moves to the Alamo City once played home games in Lubbock, Texas, San Antonio looks delightfully cosmopolitan.

For five of the first six years of the franchise's existence, the Spurs were the Dallas Chaparrals. They were so ignored that in the 1970–71 season, they became the Texas Chaparrals, adopting a regional concept with "home" games in three Texas cities. Thankfully, they had no desire to call themselves the Dallas–Fort Worth–Lubbock Chaparrals, which proved to be a sage decision because in their 11th Fort Worth appearance of the season, they attracted a crowd of mere hundreds. When they left town that night, they announced they would never return and the remaining Fort Worth dates were moved to Dallas.

Chappell, the Cold-Cocking Chaparral

In 1971–72, 31-year-old forward Len Chappell was making $30,000 a year in the last season of a 10-year career, the first nine in the NBA. Dallas coach Tom Nissalke was tired of his team being bullied by menacing forward John Brisker of the Pittsburgh Condors, and offered a $500 bounty to anyone who could take Brisker out of the game. Chappell—the team's sixth man—asked to start.

Chappell wasted little time. When the ball was in the air for the opening tip, Brisker watched the ball and Chappell coldcocked him, knocking him out of the game for several minutes. When Brisker returned, he made sure to stay away from Chappell.

In Dallas no one had time for what was considered minor league basketball. The Cowboys made their first Super Bowl appearance in 1971 and won the NFL title the next season. However, the Chaps did provide enduring memories.

In only their ninth game of their first season in 1967, the team played at home against the Indiana Pacers. After a late basket, they had a seemingly safe two-point lead with one second left in the game. The Pacers quickly inbounded the ball to guard Jerry Harkness, who, in desperation, simply heaved it toward the other basket 88 feet away. As the players and announced crowd of 2,115 watched, the ball descended toward the basket, clattered both sides of the rim, and dropped through. Because the shot was taken outside the three-point line, the Pacers won the game 119–118.

The Chaps were handicapped that first year after selecting limited talent in the initial ABA college draft; instead of ranking the players according to their skill level and potential, the Chaparrals' talent scout listed them alphabetically. His list was passed around the office and the general manager, who had been hired for his business expertise and had no basketball background, decided it was the time to exercise his authority. He got the list, took it to New York, and followed it faithfully.

"The problem was that the list he used was in alphabetical order," said Terry Stembridge, who was the Chaps' radio play-by-play announcer and public relations director. "The guy had no idea. If you look back at our first draft, you can see it." Indeed, a look at the Chaps' first draft reveals the round each player was drafted: 1. Matt Aitch, Michigan State; 2. Jim Burns, Northwestern; 3. Gary Gray, Oklahoma City; 4. Pat Riley, Kentucky. (Yes, that Pat Riley); 5. Jamie Thompson, Wichita State.

The Chaparrals also had an impact on game presentation. They are believed to have had the first pro sports team mascot. "We had Miss Chaparral, Brenda Dorney," Stembridge said. "Then we dressed up a little girl in an outfit that looked like a chaparral. She was on roller skates and would skate around the arena. All the players started cackling, making chicken sounds. That lasted one game. But we were ahead of the times. There weren't any mascots in those days."

Unfortunately for Dallas fans who supported the team, there wasn't enough entertainment or winning to create a larger fan base. In four of their six seasons, the Chaparrals had a record of .500 or better but in their other two seasons, they were 52 games under .500. They managed to make the playoffs five times—in 1970–71, they were 30–54 but eight of the 11 ABA teams made the play-offs—yet their overall record was 232–260.

After the 1972–73 season, the Dallas owners had tired of losing money and decided to sell the franchise. Ultimately, they "leased" the team to a group of San Antonio businessmen led by Angelo Drossos and B.J. "Red" McCombs. The San Antonians would have an option to buy the team at the end of the lease but the most unusual part of the offer was the amount of the lease: exactly $1 per year.

In explaining the bargain price, one of the Dallas owners said at the time, "We didn't want that sucker back."

In the end, the team could not get to San Antonio fast enough. The last game in Dallas made that 200-fan last game in Fort Worth look almost respectable. On March 26, 1973, the Chaps played their last game in Dallas, a 112–110 victory over the Carolina Cougars. A total of 130 fans were there to say good-bye.

76 The Baseline Bums

Not long after the Spurs arrived in San Antonio, a group of rowdy fans gained notoriety around the ABA as one of the most vocal and fun-loving fan bases in the league.

Though they did not sit on the baseline—rather, they were located above an entryway to the visiting team's locker room—they became known as the Baseline Bums.

The Bums began as a loosely organized group that threw tailgate parties before and after games and joined in raucous celebration of the team at every game at HemisFair Arena. Spurs ticket manager John Begzos recognized their potential as a draw and had "Baseline Bums" T-shirts made up. Begzos helped organize postgame parties in the parking lot, and the Bums often were joined by players and other personnel as they celebrated wins.

In the official *History of the San Antonio Spurs*, commissioned by the franchise to help celebrate its 40th anniversary in 2013–14, author Jan Hubbard describes the original Baseline Bums as "a small but very loud group of mischievous humorists."

Examples of their mischief included a litany of taunts that included:

"Rooty-toot-toot, rooty-toot-toot, who's that ass in the referee suit?"

"Motor boat, motor boat, putt, putt, putt. Come on Spurs, kick their butt."

"Big George" Valle was the unofficial leader of the Bums. Before player introductions he waved a large Texas state flag to incite the crowd. Leading scorer George Gervin credited him with motivating the players, as well.

"We'd look up in the stands and he'd be waving that big old flag," Gervin told the *San Antonio Express-News'* Tom Orsborn. "We'd say 'Big George is ready so we had better go on and be ready.'"

Spurs management embraced the Bums and owner Angelo Drossos encouraged players to interact with them. The club sponsored a monthly picnic for the group and many players attended the gatherings.

Valle, who passed away weeks before the start of the 2015–16 season, recalled the picnics for Hubbard in a 2013 interview.

"We'd all sit around eating barbecue and drinking beer," Valle said. "You'd actually develop relationships with the players. I ended up being good friends with Artis Gilmore. We went out to party somewhere after almost every game."

The Bums gained national notoriety—and infamy—for pouring a big bowl of guacamole on Larry Brown as he walked through the entryway after a Spurs-Nuggets game in 1975. This was back in the wild, wooly ABA days and Brown, then the coach of the Nuggets, had been quoted as saying there was nothing he liked about San Antonio except for the guacamole salad.

It was hardly a coincidence that the infamous guacamole game was on 10-cent beer night. The Bums gave him all the guacamole he could handle on his way out to the locker room.

Members of the group, including a few from the very beginning, still gather before and after games and sit in a designated "Baseline Bums" section at the AT&T Center.

77 Salary Sacrifice

When it comes to NBA contracts, one basketball operations executive summed up the approach taken by players and their agents this way: "Greed," he said, "is undefeated."

Greed, meet Tim Duncan.

At age 37 and after 15 seasons that had established him as one of the greatest big men in NBA history, Duncan in 2012 signed a two-year contract that proved, yet again, his willingness to do whatever it took for the Spurs to remain a championship contender.

The team captain took a salary cut of more than 50 percent—from $21.16 million to $9.64 million—so the team could do what it deemed necessary to remain in the thick of the championship race.

Duncan's salary sacrifice enabled the Spurs to re-sign free agents Danny Green ($854,389 to $3.5 million) and Stephen Jackson (for just over $10 million). He went from the team's highest-paid player to third on the team's salary list behind Manu Ginobili ($14.1 million) and Tony Parker ($12.5 million).

And when it came time for Duncan to re-sign with the Spurs for the big rebuild 2015–16 season, he sacrificed, yet again. This time, his salary dropped from $10 million to $5.25 million, a major help as the Spurs got under the league salary cap to make a maximum contract offer to prized free agent LaMarcus Aldridge.

Always one to set an example for his teammates when it came to conditioning, practice habits, and acceptance of Gregg Popovich's occasionally abrasive authority, Duncan's selfless approach to his salary rubbed off. Ginobili re-signed for 2015–16 at just $2.8 million, a pay cut of $4.2 million. Despite projections that placed his value at upwards of $60 million over four years, Danny Green took himself off the free-agent market when the Spurs offered a four-year deal at $10 million per season.

Ultimately, free-agent power forward David West, a former All-Star who had helped the Indiana Pacers get to the Eastern Conference Finals in 2012 and 2013, made one of the greatest salary sacrifices of all. Opting out of the final year of a Pacers contract that would have paid him $12.6 million, West told his agent that money didn't matter to him because he wanted to play for a championship contender. Though he had other options that would have paid a lot more, he signed with the Spurs for the veteran free-agent price of $1.5 million.

78 The Larry Tour

Because of his upbringing in Concord, New Hampshire, which considers Boston a mere suburb, Matt Bonner grew up a fan of the NHL's Bruins. The longtime Spurs backup big man is also a citizen of both the United States and Canada, where he played his first two pro seasons for the Toronto Raptors.

After the Spurs won their fifth championship in 2014, Bonner approached Spurs general manager R.C. Buford and coach Gregg Popovich with an idea: might it be possible for him to take the Larry O'Brien Trophy home to New Hampshire for a few days? He'd like to show it to the kids who attend his annual basketball camp in Concord.

Buford and Popovich loved the idea as did Spurs chairman Peter Holt. Soon, Bonner's notion became "The Larry Tour," as each Spurs player was offered a chance to take the trophy home for about a week.

For the NBA's most international of teams, that meant a summer tour for "Larry" of slightly more than 87,000 miles, including stops in Concord, Toronto, Buenos Aires, Rio de Janeiro, New York City, Paris, Sydney, Milan, San Diego, and Phoenix, among others.

The Larry Tour was patterned after the NHL's annual Stanley Cup tradition, in which each member of the NHL championship team is given a chance to take the trophy for a day. The Stanley Cup, perhaps the most venerated of all professional sports trophies, even has a full-time handler who never leaves its side during the annual tour.

For the Spurs' Larry Tour, "handler" duties fell to the media relations staff run by veteran Tom James. Mitch Heckart was tapped for most of the tour, which meant getting the first passport of his life. Kris Davis, a colleague in the media relations department, took two trips, one to Paris, a second to New York City.

By the end of the tour, Heckart's new passport had been stamped in France, Italy, Argentina, Brazil, Canada, and Australia. He had logged 73,000 air miles.

Heckart, now the basketball sports information director at the University of Oklahoma, enjoyed the experience but worried about changing planes on flights when he had to check "Larry" as luggage.

"Guarding it and being personally responsible for it is crazy," Heckart told the *San Antonio Express-News* after the conclusion of the tour.

Deadly serious about his summer task, Heckart consulted Phil Pritchard, the full-time "Keeper of the Cup" for the NHL.

Heckart's favorite trip with Larry was a 10-hour flight to Rio de Janeiro. When the pilots of his flight discovered he was bringing Larry on board, they requested that Larry fly with them in the cockpit, strapped into a jump seat. Then they arranged a business class seat for Heckart.

"Best flight of the whole tour," Heckart said.

So popular was the Spurs' Larry Tour that the NBA plans to make it an annual event for each successive champion. The Golden State Warriors continued the tradition, though scheduling difficulties prevented Larry from making a return trip to Australia with Warriors center Andrew Bogut.

Bonner's simple desire to share the trophy with youngsters at his basketball camp has become a very big deal.

79 The Whopper

Start with one of the better nicknames in franchise history and the fact he was the league leader in blocked shots in the final season of the ABA's existence, and Billy Paultz's four-plus seasons in silver and black should be something every Spurs fan knows. In fact, he is a candidate for one of the most underappreciated players in club history.

Paultz's wide body—he was officially listed at 6-foot-11 and 235 pounds but likely tipped the scales past 250 pounds—made him a legendary setter of screens and accounted for his nickname.

By his own admission "The Whopper" was far from a natural player. He was not recruited after a high school career in Bergen County, New Jersey, instead playing two years of junior college ball. Lou Carnesecca brought him to St. John's for his final two college seasons. Though he averaged 14.4 points per game as a senior he was not taken in the 1970 draft until the seventh round. Instead, he opted for training camp with the New York Nets. He made the team and immediately proved he belonged, averaging 14.7 points and 11.3 rebounds per game as a rookie. He was named

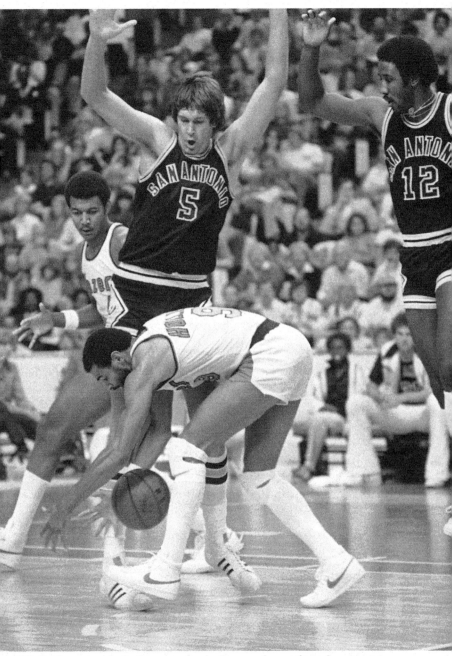

Billy Paultz was a physical presence for the Spurs and spent four-plus seasons in silver and black.

an ABA All-Star in 1973, when he averaged 16.7 points and 12.5 rebounds.

Paultz signed a free-agent contract with the Spurs before the ABA's final season in 1975–76 and immediately established himself as a valuable starter at both ends of the floor. He led the league in blocks per game (3.0) and held the club record for 14 years until David Robinson averaged 3.9 blocks in his rookie season. Paultz and Robinson remain the only Spurs to have led their respective leagues in blocks.

"He was just a terrific player, a very underrated center," said Doug Moe, who coached Paultz through four Spurs seasons after they entered the NBA. "Good passer, good shooter, good rebounder, and what a pick he set. And a very easy guy to coach and be around."

But it was at the offensive end where Paultz really proved his worth to the Spurs. His rock-solid screens freed George Gervin, Larry Kenon, and James Silas for open shots in Moe's free-flowing offense, and he was a productive offensive rebounder adept at putbacks.

It was no coincidence that the Spurs won 194 games in Paultz's first four seasons with the club. He was a key contributor in their run to the 1979 Eastern Conference Finals, where they took a 3–1 series lead over the Washington Bullets before dropping the final three games, including a controversial Game 7 in Landover, Maryland.

Moe was particularly incensed during the game about a late foul call on Paultz and twice when he believed Paultz was flagrantly fouled without a call being made. When he complained that referees Paul Mihalik and John Vanak had "stolen" the game, he was fined $5,000 by NBA commissioner Larry O'Brien.

Paultz merely expressed his regret about the Spurs having blown a double-digit lead in the fourth quarter after leading through most of the game.

"What hurt is we dominated the game," Paultz told the *San Antonio Express-News*. "I feel like we should have been in the Finals."

Midway through a disappointing 1979–80 season that cost Moe his job as head coach, general manager Bob Bass traded Paultz to the Houston Rockets for big man John Shumate. The Whopper returned for the final six games of the 1982–83 season and also appeared in all of the team's 11 playoff games.

80 Duncan's Partners

Since David Robinson retired after the 2002–03 season that earned him his second championship ring, the Spurs have spent the next dozen seasons searching for a low-post partner to team with Tim Duncan.

Replacing a first-ballot Hall of Famer was not easy. In all, 10 players have started at center alongside Duncan, though it should be noted that since the start of the 2003–04 season Duncan has jumped center for the opening tip nearly every game he has played and has defended many of the league's best centers. Asked before Game 1 of the Spurs' 2015 playoff series against the Clippers which player would be his starting center, Gregg Popovich famously responded, "Tim Duncan, just like he has for the last 14 years."

Here is a rundown of the players who have started alongside Duncan at center and/or power forward, depending on circumstance and any fan's personal point of view:

Rasho Nesterovic: The Spurs signed the 7-foot center from Slovenia to a free-agent contract a few weeks after Robinson's retirement became official in 2003, and he went straight into the starting lineup next to Duncan. He was a solid defender in the post but never averaged more than 8.7 points or 7.7 rebounds per game. He lost his starting job when the Spurs acquired Nazr Mohammed at the 2005 trade deadline. He played a minimal role in the playoff run to the 2005 championship and on June 21, 2006, was traded to the Toronto Raptors for Matt Bonner, Eric Williams, and a future second-round draft pick.

Nazr Mohammed: The deal that made Mohammed the starting center for the Spurs for the final six games of the 2004–05 season (and all of the championship playoff run) also made him one of the team's most unpopular players. That's because the trade sent Malik Rose, Tim Duncan's closest friend among his teammates and one of the most popular players among Spurs fans, to the New York Knicks in exchange. Mohammed responded with solid play as the team's starting center during a grinding playoff run that resulted in the 2005 NBA title. His best game of the playoffs was a big one—19 points and seven rebounds in a Game 5 win over Seattle that gave the Spurs a 3–2 series lead.

Mohammed lost his starting job the next season and signed a free-agent contract with the Detroit Pistons on July 18, 2006.

Fabricio Oberto: Oberto was 30 years old by the time the Spurs signed the center from Argentina for the 2005–06 season. It took him a full season to acclimate to the Spurs' system but once he figured things out he became the starter during the playoff run to the 2007 championship and one of the team's all-time favorite teammates. Though his numbers were pedestrian—he never averaged more than 4.8 points or 5.2 rebounds—he was a slick passer and a solid interior defender.

Francisco Elson: He played only 111 games in silver and black but earned a championship ring on the 2006–07 title team, for which he started 41 regular-season games and eight playoff games.

Ian Mahinmi: The team's first-round draft pick in 2005, the athletic, 6-foot-11 Mahinmi was signed for the 2007–08 season with great anticipation. By the time the Dallas Mavericks signed him as a free agent on July 13, 2010, he had missed an entire season with a knee injury and played only 32 games in silver and black.

Antonio McDyess: An All-Star and an Olympic gold medalist, the 6-foot-10 center-forward signed with the Spurs for the 2009–10 season as a 35-year-old veteran hoping for a shot at the championship ring the Spurs had denied him when he was a starter on the 2004–05 Detroit Pistons. In two seasons in San Antonio, he started 66 of his 150 games but retired after one of the team's most disappointing playoffs, the 2011 first-round elimination by the No. 8 Memphis Grizzlies.

DeJuan Blair: Though he was only 6-foot-7, Blair was a ferocious rebounder who came to the Spurs with the 37th pick of the 2009 draft and started 166 games alongside Duncan, mostly as a center. He once grabbed 23 rebounds (and scored 27 points) in a game against the Dallas Mavericks. Blair signed a free-agent contract with the Mavs on August 7, 2013.

Tiago Splitter: The Spurs drafted the 6-foot-11 Brazilian in 2007 but he was under contract to play in Spain until the Spurs finally signed him for the 2010–11 season. In five seasons he started 151 games and averaged 8.3 points and 5.3 rebounds. One of the better interior defenders of the post-Robinson years, Splitter regularly frustrated Spurs fans who preferred a more forceful finisher. On July 9, 2015, he was traded to the Atlanta Hawks for a future draft pick to clear salary cap space in order to sign LaMarcus Aldridge, the All-Star big man who began play alongside Duncan in the 2015–16 season.

81 Spurs in the Olympics

Because so many outstanding international players have worn silver and black, the list of Spurs players who have competed in the Olympics is long. Additionally, three Spurs coaches have been on Olympic benches, two as head coaches.

Though five Spurs players and one Spurs coach have won Olympic gold medals the greatest player in franchise history, Tim Duncan, did not.

The first Spur to earn Olympic gold? Though it would be 20 years before he became San Antonio's head coach, Larry Brown was a member of the United States Olympic team that won gold at the Tokyo Olympics in 1964.

Decide for yourself if that counts as a gold medal for a Spurs representative.

Next, Arkansas guard Alvin Robertson, a first-round Spurs draft pick, played for the U.S. Olympic team that swept through the 1984 competition in Los Angeles.

NBA players from the United States did not begin competing in the Olympics until the famous 1992 "Dream Team," which included Spurs center David Robinson. The Admiral also had been a member of the 1988 U.S. team that had to settle for the bronze medal in the 1988 Olympic tournament in Seoul, Korea. A loss in the semifinal game to the Soviet Union, led by future NBA standout Lithuanians Arvydas Sabonis and Sarunas Marciulionis, relegated the U.S. team to third place. Robinson would go on to win a second gold medal at the Atlanta Games in 1996.

Already an All-NBA first-team selection and MVP of the 1999 NBA Finals, Duncan was selected for the U.S. Olympic team that would win the gold medal at the 2000 Games in Sydney, Australia. Unfortunately, he had to withdraw after knee surgery was required to repair a torn meniscus in his left knee, an injury suffered late in the 1999–2000 season.

USA Basketball, the United States governing body for FIBA competitions, replaced Duncan with Denver Nuggets All-Star power forward Antonio McDyess on the 2000 team. McDyess ended up making one of the biggest plays of the Olympic tournament in Team USA's 85–83 win over Lithuania in the semifinals, rebounding a missed free throw by Kevin Garnett and putting it back for an 84–81 lead with 25 seconds remaining. McDyess then jumped high to contest a buzzer-beating three-point shot by Sarunas Jasaikevicius. Duncan's replacement altered the shot that could have ended Team USA's gold medal dreams.

McDyess spent the final two seasons of his NBA career with the Spurs, playing 150 games as a valued reserve and sometimes starter (66 games).

Coaches don't receive Olympic medals but Brown enjoyed his second gold medal Olympic experience as an assistant for U.S. head coach Rudy Tomjanovich.

Duncan finally had his Olympic experience four years later as a member of the ill-fated U.S. team at the 2004 Games in Athens. It would be Gregg Popovich's only experience on an Olympic team bench, as well. He served as an assistant for his good friend Brown, but the U.S. team never jelled for its head coach, who clashed with Allen Iverson, his best player during six seasons as head coach of the Philadelphia 76ers.

Duncan clashed with the international referees, saddled with foul trouble through much of the competition. His dream of Olympic gold ended in the tournament semifinals, when Team USA fell to Argentina 89–81. Duncan, who fouled out twice in eight Olympic games, had three fouls in the first half against Argentina and scored only 10 points

Asked about his Olympic experience after the tournament ended, Duncan did his best to be diplomatic. "To be honest," he said, "it wasn't fun. FIBA sucks."

Future Spurs forward Richard Jefferson, then with the New Jersey Nets, also played on the 2004 team.

Of course, Duncan's loss was Manu Ginobili's gain during those same Olympics. The Spurs guard played one of the best games of his career at any level, scoring 29 points to lead Argentina to a semifinal victory over Team USA. An easy win over Italy in the gold medal game made Ginobili the undisputed leader of what Argentines still venerate as *Generacion Dorada*—the Golden Generation.

Another leader of the Golden Generation, center Fabricio Oberto, became a Spur in 2005 and added an NBA championship to his Olympic gold medal achievement. Ginobili and Oberto would add bronze medals at the 2008 Olympics in Beijing.

Leaders of the French national team that has become a European powerhouse, Tony Parker and Boris Diaw played on the French Olympic team in 2012.

Signed by the Spurs in 2011, Patty Mills played for the Australian Olympic team in Beijing and again in 2012, when he was the leading scorer in London with an average of 21.2 points per game.

Aron Baynes, who won an NBA championship ring with the 2013–14 Spurs, also played for Australia at the London Games.

Then a Spurs assistant coach, Brett Brown was head coach of the 2012 Australian Olympic team. Brown entered the 2015–16 NBA season as head coach of the Philadelphia 76ers.

Tiago Splitter, a Spur for five seasons before being traded to Atlanta in 2015, played for Brazil in the 2012 Olympic tournament.

82 The Coyote

When mascots became a "thing" in the NBA, the Spurs joined in. Sticking with the team's Wild West theme, the organization in 1983 made "The Coyote" its mascot, with the agile Tim Derk inside the costume.

Derk developed dozens of ingenious, acrobatic skits designed to fire up the crowd and ridicule opposing teams. In short order the Coyote was regarded as one of the league's best, rivaling the Phoenix Gorilla and Denver's Rocky the Mountain Lion.

From 1983 to 2004, the Coyote made more than 5,000 appearances at Spurs games and events around South Texas, becoming one of the team's most recognized personalities, as popular as most of the players.

Derk suffered a stroke on February 13, 2004, and could not continue as the team's mascot. He became manager of mascot development for Spurs Sports & Entertainment, training and working with the mascots for the Spurs, the WNBA's Silver Stars, the American Hockey League's Rampage, and the Austin Toros of the NBA D-League, re-named the Austin Spurs in 2015.

"Tim Derk has touched the community in so many ways and we are thrilled that he will remain an important part of the Spurs family," said Russ Bookbinder, executive vice president of business operations for Spurs Sports & Entertainment in announcing Derk's new assignment. "We are really excited to utilize Tim's creative talents to elevate all of the franchise mascots to a higher level. His knowledge, humor, and creativity will have a great impact on all three of our mascots."

Derk also picked his successor as The Coyote but the organization keeps his identity a secret.

The new Coyote portrayer maintained the same mascot personality Derk had worked so hard to perfect and in 2007 was named to the Mascot Hall of Fame. In 2014, the Coyote was named Mascot of the Year.

When the Spurs travel internationally the Coyote usually accompanies them, most recently to their 2015 training camp in Berlin and to exhibition games in Berlin and Istanbul, Turkey. The mascot even showed up in Johannesburg, South Africa, when Gregg Popovich coached in an exhibition game pitting NBA players from Africa against NBA players from around the world.

83 Gregg Popovich's Coaching Tree

As one of the most successful and longest-tenured coaches in NBA history, it was only natural that coaches who served Gregg Popovich as assistants would land jobs as head coaches for other NBA teams. Even players who were greatly influenced by him have become coaches.

As of the summer of 2016, 10 men with close ties to Popovich had gone on to become NBA head coaches. Three of them—Avery Johnson, Mike Budenholzer, and Steve Kerr—have earned Coach of the Year honors. Also, Kerr coached the Warriors to the 2015 NBA championship.

Here are the branches of the Popovich coaching tree:

Brett Brown
Popovich hired Brown as director of player development in 2002 and elevated him to a bench assistant coach in 2007, where he remained until he was hired as head coach of the 76ers after the 2012–13 season.

NBA Coaching Record
76ers (2013–16): 47–199

Mike Brown
After serving five seasons in various basketball operations positions with the Denver Nuggets, Brown was hired as a Spurs assistant in 2000 and remained on the staff until 2003, when Rick Carlisle made him top assistant on his Indiana Pacers staff.

NBA Coaching Record
Cavaliers (2005–10): 272–138
Lakers (2011–14): 42–29
Cavaliers (2013–14): 33–49

Mike Budenholzer
Popovich gave him his first NBA job as video intern with the Warriors in 1992, then hired him as video coordinator after he became general manager of the Spurs in 1994. After he became Spurs head coach in 1996, Popovich added Budenholzer to his coaching staff before his first full season, 1996–97. Budenholzer was lead assistant from 2007–13.

NBA Coaching Resume
Hawks (2013–16): 146–100

P.J. Carlesimo

After coaching Seton Hall University from 1982 through 1994, Carlesimo was an NBA head coach in Portland (1994–97) and Golden State (1997–2000) before joining Popovich's Spurs staff (2002–07). He was top assistant beginning in 2005.

NBA Coaching Record
Pre-Popovich
Trail Blazers (1994–97): 137–109
Warriors (1997–2000): 46–113
Post-Popovich
Sonics-Thunder (2007–09): 21–74
Nets (2012–13): 35–19

Vinny Del Negro

Played two seasons under Popovich, 1996–98, starting 91 games.

NBA Coaching Record
Bulls (2008–10): 82–82
Clippers (2010–13): 128–102

Avery Johnson

As Spurs general manager in 1994, Popovich signed Johnson to a free-agent contract. He started 478 games at point guard, 286 of those after Popovich became head coach.

NBA Coaching Record
Mavericks (2004–08): 194–70
Nets (2010–13): 60–116

Steve Kerr

Played under Popovich from 1998 to 2001, and again in his final NBA season, 2002–03. Earned two of his five NBA championship rings under Popovich on Spurs' 1999 and 2003 title teams.

NBA Coaching Record
Warriors (2014–16): 140–24, won 2015 NBA championship

Quinn Snyder

In 2007 the Spurs hired Snyder to coach their NBA D-League team, the Austin Toros, and he helped direct the franchise's summer league teams and assisted with coaching during training camp.

NBA Coaching Record
Jazz (2014–16): 78–86

Jacque Vaughn

Signed as a free agent with the Spurs in 2006 and played three seasons as backup point guard, appearing in 168 games. After playing career ended he became an assistant coach under Popovich until he was hired by the Magic in the summer of 2012.

NBA Coaching Record
Magic (2012–15): 58–158

Monty Williams

Williams was on the first Spurs team Popovich coached, in 1996–97, and played 72 games for him in 1997–98. After his playing career ended he was a coaching intern on Popovich's staff from 2003 to 2005.

NBA Coaching Record
Hornets/Pelicans (2010–15): 173–221

84 Dennis Rodman

Dennis Rodman played only two seasons for the Spurs but they were memorable ones. In addition to leading the league in rebounding both seasons he wore silver and black (17.3 per game in 1993–94 and 16.8 in 1994–95), he also made the All-Defensive team both seasons (second team in 1993–94, first team in 1994–95).

Nobody questioned Rodman's amazing skill set. He was one of the most intense and effective defenders in league history, selected to the All-Defensive team eight times. Without question, he was also the greatest rebounder under 6-foot-9 in league history. He led the league for seven straight seasons, 1991–92 through 1997–98. As a member of the 1991–92 NBA champion Detroit Pistons "Bad Boys," he averaged a league-best 18.7 rebounds per game. To truly appreciate that feat, consider that only Wilt Chamberlain and Bill Russell have recorded higher per-season averages.

It was Rodman's quirkiness that ran him afoul of Spurs management. It wasn't just his multicolored hair or his numerous piercings that bothered team officials, especially club chairman Gen. Robert McDermott. He routinely violated team standards, including chronic tardiness for practices. His teammates loved his on-court intensity but were offended by his "do my own thing" approach.

Rodman was a major factor when the Spurs rolled to the best record in franchise history in 1994–95, 62–20, and advanced to the Western Conference Finals against the Houston Rockets. By the end of that series, however, he had become such a distraction he virtually guaranteed the end of his playing days in silver and black.

It was his behavior before, and during, Game 5 of that series that was the last straw. Rodman had grabbed 19 rebounds and scored 12 points to help the Spurs to a 103–81 Game 4 victory in Houston, knotting the series at two games apiece. But then he showed up 35 minutes late for a practice session back in San Antonio at which the team focused on preparations for Game 5.

Rodman doubled down on his defiance when he turned up in the team's locker room at 7:08 PM for an 8:00 PM Game 5 start. His teammates had shown up well before the 6:30 PM deadline, standard operating procedure for all NBA teams.

Coach Bob Hill's response: sitting Rodman on the bench until the 4:49 mark of the first quarter. By that time the Rockets had raced to a 16-point lead they would never relinquish in what became a 111–90 Houston win.

After tolerating his antics for two seasons, Dennis Rodman's behavior during the 1995 playoffs proved to be too much for the Spurs to swallow. He was traded to the Chicago Bulls that off-season.

Rodman played but refused to participate in team huddles during timeouts, sitting at the end of the bench and removing his shoes. During the fourth quarter he engaged in a lengthy shouting match with assistant coach Dave Cowens and when the game ended he remained on the floor, slumped against a chair for several minutes while his teammates went to the locker room.

Afterward he told reporters he did not understand why he had been benched.

"Don't ask me why I didn't start," he said. "I'm not the coach. I'm not in charge. Don't ask me. Ask him. That's the way it is. That's the way it stands. End of interview."

Hill's defense was terse and to the point: "He was 35 minutes late for practice with no call in the Western Conference Finals."

Team captain David Robinson agreed Rodman had become a distraction, saying he and his teammates had tired of the "media circus" that surrounded their teammate.

When club chairman Gen. Robert McDermott hired Gregg Popovich as the team's general manager after the 1993–94 season he did so with a caveat: find a way to get Rodman off the roster. After his antics the only question about Rodman's future was who and what Popovich might be able to get for him in a trade.

As training camp for the 1995–96 season opened, Spurs fans had their answer. Popovich sent Rodman to the Chicago Bulls for center Will Perdue.

Rodman teamed with Michael Jordan and Scottie Pippen to help the Bulls win three championships in 1996, 1997, and 1998.

Perdue became Robinson's primary backup at center and earned his fourth NBA championship ring as a member of the Spurs' 1999 title team.

85 Alvin Robertson

Alvin Robertson was one of the best players in Spurs history. He is also one of its most infamous.

One of the three players in franchise history recognized as Defensive Player of the Year (1985–86) and a three-time All-Star while playing with the Spurs, it is Robertson's legal troubles after the end of his NBA career that are hard for Spurs fans—and the organization as a whole—to stomach. He has pled guilty to misdemeanor domestic violence and been convicted of various charges, including burglary with intent to commit theft and violation of an order of protection. He has spent a year in prison for a parole violation and was arrested for a variety of sexual assault charges in 2010. Robertson was found not guilty on all those counts in 2015.

Robertson's legal woes are part of his history but so is his outstanding play on the court, and of that there can be no denial.

Drafted by the Spurs in 1984 with the seventh selection in one of the greatest draft classes in NBA history—it included Hall of Famers Hakeem Olajuwon, Michael Jordan, John Stockton, and Charles Barkley—Robertson won a gold medal with the 1984 U.S. Olympic team after an outstanding career at the University of Arkansas under Eddie Sutton. He had a solid rookie season, followed by a breakout second season in which he earned the NBA's Most Improved Player Award and Defensive Player of the Year after he averaged 3.67 steals per game, which still stands as the NBA single-season record. Only seven players have averaged at least 3.0 steals per game in a season, including Jordan, Stockton, and Magic Johnson, all Hall of Famers. Robertson did so three times, the last being his 1991–92 season with the Milwaukee Bucks. No player has done so since.

Robertson is part of an even more exclusive NBA club: one of four players who have accomplished a quadruple-double. On February 18, 1986, Robertson scored 20 points, grabbed 11 rebounds, handed out 10 assists, and had 10 steals in a 120–114 Spurs win against the Suns at HemisFair Arena. The other three members of the quadruple-double club all are centers and in the Hall of Fame: Spurs great David Robinson, Houston's Hakeem Olajuwon, and Golden State's Nate Thurmond.

Robertson represented the Spurs in the NBA All-Star Game in three straight seasons, 1985–86, 1986–87, and 1987–88, and in 1985–86 was named second team All-NBA.

Though his legal woes have made Robertson *persona non grata* to the Spurs organization, the records he set while wearing silver and black can't be expunged from the team's books. Perhaps they should not be celebrated but they must be acknowledged.

86 Visit the Basketball Hall of Fame

Every basketball fan should make a pilgrimage to Springfield, Massachusetts, to visit the Naismith Memorial Basketball Hall of Fame.

If they haven't already made the trip, Spurs fans may want to wait a few years to see a new pack of inductees. Since 1994, when George Gervin became the first Spurs player inducted, only three players who wore silver and black long enough to be associated with the Spurs have been enshrined.

Wait a minute.

How can a franchise that has won five championships and is universally acknowledged as one of the most successful pro sports

Popovich and the Hall

When he retires from coaching, Gregg Popovich is certain to enter the Naismith Memorial Basketball Hall of Fame as one of the greatest coaches in basketball history.

Spurs fans wonder why he has not yet been inducted.

The Hall of Fame's rules for when coaches are eligible for induction differ from those that govern the eligibility of players. Whereas players must wait for five years after they retire from active play to be considered, coaches can be considered after 25 years of coaching—either as a head coach or an assistant. After his time at the Air Force Academy, Pomona-Pitzer, and with the Golden State Warriors and the Spurs, Popovich has been coaching, non-stop, since 1973.

So why has he not been inducted?

The answer is simple: he simply won't allow his name to be put forward for nomination while he remains active.

franchises of the past 25 years have only four representatives in the Hall of Fame?

How can this be?

The answer lies within the rules of the Hall of Fame and the longevity of the Spurs' biggest stars. Players are not eligible for consideration by the Hall of Fame's selection committees until they have been retired from basketball for five years. That means Tim Duncan, Manu Ginobili, and Tony Parker—certain future inductees—won't be enshrined until the dawn of the next decade, at the earliest.

For the time being, Spurs fans visiting the Hall of Fame must content themselves with visiting the shrines to these players:

David Robinson: Enshrined in 2009, Robinson was a first-ballot selection after a 14-year career with the Spurs that included the 1994–95 Most Valuable Player Award, the 1989–90 Rookie of the Year Award, nine All-NBA selections, eight All-Defensive selections, and 10 All-Star Game appearances.

Artis Gilmore: That it took 23 years after his retirement in 1988 for Gilmore to enter the Hall of Fame was a travesty. It took the creation of a special ABA selection committee to right the wrong. The fact he was the very first player chosen by the ABA committee, which is allowed to directly elect one ABA player, coach, or executive each year, was entirely appropriate, for Gilmore was, without question, the greatest true center in ABA history, leading the league in rebounding in each of his five ABA seasons. But he was also a six-time NBA All-Star, twice during his five solid seasons in silver and black.

Louie Dampier: The all-time leading scorer, assist maker, and three-point shooter in ABA history, Dampier had to wait even longer than Gilmore for induction in the Hall of Fame (36 years). The special ABA committee put him in the Hall's 2015 induction class in recognition of his stellar play in nine seasons with the Kentucky Colonels, his career spanning the entirety of the ABA's existence. When Kentucky was left out of the NBA in the 1976 NBA-ABA merger, the Spurs selected him in the dispersal draft and he was a solid backup to point guard James Silas. Sadly, the NBA did not adopt the three-point shot, Dampier's specialty, until the season after his retirement.

Author's Note: Dominique Wilkins, inducted in 2006, played one full season with the Spurs, 1996–97. He played 63 games, starting 26, and led the Spurs in scoring, at 18.2 points per game. Since he played only one of his 17 seasons in silver and black, it is too far a reach to include him among Spurs in the Hall. The late Moses Malone, inducted in 2001, played the final season of his great career as a Spur. His 17 games in silver and black constitute only 1 percent of his career. That's hardly enough to include him among Spurs Hall of Famers.

87 Build a Spurs Library

If you're reading this book, you've already started to create your own Spurs library. Next, find a copy of *The Official History of the Spurs*. Commissioned by the team to commemorate its 40th anniversary and written by longtime NBA writer Jan Hubbard, this book is a comprehensive look at the team's history, including its early days as the Dallas Chaparrals. It was a valuable resource in compiling the book you hold in your hands.

Now add a copy of Terry Pluto's *Loose Balls*, an oral history of the ABA. Plenty of Spurs lore included there, as well, and you get a feel for the outlaw league and why it was embraced by basketball-starved fans in the Alamo City.

Finally, see if you can find a copy of *NBA Rookie Experience*, issued by NBA Publications after the 1997–98 season. The book chronicles the disparate experiences of six members of the first round of the 1997 draft class. Two chapters and 64 pages are devoted to No. 1 overall pick Tim Duncan, and the cover features a photo of Duncan defending the No. 2 pick of 1997, the Nets' Keith Van Horn, a player some believed had as much star potential as Duncan. Ironically, two other 1997 rookies featured in the book, Tracy McGrady and Jacque Vaughn, finished their playing careers in silver and black.

Full disclosure: the author of *NBA Rookie Experience* is yours truly.

88 Terry Cummings

When Larry Brown took over as head coach of the Spurs for the 1988–89 season, he understood he was betting on the team's future. David Robinson, the franchise-changing No. 1 overall pick in the 1987 draft, would be completing his final season of active duty in the U.S. Navy, and the team Brown inherited did not have a reliable scorer in the post. Guards Alvin Robertson, Johnny Dawkins, and small forward Willie Anderson were the top scorers in Brown's first season, when the team went 21–61, still the worst record in franchise history.

A big change was needed on the front line, even with Robinson on his way.

On May 28, 1988, general manager Bob Bass pulled the trigger on one of the biggest trades in club history, sending Robertson, a former Defensive Player of the Year, an All-NBA and All-Defensive pick, and the team's top scorer, to the Milwaukee Bucks for All-Star power forward Terry Cummings. Bass even had to throw in center Greg "Cadillac" Anderson, his team's leading rebounder

At age 28, Cummings was in his prime when he arrived and teamed with Robinson to give the Spurs a one-two punch. In their first season together they were the most productive low-post tandem in the NBA; Robinson averaged 24.3 points per game, Cummings 22.4 per game. With rookie Sean Elliott (the No. 3 overall pick in the 1988 draft) showing the potential that would ultimately get his No. 32 retired by the Spurs and raised to the rafters, the Spurs produced a 56–26 record that represented the greatest single-season turnaround in NBA history.

Even after suffering a heartbreaking Game 7 overtime loss to the eventual Western Conference champion Portland Trail Blazers in the conference semifinals, it looked like the team's starting front line would be the basis for championship contention for the next five or six years.

When Elliott assumed more of the scoring load in his second and third seasons, averaging 15.9 and 16.3 points per game, Cummings production dipped a bit but he remained a solid side-kick to Robinson, who was on his way to becoming an MVP.

Everything changed for Cummings in the summer that followed the 1991–92 season. Playing in a summer pickup game he suffered a serious injury to his left knee. He missed all but eight games of the 1992–93 season and lost the athleticism that had made him an All-Star. He never again averaged more than 7.3 points per game for the Spurs. When he became a free agent after the 1994–95 season, the team did not offer him a contract. He returned to the Bucks for the 1995–96 season and played a reserve role for four more teams before retiring in 2000.

An ordained Pentecostal minister and an accomplished musician, Cummings became one of the Spurs' most popular players during his six seasons in San Antonio. He performed musically around town and sometimes wrote and performed songs about the Spurs. In 1993, he presided over the marriage ceremony of teammate Sean Elliott.

89 U.S. Air Force

Gregg Popovich's values were shaped by the totality of his life experiences but few experiences had more of an impact than the years he spent in the United States Air Force, including four as a cadet at the U.S. Air Force Academy.

Popovich had to prove himself to legendary Air Force Academy head coach Bob Spear and his assistant, Hank Egan, who would test Popovich's resolve by keeping him on the junior varsity when Popovich believed he deserved to be playing on the varsity roster.

Popovich became team captain and leading scorer for the Falcons as a senior in 1969–70 and, after graduating, with a commission as a second lieutenant in the U.S. Air Force, he played on U.S. Armed Forces All-Star teams that toured in Europe and the Soviet Union. He served as captain of the Armed Forces team that won the AAU championship in 1972, which earned him an invitation to the U.S. Olympics tryouts in Colorado Springs. Though he didn't make the team he made an impression on many of the coaches who were there, including Larry Brown.

It was Egan, after taking over on the Falcons bench after Spear retired in 1971, who brought Popovich back to the Air Force Academy as an assistant coach in 1973. He had been Popovich's freshman and junior varsity coach during his first two seasons at Air Force and had seen his discipline, determination, and basketball IQ.

Popovich's first coaching assignment, at age 24, was as head coach of the Air Force Academy Prep School, a one-year "junior

Basic Training

After the heartbreak of the 2013 NBA Finals, Gregg Popovich decided to do something different for training camp. He took his team to his old Air Force Academy stomping grounds where, in addition to their daily training camp grind, they dined alongside cadets in the dining hall named after "father of the Air Force" General Billy Mitchell. They also spent some time on the obstacle course that is used during basic training.

It was an exercise in bonding that helped the team focus on execution and began the process of redemption: the 2014 NBA title.

In 2008, Popovich received the Air Force Academy's Distinguished Graduate Award, an honor he said he felt unworthy of but one he regards as one of the highest honors he ever has received.

college" for potential cadets unable to qualify for appointments to the Academy straight out of high school.

A few weeks before returning to Colorado as head coach in the 2005 NBA All-Star Game in Denver, Popovich recalled for the *San Antonio Express-News* a story from his first season with the prep school that illustrates his history of encouraging his players to experience life, in all its forms and quirks.

His team was on a long, springtime bus ride to Alamosa, Colorado, to play Adams State College. The highway snaked along the roaring Arkansas River, fed by melting snow. One of his big men had sprained an ankle, so Popovich ordered the bus driver to pull off the highway and park near the river.

On the pretext of giving his injured player a chance to ease the swelling in his ankle, Popovich ordered the entire team to shed their shoes, roll up their slacks, and wade in the icy water. Of course, he joined them in the river walk.

In 2005 he admitted that the wade in the water was not about icing an injury. Rather, it was so the players would have an experience they always would remember.

"I'm sure to this day they probably laugh at me about that," he said.

Egan moved Popovich up to a bench role for the Falcons in 1974 because he recognized his potential as a coach.

"He's a basketball junkie, for one thing," Egan said. "He had a passion for it and he thought about it in an intelligent way."

When he became general manager of the Spurs in 1994, Popovich hired Egan as an assistant on Bob Hill's coaching staff. Egan remained with the Spurs through Popovich's first five seasons on the Spurs bench.

90 The Bruise Brothers

Long before the Detroit Pistons decided to call its roster of hard-nosed, mayhem-making players "The Bad Boys," the Spurs had their own version of nasty basketball featuring a core of big men who weren't afraid to throw their bodies, and perhaps an elbow or two, into the action.

The physical approach followed the 1979 dismissal of head coach Doug Moe, whose Spurs teams led the league in scoring all but one of his three-plus seasons on the bench. They were last in the league in defense (points allowed) when general manager Bob Bass, himself a coach in the ABA, finished out the 1979–80 season after owner Angelo Drossos insisted that Moe be fired. Bass called on another former ABA coach, Stan Albeck, to coach the Spurs in 1980–81. Albeck wanted improvement on defense and Bass brought in the group of lumberjack types he believed could defend the paint and get rebounds.

"The Bruise Brothers" were center Dave Corzine, 6-foot-11 and 250 pounds; power forward Paul Griffin, 6-foot-9 and 215; center George Johnson, 6-foot-11 and 205; power forward Reggie Johnson, 6-foot-9 and 205; small forward Kevin Restani, 6-foot-9 and 225; and small forward Mark Olberding, 6-foot-8 and 225.

The wildly popular movie *The Blues Brothers*, starring *Saturday Night Live* comedians John Belushi and Dan Aykroyd, had been released on June 20, 1980. Belushi and Aykroyd portrayed Jake and Elwood Blues, who dressed in black suits, wore black Fedora hats, and sported black sunglasses. The Spurs picked up on the theme when their rugged bigs began terrorizing opposing players and the Bruise Brothers nickname was launched. The club even produced a Bruise Brothers poster, the six menacing-looking Spurs posed against a brick wall wearing dark fedoras, dark sunglasses, and skinny black ties.

Jake and Elwood Blues would have been proud.

In 1980–81 the Bruise Brothers left most of the scoring up to guards George Gervin (27.1 points per game) and James Silas (17.7). Olberding was the most productive of the Brothers, averaging 12.3 points and 5.7 rebounds, and Corzine averaged 10.5 points per game and 7.8 rebounds. Combined, the six Brothers averaged a solid 34.2 rebounds per game and 17.3 fouls, plenty of them of the old-school variety.

Moved into the Western Conference after playing in the East in their first four seasons in the NBA, the Spurs won the Midwest Division with a record of 52–30 but were beaten by the Houston Rockets in the first round of the playoffs.

The six Brothers returned for the 1981–82 season and helped the Spurs advance to the Western Conference Finals against Kareem Abdul-Jabbar and the Los Angeles Lakers. After Abdul-Jabbar dominated in a 4–0 sweep, Bass negotiated an off-season trade for 7-foot-2 center Artis Gilmore, sending two of the Brothers, Corzine and Olberding, to the Bulls.

Many Spurs fans were disappointed to see the Bruise Brothers broken up but happy to have Gilmore, one of the most dominant players from the ABA.

Gilmore was a dominant big man and an 11-time (ABA-NBA) All-Star but he had no more luck getting the Spurs past Abdul-Jabbar and the Lakers. Matched up against the Lakers in another series in 1982–83, Gilmore managed to lead the Spurs to two wins but the Lakers prevailed in six games.

91 Go to a Spurs Road Game

As the Spurs' national (and international) following has grown during the Popovich-Big Three era, it is not unusual to see hundreds—sometimes thousands—of Spurs fans in attendance at the team's road games. They are easy to spot in their silver-and-black Spurs attire, often wearing NBA authentic jerseys of their favorite Spurs players.

Single-game tickets are easier to obtain in the digital age, available on team websites and through secondary ticket sites like StubHub.com.

For San Antonians, the four regular-season games the Spurs annually play in Houston and Dallas—two each—are especially popular for literal road trips. The drive from San Antonio to Houston on Interstate 10 takes about three hours but anyone who has ever made the drive during commuter rush hour understands that traffic congestion clogs the roads from mid-afternoon to early evening, so plan accordingly.

The drive to Dallas on Interstate 35 is about five hours but the addition of about 131 miles of tollways on State Highway 130 has alleviated the horrific congestion on Interstate 35 through Austin (the L.A. Freeway System of Texas). The speed limit for all but 41 miles of the toll road is 80 miles per hour. For the stretch of the toll road from Seguin to Mustang Ridge, the speed limit is 85 miles per hour, the highest posted speed limit in the United States.

But there are Spurs fans everywhere and they show up in every NBA city to see their favorite team play. At one sparsely attended game at Denver's Pepsi Center in 2014—the Nuggets had gotten off to such a bad start their attendance sagged dramatically—about a thousand Spurs fans began the familiar "Go Spurs Go" chant during the game. It got so loud the Nuggets public address announcer used his microphone to initiate a "Let's Go Nuggets" cheer in a futile attempt to drown out the Spurs supporters.

Spurs players acknowledge that the presence of their supporters on the road often inspires them. A national hero in his native Argentina, Manu Ginobili knows there will be large groups of Argentines at games against the Jazz in Salt Lake City and Denver. Hundreds of his young countrymen who work at ski resorts in South America—mostly in Chile—during the South American winter emigrate to Utah and Colorado to work at ski resorts there during the North American winter. Ginobili typically greets them after games, posing for photos and signing autographs.

92 The Good, the Bad, and the Ugly

What are the best, worst, and ugliest seasons in Spurs history?

Spurs fans can decide for themselves, but start with these candidates:

The Best: Every Spurs fan knows Gregg Popovich has the best winning percentage in franchise history and more wins (and championships) than any Spurs coach. Which of his seasons ranks as best in franchise history? The 2015–16 Spurs won more games (67) than any Popovich-coached team but lost in the second round of the playoffs. Thus, the 2013–14 Spurs, with 62 regular-season wins and the most dominant Finals victory in NBA history, get the nod as the greatest of any Spurs team.

The Worst: Larry Brown would love to forget the 1988–89 season ever happened. Awaiting the arrival of David Robinson after the team's 1987 No. 1 draftee completed his tour in the U.S. Navy,

Brown knew his first season replacing Bob Weiss as Spurs head coach was going to be tough. He probably didn't think his 21–61 record would stand as the worst in club history. The flip side of that worst single season: with Robinson in the fold for the 1989–90 season, Brown's Spurs went from 21 wins to 56. At the time it was the best single-season turnaround in NBA history.

The Ugliest: This is a matter of subjective conjecture but the season that included Jerry Tarkanian's brief career on the Spurs bench jumps off the pages of Spurs history. Owner Red McCombs admits that he liked to make a splash when hiring coaches and his hiring of Tarkanian in 1992 definitely got national headlines. Tarkanian arrived with a reputation for playing a pro-style game that had made his UNLV Runnin' Rebels the highest scoring team in college basketball for 18 seasons. He had accumulated an amazing 509–105 (82.8 percent) winning record and one NCAA championship.

There was one problem: when Tarkanian took over the Spurs he failed to adapt to the differences between the college game and the pro game, including misunderstanding the rules. It didn't take McCombs long to understand he had made a terrible mistake. Tarkanian's record wasn't all that bad—9–11—but it was clear he had lost the confidence of his players and McCombs realized his experiment had gone terribly wrong. He fired Tarkanian and made another bold move, hiring former NBA All-Star John Lucas, who had battled substance abuse through the latter years of his NBA career.

Lucas did a terrific job putting the pieces back together and the Spurs went 39–22 under his guidance. (Tarkanian assistant Rex Hughes won his one game as interim coach after Tarkanian was dismissed). Nevertheless, the Season of the Shark clearly is the leading candidate for ugliest in franchise history.

93 Greet the Spurs

The team's charter flights embark from and return to the commercial aviation side of the San Antonio International Airport, located near the intersection of U.S. Highway 281 and Loop 410, one of two highways that circle the city.

Small crowds of Spurs fans often gather along the roadside to welcome the team home from important road trips—the annual rodeo road trip and playoff trips, for example—and fans often sport supportive signs. It is not unusual for large crowds to gather in the wee hours of the morning to show their support, and the coaches and players sincerely appreciate it.

This was the case after the Spurs returned from Miami after two of the most frustrating losses in franchise history, Games 6 and 7 of the 2013 NBA Finals. Hundreds of Spurs fans were waiting the next day to let the players and coaches know they felt their pain and still loved them.

Stuck on the Tarmac

After one of their finest playoff series wins ever—a seven-game grind against the New Orleans Hornets that culminated in a Game 7 win at New Orleans Arena in 2008—the Spurs ended up stuck on their team plane at New Orleans International Airport because of a mechanical problem on the aircraft. It was Jazz and Heritage Festival time in New Orleans and every hotel room in the city was filled. There was nothing for the Spurs to do but try to get some sleep on their plane.

After they finally made it to Los Angeles, Spurs players talked about the experience on the plane.

Said Manu Ginobili, "I'll always remember Pop walking through the aisles, covering us with blankets, concerned about getting us to sleep. Nobody could sleep."

The same thing happened after one of the most heartbreaking losses in recent years, the 111–109 Game 7 loss to the Clippers during the first round of the 2015 playoffs, when an acrobatic basket by Clippers guard Chris Paul with one second remaining knocked the Spurs out of the playoffs.

Gregg Popovich's response: "I'd like to thank the hundreds of fans who were at the airport. It actually made me feel worse, to be honest, how much they enjoy the players and the Spurs. It was really heartfelt and gratifying, but it really made us feel like we let them all down. So it was a double-edged sword. But thank you very much."

94 The $250,000 Fine

Gregg Popovich didn't invent the concept of managing or limiting the playing time of veteran players. Utah Jazz coach Jerry Sloan, one of Popovich's role models, gets much of the credit for the concept, which he used to extend the careers of Utah's Hall of Fame duo of John Stockton and Karl Malone. Stockton, the NBA's all-time leader in assists, played through age 40. So did Malone, the NBA's No. 2 all-time scorer.

By the time Tim Duncan turned 35 during the 2012 NBA playoffs, Popovich was fully committed to a program of minimizing his playing time. The Spurs coach also was acutely aware that the other two members of the Spurs' Big Three, Manu Ginobili and Tony Parker, had been pros since the age of 15. All three were in line for an occasional game on the sideline and Popovich chose such games with care. Typically, he would sit one of his veteran stars—and sometimes all three—during the second games of back-to-back sets, especially if such games came at the end of a particularly grueling stretch.

On November 29, 2012, the NBA's schedule makers presented Popovich with a perfect storm of schedule-induced fatigue, prompting a decision that incensed NBA commissioner David Stern so much he levied the largest league fine ever against the club: $250,000.

The Spurs' schedule in the final week of November during the 2012–13 season began with a Sunday night road game against the Toronto Raptors, which turned out to be a double-overtime victory for the Spurs. That was followed by another road game on Monday night against the Washington Wizards. Tuesday was an off day, but the schedule picked back up with a third straight road game, this time against the Orlando Magic. It was the fifth straight road game for the team and produced a fifth straight road win.

Next up after Orlando was a game the very next night against the defending NBA champion Miami Heat. It would be the team's fourth game in five nights and the second game of another set of back-to-back games. Even worse, the Spurs would have but a single day off on their return to San Antonio after the Miami game, with Midwest Division rival Memphis on the schedule.

For Popovich there was only one thing that made sense: send his Big Three stars back to San Antonio after the game in Orlando so they could be fresh for the game against the Grizzlies. Starting guard Danny Green was added to the list of players sent home for extra rest.

The game in Miami was the featured TV game for the TNT network, one of the NBA's broadcast partners, and neither network officials nor Stern were happy to discover that a game they had promoted as one of the most compelling of the season would be denied some of the league's top stars.

Stern issued a statement and announced that the Spurs would be fined for holding the four players out of the game.

"The result here is dictated by the totality of the facts in this case," Stern said in a statement. "The Spurs decided to make four of their top players unavailable for an early season game that was the team's only regular-season visit to Miami. The team also did this without informing the Heat, the media, or the league office in a timely way. Under these circumstances, I have concluded that the Spurs did a disservice to the league and our fans."

Teams are required to report as soon as they know a player will not travel because of injury. The league's statement said the Spurs were in violation of league policy reviewed with the board of governors in April 2010 against resting players in a manner "contrary to the best interests of the NBA."

Popovich's starters against the Heat were Patty Mills, Nando De Colo, Boris Diaw, Matt Bonner, and Tiago Splitter. His four bench players—DeJuan Blair, Gary Neal, Cory Joseph, and James Anderson—each played no fewer than 14:57.

Somehow, the short-handed Spurs took a three-point lead into the fourth quarter and led by five points, 98–93, with just 2:14 remaining in the game.

Miami's LeBron James, Dwyane Wade, and Ray Allen sparked a late rally to pull out a 105–100 win for the Heat.

Popovich said he was disappointed in the league's decision to levy the hefty fine.

"What I do from my perspective is from a coaching perspective," he said. "And I think the league operates from a business perspective and I think that's reflective in the action that they took."

Ultimately, Popovich's action helped illuminate the challenge of scheduling that often leads to fatigue of players, veteran and otherwise. Beginning with the 2014–15 season, the NBA extended the season by about a week in an effort to reduce the number of back-to-back games and four-games-in-five-nights stretches. In the 2015–16 schedule, the number of stretches in which teams have to play four games in five nights was reduced dramatically, from 70 to 27. Back-to-back sets also were reduced and the Spurs were one of the prime beneficiaries. They were not scheduled for a single four-in-five stretch and their back-to-back games went from 21 in 2014–15 to 16.

The $250,000 turned out to be money well spent.

95 Find an Iceman Poster

You can make a case that the "Iceman" poster Nike produced to promote George Gervin is the coolest basketball poster of all time. Pun intended.

As if a scoring title weren't enough to make Gervin a legend, Nike did the rest, producing what may be the most iconic basketball poster ever: the Iceman, wearing silver warmups and seated on a throne of ice, legs crossed, a silver basketball in each hand.

"They flew me into Seattle and into this ice house, this little warehouse, and once I got there they started building that ice throne," he said. "People always say, 'Was that real ice?' Oh, yeah, that was real ice, now. And they had to take thousands of pictures of me sitting on that ice. I never knew that poster would be as iconic as it is.

"Everywhere I go today people tell me, 'I had that poster on my wall. I had Farah Fawcett and the Iceman posters right next to each other.'

"That's still kind of special."

By the way, Nike produced a special version of the poster for Gervin's many Hispanic fans in and around San Antonio. It read EL HOMBRE DE HIELO (The Man of Ice).

Still one of the most memorable posters to ever feature an NBA player, George Gervin's collaboration with Nike is a worthy Spurs fan collectible.

In 1994, Nike commemorated the poster in the first of its "Barbershop" TV commercials, with various NBA greats gathered in a real-life barbershop. The spot begins with Gervin and fellow Spurs great David Robinson walking down a street toward the barbershop. With the intro music from Curtis Mayfield's "Superfly" playing in the background, the spot cuts to the interior, with point guard Tim Hardaway sitting in a barber chair and talking about the Iceman poster.

"Nineteen seventy-seven, butterfly collar," Hardaway says as the poster appears on screen. "Walk outside with that on in San Antonio now you'll burn up."

Eventually, Hardaway asks Gervin to tell the group in the barbershop about his "finger roll from the free throw line."

Gervin's response: "You know, that was my patented...my patented shot. One thing I could do...was finger roll."

The barbershop erupts in laughter, but the spot seriously enhanced the status of the Iceman poster as a true collector's item, especially for Spurs fans.

It is still possible to find the poster for sale online. A recent check of eBay revealed Iceman posters on sale for prices ranging from $5.25 to $75.

Caveat emptor.

The 1979 Eastern Conference Finals

After the NBA finally agreed to absorb four of the ABA's remaining six teams into the older league, it was the Spurs who made the first serious run at an NBA title. Playing in the Eastern Conference upon entering the NBA, the Spurs in 1979 survived a Game 7 shootout between George Gervin and an old ABA rival, Julius Erving, to win a semifinals matchup and advance to the conference finals against the Washington Bullets.

A trip to the NBA Finals seemed close enough to touch when the Spurs took a 3–1 lead in the best-of-seven series with a 118–102 win at HemisFair Arena.

Afterward, Bullets coach Dick Motta stole a line from *San Antonio Express-News* sports columnist Dan Cook and reminded the world that "the opera isn't over until the fat lady sings."

Motta was right and the last act of what would be regarded in San Antonio as a tragic opera was Game 7 at the Capitol Center, the Bullets' home court in Landover, Maryland.

The win that would put the Spurs in the NBA Finals for the first time seemed even closer in that game when they took a 10-point lead in the fourth quarter before the lights suddenly went out in the arena.

It took nearly 20 minutes for arena officials to get the lights turned back on. There were accusations that the Bullets had intentionally turned them off in an attempt to change the game's momentum but those never were proved. Nonetheless, the momentum did change. The Spurs missed 10 of their last 14 shots and the Bullets rallied for a 107–105 win.

Washington's Bobby Dandridge scored 37 points, including a jumper with eight seconds left that he launched over three Spurs defenders.

Bullets center Elvin Hayes blocked James Silas' attempt to tie the game and the Spurs left the court to ponder what might have been.

"We made history backward," Gervin would tell the *San Antonio Express-News* 35 years later. "We were showing the NBA we belonged back then. It was the (third) year we were in the league and we had a chance to be in the Finals. I think we got a little bit ahead of ourselves. We just didn't know how to close it out."

500,000 pennies

The heartbreaking loss to the Bullets—George Gervin admitted to shedding tears in the locker room afterward—was all the more difficult for the Spurs and their fans to accept because of the differential in fouls in the deciding fourth quarter, when the Spurs let a double-digit lead slip away. To pay the subsequent fine levied against coach Dough Moe after he criticized the referees, a local radio station ran a promotion to collect 500,000 pennies to pay the fine and Spurs fans responded. The pennies were collected and sent to the league office.

Gervin scored 42 points in the game but shook his head as he recalled the Spurs' inability to get defensive stops as their lead vanished.

"It just goes to show you it isn't all the time about how many you score and I think what makes this (Spurs) team special today is they get stops when it's time. That's what we didn't do," Gervin said. "We didn't get stops when it was time but we had all the manpower and the leadership in the coaches to get it done.

"It just didn't happen."

Gervin acknowledged that the power failure, intentional or otherwise, had an effect on the Spurs but said the credit for the outcome really belonged to Dandridge, who was unstoppable in crunch time.

Moe saw things a little differently in the immediate aftermath of the crushing loss. He didn't say anything about the power failure but he had plenty to say about the officiating of John Vanak and Paul Mihalik. The two referees had sent the Bullets to the foul line for 15 fourth-quarter free throws. The Spurs shot only four foul shots in the final period.

"The refs stole it," he told reporters after the game. "John Vanak and Paul Mihalik wouldn't make a call for us at the end. It was a great-refereed game and then they stole it at the end.

"It makes you wonder if it was on purpose. They should be set before a firing squad. (The Bullets) stole their way into the Finals. Who knows if it's personal."

NBA commissioner Larry O'Brien fined Moe $5,000 for his remarks, at the time one of the largest individual fines in league history.

97 Bob Hill

One of the most successful coaches in franchise history—his record in two-plus seasons was 124–58, a winning percentage of 68.1, second only to Gregg Popovich (69.2) in franchise history—Bob Hill is recalled by most Spurs fans for being fired by Popovich 18 games into the 1996–97 season, just as All-Star center David Robinson was about to return from the injured list.

A snappy dresser with perfectly coiffed hair—he favored a Pat Riley–like pompadour cut—Hill became a fan favorite. Despite losses in the 1995 Western Conference Finals (to Houston) and the 1996 semifinals (to Utah), Hill sought a contract extension. Little did the fans know Popovich had denied it because he was convinced the team needed more toughness and a greater commitment to defense.

After the Spurs fell to 3–15 with a blowout loss to the Golden State Warriors on the heels of an embarrassing loss to the NBA's worst team, the Vancouver Grizzlies, Popovich met with club chairman Peter Holt and club president Jack Diller to discuss firing Hill. The loss to the Grizzlies—their second of the young season to Vancouver—put them at 1–9 against teams that had been in the NBA's draft lottery in June.

The conclusion of the three executives: it was an untenable situation that demanded immediate action.

Holt and Popovich announced Hill's dismissal at a press conference the day after the Golden State loss. They were asked about Robinson's impending return to the lineup.

"I know nobody will believe this and I understand that," Holt said, "but it really was somewhat of a coincidence. If they had told us yesterday that David couldn't come back for another two weeks we still would have made this decision and made it now."

Popovich understood how the decision looked but didn't care because he knew a change had to come.

"When you decide on something as difficult as this and feel that it is the right thing to do, it is best to do it right away," he said. "I fully realize that the timing might look bad. The fact that David is coming back is a coincidence.

"At this point I thought a change in direction was necessary. The decision wasn't made in a knee-jerk way. It was made with a lot of thought and a lot of counsel and a lot of heartache."

Nevertheless, there was outrage in some quarters of the media and among the team's fans. Even Robinson questioned the move when it was announced.

"Do I agree with the decision?" he said in an interview with the *Express-News*. "No. But it's not my decision to make. I feel like if we have some adversity we should try to stick it out together."

Hill denied that his players had not responded well to his leadership.

"That's absolutely ridiculous," he told the *San Antonio Express-News*. "We had so many injuries. We were undermanned every night because of the injuries. They were doing the best they could."

Hill returned to coaching in 2005 with the Seattle SuperSonics, but was replaced after the Sonics went 53–81 in his two seasons on the bench.

98 The 1975 ABA All-Star Game

By 1974–75, all it took for one of the American Basketball Association's 10 remaining teams to host the league's All-Star Game was a willingness to do so.

Spurs co-owner and club president Angelo Drossos went to the league meeting the summer before the team's second season and when the All-Star Game was brought up none of the other franchises seemed eager to host.

Believing an All-Star Game would generate just the sort of attention San Antonio's new team needed, Drossos was the only owner to raise his hand when those assembled were asked which franchise might like to host that season's game.

"I do not have a clue how we ended up with the game," recalls Wayne Witt, former director of media relations. "I went to work for Angelo in May of 1974 and there were only four of us in the front office then. There was Bernie Lareau, the trainer-business manager-traveling secretary; John Begzos, the sales manager; Terry Stembridge, the broadcaster and radio-TV ad salesman; and me, the PR guy. A little later, Jeff Carmody came on to the sales staff and handled season tickets.

"Bernie had a condo across the street from Blossom Athletic Center and we used to meet Angelo in his kitchen on Monday mornings to figure out what we were going to do next. On one of these mornings in midsummer of 1974 Angelo looked at me and said, 'Wayne, you are going to be general chairman of the 1975 All-Star Game.'

"I said, 'Angelo I've never even been to an All-Star Game,'" Witt said.

"He said, 'Don't worry, Wayne, we'll help you.'"

Planning for the game focused on how to fill the arena and how best to showcase San Antonio to a national TV audience.

Tickets for the All-Star game were hawked at every Spurs home game, with little advertising or outside marketing.

"It was like any advance sale," Witt said. "We sold them during the game and did some telemarketing. "

The tiny front office core didn't have to debate a theme for the weekend.

"We wanted to make the whole shebang as Texas as possible," Witt said.

When players and team officials arrived at the Hilton Hotel, the official ABA All-Star hotel, they found their beds covered with Lone Star State souvenirs, including six-packs of Lone Star Beer.

In keeping with the Texas theme, Willie Nelson was hired to perform at a pregame gala scheduled for the Saturday night before the game. Nelson had just recorded *Red Headed Stranger*, the concept album that would make him a crossover star, but it would not be released until May of 1975. Most of the ABA players were befuddled when he was introduced at the party, held at the San Antonio Convention Center.

Dan Issel, the Hall of Fame big man who then played for the league's best team, the Kentucky Colonels, recalls Nelson's performance.

"They said, 'Ladies and gentlemen, Willie Nelson!'" Issel remembers. "I looked around and every player was saying the same thing: 'Who the heck is that?'

"I've got to say I was blown away by Willie and became a huge fan."

Nelson had agreed to perform for free at the gala as long as he could sing the national anthem at the game, being televised nationally by the USA Network.

"He was great on game day," Witt said. "What he didn't know was that the network went to commercials during the anthem."

The game, won by the East 151–124, seemed an afterthought to some. Indiana Pacers guard Freddie Lewis scored 26 points and had 10 assists for the winning team. He was named the game's MVP.

"I can't even remember who won," said Gervin, who led the West team in scoring, with 23 points. "I played in so many of those games I can't keep track.

"What I do remember is the horse they tried to give Freddie Lewis. A horse! Wowie, that was something else."

Someone in Spurs management had gotten title to a racing quarter horse named Tuff Julie to present to the MVP, along with a hand-tooled saddle and bridle.

Lewis was expecting a trophy and maybe a car.

"Freddie didn't want anything to do with that horse," Witt said. "We agreed to auction it off and split the proceeds with him. I think he got about $1,500."

Three Spurs played in the game and accounted for nearly half the West's points. In addition to Gervin's 23, point guard James Silas scored 21 points and center Sven Nater scored 12.

99 Enjoy a Glass of A to Z Wine

No, this is not an alphabetical listing of every player to ever wear silver and black. Rather, it refers to Gregg Popovich's oenological pursuits.

A gourmand and connoisseur of fine wine, the Spurs coach began learning about wine in the early 1970s during an Air

Force posting at Moffat Field, a Naval Air Station in Sunnyvale, California, not far from the Napa Valley. He discovered his passion for wine visiting the wineries on weekend tasting trips, and when Popovich is passionate about something he is "all in." He learned anything and everything he could about wine, including how it is made.

Eventually, Popovich took his interest in wine and winemaking (oenology) to its logical end when he became an investor in the A to Z Wineworks, located in Newburg, Oregon. A friend had introduced him to A to Z owners Bill and Deb Hatcher and they became friends long before the coach became the largest single investor in their wine operation.

Popovich's interest is focused on the winery's production of a fine, affordable pinot noir. "Aristocratic Wines at Affordable Prices," each bottle of A to Z wine declares, and sophisticated wine drinkers understand that finding a bottle of fine pinot noir for less than $15 dollars definitely is a bargain.

No one need question the declaration that A to Z pinot noir is a fine wine. No less an authority than *Wine Spectator* magazine twice has put it on its Top 100 list. *Food and Wine* magazine has had it on its list of Best American Pinot Noirs Under $20.

Popovich also gets exclusive possession of the Hatchers' reserve pinot noir that Popovich formally named "Rock and Hammer." Each bottle has a back label that contains the famous Jacob Riis stonecutter quote that Popovich has made the Spurs' mantra.

You won't find Rock and Hammer at your local liquor store. It never has been offered for sale despite its reputation as one of the finest pinot noirs produced anywhere.

As detailed in YahooSports' "Ball Don't Lie" blog, in 2014 Popovich hosted a vertical tasting of every Rock and Hammer vintage from 2004 through 2012 at the Rex Hill Winery's Classic Wines Auction. Tickets for the event cost $750, with five charities benefiting. Popovich sent a bottle of Rock and Hammer home with each donor.

Oregonian sports columnist John Canzano got a description of Rock and Hammer from A to Z vineyards co-operator Deb Hatcher: "It's a fine pinot noir. It's different, year to year. Full body, richness, some spice on the finish. It has a beautiful pinot noir nose. It's always a blend. We specialize in that."

Popovich uses the small annual production for personal use, mostly to share with special friends on special occasions and as gifts and charitable donations. George Karl, for whom Popovich served as an assistant on the ill-fated USA Men's National Team that finished sixth in the 2002 FIBA World Championships in Indianapolis, regularly received a bottle whenever Popovich brought the Spurs to Denver to play Karl's Nuggets.

When Caltech snapped a 310-game losing streak in the Southern California Intercollegiate Athletic Conference, the same Division III conference as Pomona-Pitzer, once coached by Popovich, the Spurs coach shipped a case to Beavers coach Oliver Eslinger.

According to a terrific 2013 Popovich profile by *Sports Illustrated* writer Jack McCallum, there was a message attached to the case: "Congratulations to you and the players for showing the true spirit of sport you display. I am thrilled for you and as a former loser to Caltech, I wish you more wins."

100 Take This Ultimate Spurs Fan Trivia Quiz

Answer six of these 11 questions correctly if you truly want to call yourself a Spurs fan; get seven or more right and qualify to wear any Spurs authentic jersey you wish, including a No. 21 Tim Duncan or a No. 44 Gervin; get all 11 correct and count yourself the ultimate Spurs fan, worthy of being a Baseline Bum.

1. Which coach has the best winning percentage in franchise history, regardless of number of games coached?
2. Who was the first coach in franchise history?
3. Who scored the most points for the Spurs in their first season in San Antonio?
4. Who was the first Australian to play for the Spurs?
5. Which Spurs players have been MVP of the All-Star Game?
6. Who was the first coach of the San Antonio Spurs?
7. Who was the first European-born player to come directly to the Spurs without first attending college in the U.S.?
8. After the Spurs made Manu Ginobili their second pick of the second round of the 1999 NBA draft, which other foreign-born player did they acquire via trade with the Dallas Mavericks?
9. Who sang the national anthem at the ABA All-Star Game at HemisFair Arena in 1975?
10. Which player was selected immediately ahead of Alfredrick Hughes in the 1985 draft?
11. Which team finished second in the 1987 draft lottery that gave the Spurs the right to make David Robinson the No. 1 overall pick?

Answers:

1. Rex Hughes, 1–0 as interim coach after the dismissal of Jerry Tarkanian in 1992
2. Cliff Hagan
3. James Silas, 1,321 points. George Gervin had a higher scoring average (19.4 PPG) but played only 25 games
4. Andrew Gaze, who played 19 games in the 1998–99 season
5. George Gervin (1980) and Tim Duncan (co-MVP, with Shaquille O'Neal, 2000)
6. Tom Nissalke
7. Zarko Paspalj (Montenegro), 1989–90
8. Gordan Giricek
9. Willie Nelson
10. Karl Malone, No. 13, to Utah
11. Phoenix Suns

Acknowledgments

I covered the NBA for the *Denver Post* from 1985 to 2000, FoxSports.com from 2000 to 2003, and then, in 2003, I was hired by the *San Antonio Express-News* to report on the NBA and augment its Spurs coverage. That makes me something of an authority on Spurs history. Since it was former *Express-News* Spurs reporter Johnny Ludden who advocated my hire and former sports editor Steve Quintana who agreed with him, I owe both large measures of gratitude, including thanks for getting the opportunity to write this book.

Most of the research for the book was done online, especially on BasketballReference.com, an amazing source of statistical minutiae that has become the best friend of every basketball reporter. Also, the archives of the *Express-News* were mined to their depths.

I never would have undertaken this project had it not been for assurances of assistance from some of those individuals who had seen the inner workings of the Spurs organization in its very early days in San Antonio. Chief among these was Wayne Witt, the team's director of media relations from 1974 to 1991. Recently retired from the athletic department at the Univeristy of the Incarnate Word, Wayne spun tales about the Spurs' early years over plates of enchiladas and bottles of cold beer. He also guided me to others with first-hand knowledge of the early doings, and nearly everything you read about the team's first decade includes his input.

The great NBA reporter and columnist Jan Hubbard deserves special thanks. His book, *The History of the San Antonio Spurs*, was an invaluable resource and a fount of information. In his role as executive editor of NBA Publications, it was Hubbard who asked me to write *NBA Rookie Experience* about rookies from the NBA draft class of 1997, which included one Tim Duncan. Nearly everything you read about Duncan's rookie season in this book was gleaned from that book. Jan's friendship, encouragement, and guidance during the writing of the book was immensely helpful.

The many colleagues with whom I have worked as a pro basketball writer deserve pats on backs, as well. Among these, especially the aforementioned Johnny Ludden. Also: Buck Harvey, Jeff McDonald, Tim Griffin, Marc Spears, Dan McCarney, Tom Orsborn, Mark Kiszla, and Mark Rosner. Special thanks to former *Express-News* sports editor Burt Henry for signing off on my writing the book when the opportunity first was presented.

Finally, my manuscript received its first read and a lovingly deft edit from my wife, Nancy Cook-Monroe, who put to good use her elegant writing skill and her journalism degree from SMU.